THE
HOOP &
THE TREE

Additional praise for the new edition

Chris Hoffman's new version of *The Hoop and the Tree* is even more beautiful and enlightening. You'll be uplifted as he distills world spiritual and wisdom traditions, including modern psychology, into practical guidance for a life of connectedness with all our relations. Come away feeling more grounded at home on our Mother Earth. Enjoy!

—Anita Sanchez, PhD, author of *The Four Sacred Gifts: Indigenous Wisdom for Modern Times*

The new and revised edition of *The Hoop and the Tree* offers deeply thoughtful and wise advice. The symbol that serves as an inner compass, drawn from ancient traditions from around the world, is especially relevant for these troubling times. I couldn't put the book down.

—Erica Elliott, MD, author of *Medicine and Miracles in the High Desert: My Life Among the Navajo People.*

Our personal, social, spiritual, and ecological dis-ease these days makes the call for living in harmony with one another, the Earth, and the Divine more pressing than ever. The second edition of *The Hoop and the Tree* offers an early roadmap for how we might go on. Re-grounding us in story, spiritual teaching, and science, it reminds us of the profound wisdom of the hoop-and-tree metaphor, the gifts it has offered others, and the potential it holds for us all. It highlights archetypal initiations through which we can learn to care for one another, the earth, and future generations; and it introduces concrete practices that promote personal, organizational, social, and ecological wholeness.

—Amanda Trosten-Bloom, coauthor of *The Power of Appreciative Inquiry*, cofounder, Rocky Mountain Center for Positive Change

Poetry by Chris Hoffman
On the Way • *Realization Point* • *Cairns*

THE
HOOP &
THE TREE

A COMPASS FOR FINDING A DEEPER
RELATIONSHIP WITH ALL LIFE

CHRIS HOFFMAN

COUNCIL
OAK
BOOKS

Chicago

Published by Council Oak Books
An imprint of Chicago Review Press Incorporated
814 North Franklin Street
Chicago, Illinois 60610
ISBN 978-1-64160-494-9

Grateful acknowledgment is made for permission to quote from the following: All Bible quotations are from the Revised Standard Version of the Bible, copyright © 1952 [2nd edition, 1971] by the Division of Christian Education of the National Council of the Churches of Christ in the United States of America. Used by permission. All rights reserved. Lines from "Hades and Euclid" (first version) by Harry Martinson. Reprinted from *Friends, You Drank Some Darkness: Three Swedish Poets: Martinson, Ekelof, and Transtromer*, Beacon Press, Boston, 1975. Copyright © 1975 by Robert Bly. Reprinted by permission of the author. "A Love Letter" by Nanao Sakaki, copyright © Nanao Sakaki, from *Break the Mirror: The Poems of Nanao Sakaki*, Blackberry Books, Nobelboro, ME. "I live my life in growing orbits," from *Selected Poems of Rainer Maria Rilke*, edited and translated by Robert Bly, copyright © by Robert Bly. Reprinted by permission of HarperCollins Publishers, Inc. Excerpt from *Emotional Intelligence* by Daniel Goleman, copyright © 1995 by Daniel Goleman. Used by permission of Bantam Books, a division of Random House, Inc.

Library of Congress Cataloging-in-Publication Data
Is available from the Library of Congress.

Cover design: Jonathan Hahn
Cover photographs: Circle, MirageC/Moment/Getty Images; tree, Jeremy Bishop/Unsplash.
Typesetting: Nord Compo
Image credits: Frontispiece: Yggdrasill, the Mundane Tree, Frontispiece of *Northern Antiquities* by Bishop Thomas Percy, 1847, Public domain. Chapter 1: Stupa at Boudnath, Photograph by the author. Chapter 2: Yin-yang symbol, Public domain. Chapter 3: The Fruitful Tree, After an engraving dated 1512, Public domain. Chapter 4: Whirling Dervish, cover photograph from the book *Rumi and Sufism* by Eva de Vitray-Meyerovitch, used by permission of the Post-Apollo Press. Chapter 5: The Tree of the Great Peace, Cover design of *The Great Peace . . . The Gathering of Good Minds* CD-ROM, Original artwork by Raymond R. Skye (Tuscarora) and Donald Gibson, Used by permission of GoodMinds.com, Six Nations of The Grand River Territory, Brantford, Ontario, Canada. Chapter 6: Original art used by permission of workshop participant.

Printed in the United States of America
5 4 3 2 1

To my son, Benjamin.

The Hoop and the Tree as the shape of wholeness in the universe: In Norse Myth the great Tree Yggdrasill grows through the center of the universe, penetrating the three worlds—lower, middle, and upper. Yggdrasill, the whole world itself, and the great ocean around it, are surrounded by an enormous serpent biting its own tail, making the shape of the Hoop.

Contents

One of many Hoop-and-Tree images of wholeness from the world's wisdom traditions, the Buddhist stupa takes the form of the Tree when viewed from the side, and of the Hoop mandala when viewed from above. *Stupa at Boudnath, near Kathmandu, Nepal.*

1

The Shape of All Shapes

WE HUMAN BEINGS ARE STORYTELLING ANIMALS. We venture into the world—the outer world of science and facts and data and ineffable mysteries, or the inner world of feelings and thoughts and dreams and ineffable mysteries—and return to tell each other about it. None of our stories is "The Truth." There is an old Zuni saying that there are no truths, only stories. The truth is beyond stories. But stories teach us and help us to live this precious life we have been given. We tell each other what we have learned about planting corn, about the best way to program a computer, bake bread, or handle a wrench. We also tell each other about ways to navigate the emotional and spiritual rapids of life: birth, initiation, marriage, fruitfulness, loss, success, death. These are the stories we live by. They come from science, history, literature, and the great spiritual traditions of the world. The stories we live by have the power to shape our destiny.

This book is about a robust story, one that has been told in many versions and tongues over the years. It is a story about what we all desire: to lead lives of balance and fulfillment. It offers an image of the deep structure of health and wholeness, both in the universe and in the human psyche and soul, an image of the beauty at the heart of everything.

I first encountered this image many years ago. I didn't pay a lot of attention to it then, but it lodged in me like a seed in the ground. Over the years, as I've tried to help my counseling and consulting clients and to make sense of my own life, the seed has sprouted and grown to the extent that it helps me enormously in my efforts to be a useful and loving human being.

The image first revealed itself to me in a story of the Oglala Lakota.

In the summer of 1873, a band of Lakota was slowly making its way across the high plains of North America toward the Rocky Mountains. One evening in camp a nine-year-old boy was eating with an older friend when the boy suddenly heard a voice saying to him, "It is time; now they are calling you." So loud and so real was this voice that the boy stood up and followed it out of the teepee. As he went out, both of his thighs began hurting him, and, as he tells it, "it was like waking from a dream, and there wasn't any voice." The older man was amazed and concerned by the boy's behavior, for the man had heard nothing.

The next day the boy went riding with some other boys. When he got off his horse to get a drink from a creek, his legs suddenly crumpled under him. He couldn't walk. The other boys had to help him back to camp. The following day the boy had to travel in a pony drag; his arms, legs, and face were so swollen he couldn't move.

That evening as he was lying in his family teepee, he saw through the doorway two men coming down from the clouds, headfirst like arrows slanting down. When they landed they called to him, "Hurry! Come! Your Grandfathers are calling you!" Then they turned and shot back up into the sky.

When the boy got up to follow them, his legs no longer hurt. He went outside the teepee where a little cloud came down and carried him up into the sky. There the spirit beings filled him with an extraordinary series of experiences. When he returned to human consciousness he found he had been gone twelve days. Although his body was still swollen, he felt healed and joyful. Soon his body too was well.

It took the boy many years to accept his vision. He spoke not a word of it to anyone until he was seventeen. When he finally confided in a respected medicine man, the elder told him he must enact his vision for the whole tribe. The ceremony was a great pageant, involving many people and sixteen horses—four each of the colors of the four directions—black, white, sorrels, and buckskins.

After this ceremony the boy lost the fear that had been troubling him for so many years, everyone in the community felt happy, and many people who had been sick were now well again. Even the horses seemed to have become healthier and happier.

The boy's name was Black Elk. The vision he received at nine years of age guided him to become a wise and respected elder who helped his people all his life. Much of what he saw in his vision was beyond the power of words to say. Yet he *was* able to tell of his glimpse of the breathtaking wholeness of the universe. As poetically summarized by John Neihardt, Black Elk's interviewer, Black Elk saw that he was:

... *standing on the highest mountain of them all, and round about beneath me was the whole hoop of the world. And while I stood there I saw more than I can tell and I understood more than I saw; for I was seeing in a sacred manner the shapes of all things in the spirit, and the shape of all shapes as they must live together like one being. And I saw that the sacred hoop of my people was one of many hoops that made one circle, wide as daylight and as starlight, and in the center grew one mighty flowering tree to shelter all the children of one mother and one father. And I saw that it was holy.*[1]

Black Elk was touched and healed by what might be called the deep structure of wholeness in the universe. It appeared to him through the image or visual metaphor of the Hoop and the Tree. This image of the Hoop and the Tree is not accidental. In the years since reading about Black Elk, I have discovered that the image appears not only in Lakota mythology but also throughout the great wisdom traditions of the world—and indeed in modern psychology and systems science—as an image of the deep structure of wholeness and health, both in the universe and in the human psyche and soul.

Moreover, the wisdom traditions teach that this pattern of wholeness lies latent within each of us, waiting as a seed waits underground ready to bring forth flowers and fruit.

The Hoop and the Tree could be said to represent two "dimensions of the soul" that must be fully developed and in balance with each other for the soul to be whole. The Hoop-and-Tree image also acts as a skeleton key that can open the door to the great variety of spiritual and mythological ways of the world without depreciating or diminishing our magnificent human diversity.

The Shape of the Model

To see how the Hoop-and-Tree model depicts wholeness, it will help to understand what these two "dimensions" represent.

All the great wisdom traditions teach the importance of aspiring toward some state of connection with the Divine or some state of wisdom or enlightenment that is ultimately unutterable. All the traditions also teach about the importance of relationship. These two types of teachings meet in the image of the Hoop and the Tree.

The Hoop dimension has to do with relationship in all its aspects. When people gather for family meals, or to sing songs, or to sit at the knee of a storyteller, they spontaneously form the shape of a Hoop. This may be why images of the Hoop, and objects or qualities that are like hoops, are familiar metaphors for relationship. We speak of our inner "circle" or our family "circle." Native Americans honor all their relations through Hoop-shaped medicine wheels and sweat lodges. Taoists use the well-known Hoop of the yin-yang symbol to represent being and flowing in right relationship with the way of nature. Psychologists heal within the "sacred circle" of the therapeutic relationship.

The Hoop of the *mandala* (Sanskrit for "magic circle") appears in all cultures and times as a way to represent wholeness. Mandala symbolism includes concentrically arranged figures, radial or spherical designs, and circles with a central point. Common examples are the sun disc and various types of wheels, including medicine wheels and the wheel of rebirth. There are even danced mandalas such as traditional round dances, the Dances of Universal Peace, developed by Murshid Samuel Lewis, and the meditative martial art of Chinese T'ai-chi Ch'uan.[2]

Although the typical mandala is a Hoop, wheel, or circle of some kind, there are other cognates or analogs of the "magic circle" that serve the same function, though they don't look round. The square, the equilateral horizontal cross, and the image of fourfoldness or quaternity are all Hoop cognates.[3] We use the fourfoldness of the four directions—north, south, east, and west—in order to describe the Hoop of the whole horizon. Other examples of fourfoldness include the four seasons, the four elements, the four archangels, and the four evangelists.

The Tree dimension has to do with aspiration and deepening for individual growth. We acknowledge this correspondence between individual growth and the Tree in our everyday language when we quote old proverbs like "Just as the twig is bent, the tree's inclined" and "The apple doesn't fall far from the tree."

The Tree dimension is a vertical dimension. Traditional wisdom and contemporary spiritual and psychological practice also associate with this dimension imagery of tree cognates, such as mountains, ladders, and pillars. Tree cognates all carry the Tree sense of verticality, while emphasizing some particular attribute of the Tree. The mountain emphasizes being central and rooted or grounded; the ladder emphasizes the route of ascent and descent; the pillar, a connection between above and below. We ascend the Tree or Tree cognate for development that at its highest reaches is spiritual development.

The Tree also involves descent for development of the soul. Images of descent along the Tree dimension have to do with exploring one's "roots" both in terms of ancestors ("The Family Tree"), and in terms of the subterranean explorations of depth psychology. A tree can grow tall only if it has sturdy and far-reaching roots.

Imagine a vertical axis running through the center of your being, from deep in the ground up to your highest aspiration or to your image of the Divine. Recall a time when you felt especially grounded or rooted. Think of your highest aspiration and what it feels like to be stretching toward that goal. This is the Tree, which roots you, centers you, and offers you a way to ascend to the light of your highest aspiration, and a way to be fruitful. Imagine also the Tree encircled by a Hoop on a horizontal plane, with the center of the Hoop pierced by the trunk of the Tree. Remember your family or some other group that encircles you with love. Recall being surrounded by the beauty of nature. The Hoop brings you into relationship with the rest of the universe. Together the Hoop-and-Tree image is a pattern or model for wholeness in the universe and in you. In this simplest abstract form it resembles a gyroscope.

A gyroscope is a little hoop spinning on a vertical axle that keeps itself balanced and upright no matter what. You can feel this almost miraculous stability yourself by experimenting with a toy gyroscope. Gyroscopes are so steady in fact that advanced gyroscopes have been used as the heart of navigational instruments for aircraft and ships. A hoop of relationship around a vertical growing core of individuality makes this same shape. Our ancestors visualized this shape as a Hoop around a Tree. And these two dimensions of the soul do form an internal gyrocompass for one's life. Having the Hoop and the Tree developed and in balance can keep you steady, balanced, and "on course."

"There are no truths, only stories": the Hoop and the Tree are metaphors, just as a gyroscope can be a metaphor. They are not "things" but together represent a fundamental pattern of energy in the universe. It is impossible to be entirely precise about what each of them "means," because they are both patterns of infinite subtlety. But it *is* possible to suggest the realm over which each holds sway.

One might summarize by saying that the Tree is the autonomous aspect of the whole self and has to do with deepening and ascending for growth, while the Hoop is the affiliative aspect and has to do with widening for growth. The vector of the Tree is *aspirational* and the vector of the Hoop is *relational*. Neither of these two dimensions of wholeness is complete in and of itself; neither is "better" than the other. They are different and complementary.

Psychology teaches that the psyche of every person has both a female aspect and a male aspect. The Hoop is associated with the female aspect of the psyche and with behaviors such as inclusion and cooperation. The Tree is associated with the male aspect and with behaviors such as self-assertion. In poetic terms we could say that the Hoop has a female tone, the Tree a male tone. Both are needed, together and in balance, for a person, or a society, to become whole.

Schematic Diagram of the Hoop-and-Tree Model

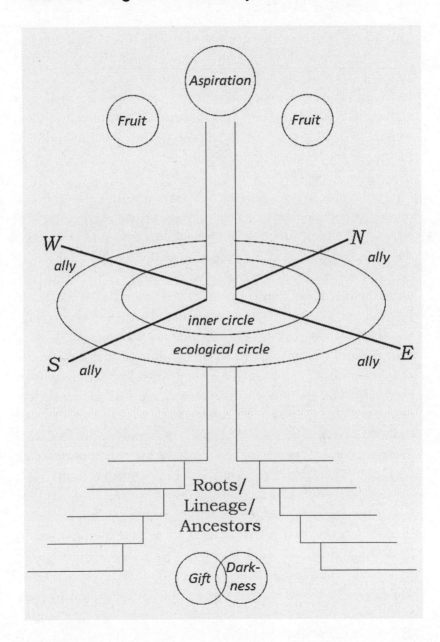

Evidence from Around the World and Throughout History

The Hoop-and-Tree pattern appears over and over in wisdom traditions ranging from ancient mythology through the world's great religions to modern psychology and systems science. While some traditions like Taoism, Wicca, and many Native American traditions emphasize Hoop and others like Judaism, Christianity, and Islam emphasize Tree, if you look closely you will see that most wisdom traditions are pointing to a model of psycho-spiritual wholeness that is Hoop and Tree together.

No human culture has ever fully embodied this wholeness, of course. As nothing human is perfect, neither Hoop cultures nor Tree cultures have been perfect. The Tree cultures tended to be lopsided one way; the Hoop cultures tended to be lopsided the other. For example, the Hoop belief in reincarnation supported the Celtic Druids in the practice of human sacrifice.[4] And we are all familiar with hierarchical (Tree orientation) excesses of slavery and oppression.

Yet if we look beyond the excesses or distortions of Hoop or Tree cultures we can learn from the wisdom of each—the trends and tendencies of Hoop and Tree from which we may make inferences about the ideal for which we are striving. This ideal may have been with us as long as consciousness itself has been with us. The earliest Hoop-and-Tree image I know of appears on a seal from the Indus Valley (Harappan) civilization and is over four thousand years old.[5] The most current image lives in your own heart.

Even a brief summary of the evidence for the Hoop and the Tree can seem overwhelming. In a sense, this is precisely the point. It is not just one path or tradition or school, but all our accumulated human wisdom that is telling us, "This way lies wholeness." By viewing the Hoop and the Tree from these many perspectives you can begin to see its splendor and perhaps also find the permutation of this key that is the right size and shape to open the door to your own wholeness.

Each of these wisdom traditions—world religions, lesser-known spiritual practices, psychological and scientific understanding—is like the facet of a diamond. We may peer through each of these facets to attempt to see what is at the heart of the diamond. Each facet, though, is like a pane in a seventeenth-century glass window full of wrinkles and bubbles, each one distorting our view in a different way. Even the great religions only let us see "through a glass darkly." To get the fullest understanding of what is at the heart, we must flatten our noses against many windowpanes, view through many facets.

In discussing these many traditions, most of which I approach as an outsider looking in, I am only trying to appreciate and highlight some suggestive commonalities and not intending to reduce what is rich, inestimably valuable, and complex to just a few sentences. My hope is that the Hoop and Tree image can be helpful to us all in discovering where we meet in wholeness.

Among the major contemporary world religions, Christianity obviously emphasizes the Tree with its central image of the Tree of the Cross, which powerfully represents ascent to connection with the Divine. According to tradition, Christ also descended from this Tree into Hades "to the extreme of its depth" in order to bring healing. Tradition also says that Christ brought the Tree of the Cross to Hades and planted it there as a witness to a profound truth. So the Christian Tree is the axis of the universe that runs from Hades to Paradise.

Yet the principal sacrament of Christianity is a Hoop ritual. In Holy Communion the consecrated bread and wine are shared among all. A Hoop-shaped container—a chalice or eucharistic bowl—brings the congregation into relationship in the round of community. Although the Roman Catholic Church places some restrictions on participation in this sacrament, the early Christian church and the non-Roman denominations all tend to emphasize inclusion and participation. Theologian Harvey Cox says, "Communion is like a family meal, the gathering of old and young, sick and well, around a common table and reminds all those who participate that the goods of the earth should be shared, not hoarded."[6] Holy Communion and the Holy Cross form the Hoop and Tree of the Christian world.

Jesus Christ Himself teaches the Hoop-and-Tree way to wholeness. When someone asked Jesus about the best way to live, Jesus
replied, "Love the Lord and love your neighbor" (Mark 12:30–31).
This is a summary of the Tree and the Hoop teachings—the Tree
aspiration to the Lord, and the Hoop relation to the community.
Accept Divine love (ascent/descent along the Tree axis) and then
give this love to the world (Hoop).

Each summer in the high plains of North America, hundreds
of people gather in four-day ceremonies to pray to a sacred Tree
and dance around it in a sacred Hoop. As part of these Lakota sun
dances, the dancers carry the spiritual renewal obtained from the
Tree out to the wider Hoop of community.

People of European descent come to these dances from as far
away as Australia and Germany. It's no wonder the dances resonate for them. For hundreds of years ancient Europeans danced
this Hoop-and-Tree pattern in religious observations every spring.
If you had lived in pre-Christian Europe, you might have seen
something like this:

A great procession of people ventures into the woods to visit
a particular tree. The tree has previously been selected, prayed to,
and asked if it would be willing to give its life for the benefit of
the community. Now, after further prayers and offerings, the tree
is chopped down. A line of many pairs of people, holding stout
poles between them, catches the falling tree so it won't touch the
ground. They lop off the lower branches of the tree, leaving a high
crown of foliage. Then they carry the tree between them, or pull it
on a cart behind a team of oxen, and parade it into the center of
the village with great rejoicing. Here they decorate the tree with
flags, ribbons, gilded eggshells, flowers, and perhaps with sausage
and cakes. Then the people erect the tree and in a great Hoop
round about the Tree they dance merrily to music.[7]

These "May pole" dances were performed not only in England,
but also throughout Europe, from Spain to Scandinavia, though
the timing of the festival varied somewhat, depending on the
sun's return to each latitude. This meeting of Hoop and Tree celebrated fertility and a great healing—the renewal of life—and was

for centuries one of the most important religious festivals of pre-Christian Europe.

Our Scandinavian ancestors visualized the wholeness of the universe itself in a Hoop-and-Tree form: the Hoop of the Midgard Serpent encircled the great world axis Tree, Yggdrasill, which like the Tree of the Cross extended to both the upper and lower worlds. Similarly, the ancient Greeks centered their world on the Tree cognate Mount Olympus, with Zeus ruling from above and Hades from below, while the whole cosmos was bounded on the horizontal plane by the Hoop of Oceanos, who encircled the world at its outermost limits, continuously flowing back on himself in a circle, just like the Midgard Serpent.

In the shamanic world view also, the wholeness of the universe has the Hoop-and-Tree shape. Shamanism is a form of psychological, spiritual, and physical healing that is at least forty thousand years old.[8] It has survived to the present day in many traditional cultures, and is even practiced in some contemporary psychological consulting rooms, because people continue to find it helpful. There are many varieties of shamanism, but the core technique of shamanic healing involves a psycho-spiritual journey in an altered state of consciousness. The shaman makes this journey in a universe that has at least three levels: an upper world, the earth we live on, and a lower world or underworld—all connected by a central axis.[9] Each world is a Hoop. The central axis is a Tree cognate, or most often the Tree itself.

For many shamans the goal of the journey itself is a Tree. "During their initiatory trances, some fledgling Siberian shamans find themselves being nurtured in nests high in the World Tree. The higher the nest, the more powerful the shaman will be."[10] The Tree is the teacher. For the shamans of the Conibo of the upper Amazon, "'learning from the trees' is considered superior to learning from another shaman."[11] The shaman ascends or descends the Tree for spiritual boons, for healing wisdom, and to restore the Hoop of right relationship in these other realms. Then the shaman returns to bring this benefit to the Hoop of the shaman's community.

The Tree in the Buddhist story is the bodhi tree, under which Buddha attained enlightenment. After attaining enlightenment, Buddha began carrying the blessings of his achievement out into the community. His initial work of teaching is known as turning the "Wheel of the Dharma," the Hoop. There is a form of shrine, widespread in the Buddhist world, called a *stupa*. The stupa acts as a reminder of the shape of wholeness. It is said to be "an abstract image of the state of enlightenment attainable by all beings."[12] This abstract image of enlightenment takes the form of a Hoop (mandala) extended upward along the Tree axis.

All three Abrahamic traditions (Judaism, Christianity, and Islam) refer to a Paradise, an image of wholeness, at the beginning of everything. What is this Paradise? It is a garden with a Tree at its center. The Garden of Eden is a magic circle or mandala by virtue of fourfoldness: the four rivers that rise at the foot of the Tree and flow from the Garden (Genesis 2:10–14). The shape of Paradise is the shape of the Hoop around the Tree of Life that is hidden inside the Tree of Knowledge.[13]

Judaism also reveals the Hoop and the Tree in the mystical practice of Kabbalah. Kabbalah presents a route to the Divine called the "Tree of Life," or *Etz Chaiim*. One may follow this path to wholeness by meditating on the fruit of this Tree—their qualities and interrelationships. These fruit, or *Sefirot*, are most often depicted as spheres or circles (Hoops) on the Tree. In the Kabbalistic story, the composition of the primordial ideal human, Adam Kadmon, is patterned on the Tree of Life with its Sefirot. Thus the ideal image of human wholeness has Hoops in balance on the Tree.

The Sufis of Islam actually move the shape of wholeness into the body through the celebrated dance of the "whirling dervishes" of the Mevlevi order. The dervishes start whirling slowly, spreading their arms like wings, the right palm turned upward toward the sky to gather divine grace, and the left palm turned downward to give it to the earth. The dancers whirl faster and faster to a supreme moment of union with the Divine. Each dancer turns full 360-degree circles, experiencing the Qur'an's teaching that "wheresoever you turn, there is the face of God" (II, 115). Here we have

The Tree of Life

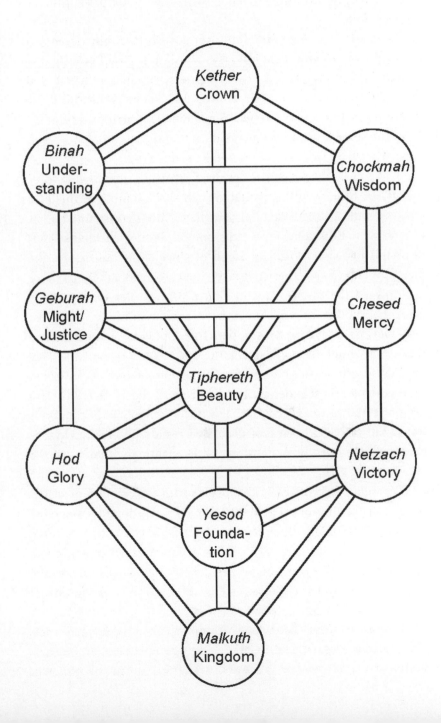

clearly the shape of the Hoop—the whirling—and the shape of the Tree—the upright bodies together with the hands passing grace from up to down.

The tantric teachings of Hinduism describe the fully developed self with a Hoop-and-Tree model. According to Hindu tantra, the human body has a set of energy centers, which are distributed along the spine. These energy centers are called *chakras*, from the Sanskrit word meaning "wheel." Since tantric practitioners understand the spine as a Tree cognate, tantra represents wholeness with these wheels or Hoops in alignment on the Tree.

The San Bushmen of the Kalahari practice a remarkable technology for healing and spiritual growth that exemplifies the Tree growing within the Hoop. This practice is the *!kia*-healing dance. (The exclamation point represents one of the four clicking sounds in their language.) Within a Hoop of singers and musicians, the practitioners of !kia experience a spiritual ascension along the Tree axis toward the divine. During !kia a practitioner may perform cures, handle fire or walk on it, have x-ray vision, see over great distances, or converse with supernatural powers. Like the good shaman or Buddhist bodhisattva, the !kia master ascends the Tree for the benefit of the community. The point is not so much in experiencing transcendence, but in bringing back its fruits. If a person were just to experience !kia without doing any healing, this would be seen as a misuse of these !kia-related powers.[14] Here as elsewhere the Tree grows within the Hoop for the benefit of the Hoop.

Contemporary Wiccan ritual begins with the creation of sacred space, the "casting of a circle." This is typically done by someone using a ceremonial implement to describe a Hoop in the space around the practitioners. Within this Hoop, Wiccan practitioners use the Tree axis to bring about healing through rituals such as the "Tree of Life" and the "Cone of Power" and by "drawing down" spiritual energy from above.[15]

Chinese Taoism and Confucianism have influenced each other over the years, and in many ways complement each other. Neither tradition was or is an exclusive tradition in the sense of, say, Christianity that at times has considered itself the one true way. Taoism with its well-known Hoop symbol of yin and yang, emphasizes the Hoop attributes of relationship, receptivity, and flow. Confucius taught self-cultivation or self-development toward becoming a "profound person" (*chun-tzu*), or sage. Achieving this goal requires the accumulation of knowledge, skills, insight, and wisdom. These are all ascending levels on the Tree axis. Confucius grounded his teaching in the *roots* of the past. It could well be said that for China, Taoism is the Hoop to the Tree of Confucianism.

In Native American Pueblo creation stories, humans emerged from a succession of three (or four) underworlds to the present world. Each world is a Hoop; the route of emergence to increasing wholeness is a Tree or Tree cognate.[16] For example, the Zuni people emerged from the "Four Wombs of the World," which were a series of caverns in the lower regions. The lowest of these was so dark and small that living conditions eventually became crowded and unbearable. Two children of the divine "Holder of the Paths of Life" came to guide the people, and led them up a Ladder (Tree cognate) to the roof of the first cave. There, using a Hoop of wood with a magic knife attached to its center, they made a hole for the people to emerge. Eventually the second cave likewise became crowded, and the people asked for help. The divine children/priests led the people up another Ladder and through a hole into the third world, lighter than the previous two, and eventually into the fourth world, where for the first time the people saw the light of the sun.[17] Here the Zuni established their home in this world at "the middle place," the center of the world. Similarly, when the Hopi third world was destroyed by flood, the survivors emerged upward through hollow reeds to find the fourth world.[18] The ancestors of the Acoma people climbed up on a pine tree.[19]

The architecture of sacred space for the Pueblo people reflects this Hoop-and-Tree pattern of emergence toward wholeness. The Pueblo *kiva* is an underground ceremonial chamber whose floor plan is a Hoop mandala. In the floor is a small hole, the *sipapu*, leading down into the first underworld. The floor mandala is the second world of the emergence story. The raised seating ledge represents the third world. The ladder (Tree cognate) pokes through the roof opening and leads up to the fourth, our present, world. Frank Waters, an expert on pueblo ceremonialism, says, "The kiva is not only an architectural symbol of the physical universe. The universe . . . is itself but a structural symbol of the mystical soul-form of all creation. And both are duplicated in man himself."[20] Like the Buddhist stupa, the pueblo kiva is an architectural expression of Hoop-and-Tree wholeness, the "shape of all shapes."

Someone once asked Sigmund Freud to say what a healthy person ought to be able to do and do well. Freud's answer was pithy: "to love and to work" ("*leiben und arbeiten*").[21] Now if we understand "to work" in the sense of working *toward* something, then Freud's definition of health was the Hoop and the Tree: the Hoop of relationship and the Tree of aspiration.

Carl Jung was even more explicit. Jung analyzed thousands of dreams in his lifetime and digested an almost unimaginable amount of the world's literature on mysticism, religion, and philosophy. One of the fruits of this prodigious labor was Jung's concept of the archetype of "the Self": an innate model of psychological and spiritual wholeness.

Jung found that images of the Self appear universally in dreams, visions, active imagination, and works of art, particularly spiritual or religious art. What does this symbol of psycho-spiritual wholeness look like? The Hoop and the Tree. Jung said, "If a mandala [Hoop] may be described as a symbol of the Self seen in cross section, then the tree would represent a profile view of it: the Self depicted as a process of growth."[22]

In the 1940s psychologist Andras Angyal examined the Hoop and the Tree using the terms *homonomy* and *autonomy*. Homonomy is the motivation to be in harmony with "superindividual units"—the family, the gang, the social group, nature, God, an ethical world order. We wish to share and participate in something regarded as being greater than our individual selves, and so we seek union with these larger units. Autonomy is the self-assertive tendency that aims at controlling or dominating the surroundings or mastering some object in order to satisfy our own needs. It aims at achievement and conquest. Angyal argued that all human behavior is co-determined by these two key tendencies.[23]

Contemporary General Systems Theory studies the principles of organization in natural systems. Systems Theory says that "there is interdependence among the systems—as with points along a net, when one is displaced, all others suffer some displacement."[24] This is the Hoop of Relationship. In fact, as we shall see later, it is an almost perfect description of a prime Hoop image: the image of Indra's Net. Systems theory also gives us Tree hierarchy: "Evolution appears to drive toward the superposition of system upon system in a continuous hierarchy. . . . Organization in nature comes to resemble a complex, multilevel pyramid, with many relatively simple systems at the bottom and a few (and ultimately one) complex system(s) at the top."[25] In other words, Systems Theory says that reality is described by a Tree hierarchy of nested systems that exhibit Hoop interdependence: the Hoop-and-Tree model of wholeness.

All these world wisdom traditions, ancient and modern, tell different versions of an eternal human story. It is the story about the path to psychological and spiritual wholeness, also called "enlightenment" or "connection with the Divine." Each story is an approximation, a different facet or cloudy window on the ineffable, expressed in images familiar and helpful to its given audience. Although the versions differ somewhat in details—the number and location of Hoops for example—they all point to an underlying Hoop-and-Tree pattern.

Perhaps the reason the world's wisdom traditions offer so many examples of the Hoop-and-Tree pattern of wholeness is because even the helix of our DNA carries the shape of an extended Hoop spiraling around a Tree axis. The pattern is coded in the very basis of life.

The Hoop and the Tree in Our Own Lives

This brief sampling of the world's wisdom makes abundantly clear that the Hoop and Tree pattern appears all over the world and throughout history as a model of wholeness. What does this model have to offer our lives today?

In headlines from Bosnia to Belfast, Cambodia to Cyprus, from the inner city as well as from the Middle East, we read of the terrible consequences of conflict. Human beings, otherwise normal, view their neighbors as somehow "other," less than human, and do unspeakable things to them. Each party to the conflict sees the other as evil in some way. Yet like all of us, every participant in the conflict wants to be happy and avoid suffering. Each one of us wants to be seen, heard, felt, and respected as who we truly are.

One way of looking at these inter-racial, intercultural, inter-religious, and international conflicts is that they are the external manifestations of different mythic systems colliding with each other. Each group has its own mythic system, which is simply to say that each group has its own way of speaking about that which is so profound that it cannot be put into words directly. The outer ways are in conflict, where the inner realities are in concert.

So it is time to listen for what might be called a *metamyth*, a myth about myths that will help us learn to live with all our amazing diversity. We need a way to penetrate all the external confusion and discover what we have in common: the underlying deep structure of our existence.

The Hoop and the Tree may or may not be *the* metamyth. It does help us see that our own spiritual paths are not so unique or separate from other spiritual paths. In any event it can arouse readiness and expectancy, can whet our appetites and sharpen our ears for whatever metamyth is emerging. Whatever the meta-myth may be, it will have to be couched in the metaphors that all humans share, metaphors of nature like the Hoop and the Tree.

Today we are also witnessing massive environmental destruction. Individuals and corporations who view the natural environment as "other" and who are unconscious of their interdependence with the natural environment, or who imagine the earth is infinitely abundant, siphon the vitality out of the earth, our home, and fill it with toxins. Yet every person loves life, at least to the extent of not wanting harm to come to themselves or to their loved ones.

The Hoop-and-Tree shape of wholeness shows clearly that to be fully developed we must become ecological beings. True psychological and spiritual healing involves establishing not only right relationships with other people but also right relationships with all of the ecosystem, and, ultimately, with all of existence. All psychology is ecopsychology. The Hoop and Tree shape of wholeness says that at our best we are all ecological beings and we all belong here. We are home.

Finally, as individuals we are each trying to live our own lives as best we can—trying to find fulfillment, to create happiness, to cope with suffering, to discover our unique gifts and bring them to fruition. Yet we often struggle to understand one another.

The Hoop-and-Tree model can help us as individuals understand how to live lives of balance, wholeness, and fulfillment. It offers a "gyrocompass" to each of us on our own Hero's/Heroine's Journey. It can also help us to see and appreciate others as who they truly are, and help us to understand and value both masculine and feminine ways of knowing.

As a counselor and teacher I have had the privilege of accompanying individuals on part of their personal journeys to wholeness. I've seen how the Hoop and the Tree has helped them. In my own life, I have felt the validity of the Hoop and Tree in my body as I practice the moving meditation of T'ai-chi and the sitting meditation of Zen. I too have used the Hoop and the Tree as an internal compass to orient me when I am facing decisions.

Hundreds of years before Black Elk experienced his healing vision, a European Christian "shaman" discovered, like many of us today, that he had "lost his way" in the middle of life's journey. Like many of us, he embarked on a journey of self-discovery. He began to question everything, inner and outer. His psychological and spiritual explorations eventually led through the lowest, most vile expressions of human nature to the highest aspirations of communion with the Divine.

Dante Alighieri expressed his vision in *The Divine Comedy*, a work that is perhaps the supreme expression of the Middle Ages and is certainly one of the great poetic achievements of all time. In Dante's vision the shape of wholeness takes the shape of Hoops-on-a-Mountain, in other words, Hoops-on-a-Tree-cognate, the "shape of all shapes."

Dante's vision begins with a descent into the lower region of the whole universe, the Inferno, which consists of a deep pit, an anti-mountain, with Hoops of circular levels stepping lower and lower. After surviving the terrors of the lower regions Dante climbs the upward—reaching the mountain of Purgatory. This too has a structure of Hoops (each one a ledge or cornice) rising higher and higher on a Tree cognate. The last section of the journey ends with Dante centered and balanced: whole. His image of wholeness is a supreme integration of instinct and intellect, Hoop and Tree. It is a wheel on an axle, like a gyroscope: "in a great flash of light . . . I could feel my being turned—instinct and intellect balanced equally/ as in a wheel whose motion nothing jars—by the Love that moves the Sun and the other stars."[26]

This sense of balance and wholeness is available to each of us, if we can only find our way through to the Hoop and Tree of our own being. The trick is to use the Hoop and the Tree as a learning device and then be willing to abandon it when the time comes. The Hoop and the Tree is a way to explore that psyche, soul, or little *s* self that is ultimately only a glimmer of the great mysterious. Though the Hoop and the Tree is a robust and fecund metaphor, it is not "the Truth." As the poet William Butler Yeats once said, human beings cannot know the truth, but they can embody it.[27] Regardless of all the wonderful images and teachings from the world's wisdom traditions, the ultimate value of the Hoop and the Tree comes when you feel its resonance in your own being. This book is about finding that resonance.

Can It Really Help?

The Hoop and the Tree is a mental model or image of wholeness. How much influence on our lives can a mere image have?

Actually, images have a huge influence. The images in our minds become, as the Buddhist *Dhammapada* says, the forerunners of all things.[28] A Zen proverb sums this up: "Sow a thought, reap an action. Sow an action, reap a habit. Sow a habit, reap a character. Sow a character, reap a destiny."

Positive images or mental models can move us away from dysfunction and toward health. Numerous techniques of psychotherapy work by helping the client change deeply held images or mental models. Various schools of therapy give these images different names—*cognitive constructs, schemas, cognitive templates, core beliefs, rational* and *irrational beliefs*—but they all refer to deeply held images about the self and about what is possible. Richard Bandler and John Grinder found that therapeutic "wizards" such as Fritz Perls, Virginia Satir, and Milton Erikson all shared a common underlying approach: "They introduce changes in their clients' *models* which allow their clients more options in their behavior" [emphasis added].[29]

Images influence whole societies as well as individuals. In *The Image of the Future*, Fred Polak examined cultures from ancient Greece to the present. He found "the positive image of the future at work in every instance of the flowering of a culture, and weakened images of the future as a primary factor in the decay of cultures.... The potential strength of a culture [can] be measured by measuring the intensity and energy of its images of the future."[30] Without a mental model of the future, societies will stagnate and decay. As Polak's translator Elise Boulding says, "You can't work for something you can't imagine."

Setting Off

So follow me more deeply into the story of the Hoop and the Tree. Parts of this story are as ancient as life itself; parts are as contemporary as modern science. All of it is about you . . . and within you.

To begin, come with me to a place in the woods. It's not near and it's not far. We walk there just before sunset along a path that slopes gently upward. The air is cool but not cold. And we find our way easily by the light of sunset filtering through the trees. We come to a grassy clearing where there are little tussocks and smooth weathered trunks of old fallen trees, comfortable to sit against. We sit with some friends in a circle, and at the center of the circle we build a small fire.

Make yourself comfortable. Feel the warmth. Smell the sweet smoke. Hear the fire pop and crackle. Watch the sparks drifting up to the dusking sky. We look around and see against the immense field of stars the dark pointy tips of the pine trees encircling us like the points of a crown.

Here is where our ancestors have come, generation upon generation—to circular clearings in the trees like this one, to rings of stone on the plains and on the grassy places, to rings of people under the night sky. We are humans, of *humus* the earth. The name Adam comes from the Hebrew for "clay" or "earth" (*adhamah*). We all are of this earth. We are all indigenous people. We all belong here. And this wilderness is the home from which we all came, generations ago. It is our mother and our father and our teacher. And our oldest human tradition is to live in balance with it. And thus for thousands of years, we have been coming to the natural world.

Our eyes follow the trail of smoke as it drifts up and disappears into the immensity of space. Like our ancestors before us, we feel small, filled with awe, and yet privileged to witness this life in its magnificence. We seek some way to heal our sense of insignificance and some way to honor and connect with that ultimately unnamable which fills us with awe. We seek the Hoop and the Tree.

There are many mythologies in the world, many ways to follow the Hoop and the Tree. These are not just old stories but keys for opening the door of this very moment.

Take as your image the Hoop of Communion and the Tree of the Cross; or take the Wheel of Dharma and the Bo Tree; or take the Kabbalistic Hoops of the Sefirot and the Tree of Life;

or take the Islamic dervish dance; or take the yin yang Hoop of Taoism and the Confucian aspiration to be a profound person; or take the Hoop of all our relations and the shaman's Tree; or take the psychological Hoop of relationship and the Tree of aspiration with its psychological roots. Sit with a Hoop of friends around a fire and watch the sparks and smoke drift up to the infinite night sky, as the fire's ashes crumble back into the earth from which we all came. These are all hints. To use a Zen image, these are all "fingers pointing at the moon," pointing at the truth. They are hints at how to live an ecological life, at home in the universe, with both wisdom and compassion. Ultimately the only Hoop and Tree that matters is the Hoop and the Tree of your own unfolding in the world.

The Taoist yin-yang symbol, surrounded by the trigrams of the I Ching arranged in a Hoop.

2

All My Relations: The Hoop

There is no object so soft, but it makes a hub for
the wheeled universe.

—Walt Whitman, "Song of Myself"

To turn, turn will be our delight
Till by turning and turning we come 'round right.

—"Simple Gifts," a Shaker hymn

MARK* WAS A TALENTED ENGINEER, considered by his vice president
to be "one of the smartest men in the company." Mark also possessed rare expertise essential for the company's success in a key
project. Yet Mark was about to lose his job. Why? He had such
poor interpersonal skills that the people who reported to him were
rebelling. When I got to know Mark better through our counseling
sessions, I found out that he also had endured a painful divorce and
was struggling in his relationship with his college-age son. Though
Mark had highly developed Tree skills and intelligence, he was failing at relationship. He lacked the Hoop.

The sense of the Hoop being wide or small is most immediate as we feel our own heart—not the physical heart, but our

---

* The names of all clients mentioned in this book have been changed.

heart-sense—expand with compassion toward others or constrict in self-focused pain. It is the practice of the widening the Hoop that begins the end of loneliness and alienation. The fully developed Hoop connects us not only with other people, but also as the "Hoop of many Hoops" connects us with the wider "ecological circle" of the rest of the universe.

A couple of images from traditional teaching stories epitomize this broader sense of relationship.

The *Ramayana* is one of the two great epics of India, occupying a place in Indian civilization roughly equivalent to the Christian Bible plus all of Shakespeare. It is a long, involved story, but the central theme concerns demonic forces that have ravaged the earth and the efforts of the hero Rama to rid the earth of the demons. The demon king has also abducted Rama's wife, and to make matters worse, proposes to eat her if she does not agree to marry him. Rama is an incarnation of the world-protecting Hindu god Vishnu; his wife is an incarnation of the goddess Lakshmi and a manifestation of the earth Herself.

Near the end of the epic there is a great battle between the forces of good and the entire demon army. Rama leads the forces of good. He is assisted by his devoted half brother Lakshmana. What others make up the forces of good? Not humans but monkeys and bears. The monkey king and the bear king lead their whole armies against the forces of evil and endure horrible suffering. In one gruesome phase of the battle a powerful demon warrior manages to slaughter the entire monkey army and the entire bear army. Only after a prodigious effort to secure some healing herbs, which involves carrying a mountain over the entire Indian subcontinent, are the animals brought back to life.

Rama grieves over all the suffering and is afraid he might lose his animal friends forever next time. He proposes to them that they all go home. He will fight on alone. They refuse to leave, in a very moving speech acknowledging the Hoop of Relationship. Hanuman, the great monkey, says, "Dear Rama, we are indeed your old good friends from long ago, and your companions of ancient days come here to help you. We are your forebears. We are your ancestors the animals, and you are our child Humanity."[1]

In the course of the Greek myth of Psyche and Eros, the human woman named Psyche becomes separated from her husband Eros, the god of love. She yearns for him, but to find him again, Psyche must succeed at several seemingly impossible tasks. One of these is to sort a whole mountain of mixed seeds—wheat, barley, poppy, flax, and many others—into separate piles, and to do so before the end of the day or die. Another is to gather some of the golden fleece of ferocious wild rams . . . and again to do it by the end of the day or die. As a mortal woman Psyche could never accomplish these tasks on her own. But relatives outside the human realm miraculously appear to help her. A colony of ants sorts the seeds for her, and a bunch of green reeds at the river's edge tell her how she can gather the fleece in safety. One of the messages of this story is that the human psyche needs relationship with the realm of animals and plants in order to become whole.

"No Man Is an Island, Entire of Itself"

—John Donne, *Devotions*, XVII

The most immediate aspect of the Hoop, however, is our relationship with other people. There is plenty of evidence that we need this aspect of the Hoop. For example, scientific research has shown that:

- People who lack strong relationships have two to three times the risk of early death, regardless of whether they smoke, drink alcoholic beverages, or exercise regularly.
- Terminal cancer strikes socially isolated people more often than those who have close personal relationships.
- Pregnant women under stress and without supportive relationships have three times more complications than pregnant women who suffer from the same stress but have strong social support.
- Social isolation is a major risk factor contributing to coronary disease, comparable to physiological factors such as diet, cigarette smoking, obesity, and lack of physical activity.[2]

Even in terms of how our bodies function, we are designed to connect with other people—through copulation, for example, and through the production of mother's milk. Human infants are born preferring sights and sounds that facilitate social responsiveness, and the ones that are touched and massaged gain weight more rapidly and develop faster neurologically than those without such contact.[3]

As babies we begin to develop our Hoop though our relationship with our principal caregiver, usually our mother or father. Psychologists refer to the strong bond that occurs in this relationship as *bonding* or *attachment*. When the parent is emotionally present, by being sensitive to what the child is doing or feeling and by responding appropriately, the child usually develops *secure attachment*.[4] Psychologist John Bowlby has looked at a huge amount of attachment research, with both human and animal subjects. He found that secure attachment as an infant not only predicts social competence as a young child, but also is essential to the health of the adult the child grows to be.

Insecure attachment, on the other hand, often foreshadows problems later in life, including chronic fear, depression, inappropriate aggression, and anxiety.[5] Psychologists have also found that severe *deprivation* of attachment tends to result in adults who are themselves incapable of forming attachment, and who have a higher than average likelihood of being abusive.[6] Much of the violence and suffering in our world today results from such broken Hoops.

The Interpersonal Ring of the Hoop: The Social Atom

A useful way to think about our relationships with other people is through a psychological Hoop concept called the "social atom." The social atom graphically depicts our sense that connections between people involve a factor of closeness or distance: significant people are "close" to us, others more peripheral, or distant.

The social atom diagram resembles a set of concentric widening Hoops, like the ripples from a stone dropped in a pond. To chart your own social atom, draw four concentric circles on a sheet of paper. Write your own name at the center, where the stone would have plunked into the pond. Write the names of the people "closest" or most important to you in the band between the inner-most circle and the next circle outward. These might be the names of your spouse, your children, your most intimate friends. This is your "inner circle."

As long as you can maintain your relationships with your inner circle, you will feel "at home" in society.[7] If one of these relation-ships were to change or vanish—for example, if your spouse or best friend were to die or move away—you would feel less than whole. You would go through a period of mourning and readjustment, trying to reestablish social equilibrium in your life.

The importance of having an intact social atom is often most evident in the lives of our elders. With illness and death of friends and loved ones a frequent occurrence, elderly people often develop gaps in their social atoms more quickly than the gaps can be filled with new relationships of equivalent quality. Sometimes an other-wise healthy elder will fail quickly within a few months or weeks after losing a lifetime partner from the inner circle.

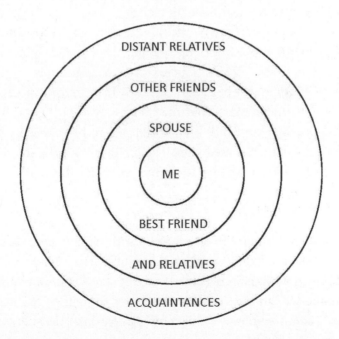

In your social atom diagram, in the next band outward from your inner circle, put the names of other friends and more distant relatives. These are the people you would be sad to lose, but whose role in your life could be filled by other people relatively easily. Proceeding outward, put names in the bands farther and farther from the center as you feel the named people are less and less essential for your psychosocial equilibrium. Often, after doing this exercise, people discover they want to change how they are living their lives—to spend more time and energy with those dearest to them or otherwise to "mend the Hoop."

Mark the engineer made some changes. Fortunately Mark was not only bright but also motivated and willing to work hard to master the art of relationship. His own emotions had been a mystery to him. He devoted himself to solving that mystery. With some coaching he explored the messages sent by his body language. He began to liberate his voice. He even thought up the idea of using his voice mail to hear how he sounded to others. In the safe Hoop of a counseling relationship he developed awareness of his own emotions and sensitivity to the emotions of others. With these skills he began to repair his relationships.

Thanks to Mark's hard work this story has a happy ending. Mark's immediate boss and the people who worked for Mark reported that Mark became much easier to communicate with. Mark kept his job and began to flourish. In a follow-up session several months later Mark told me that his relationship with his son had improved, and that he was engaged to be married. Mark began with a well-developed Tree. His life improved greatly when he learned how to bring his Hoop into balance with it.

The Wider Hoop

The Hoop is not limited to relationship with other human beings. In March 1989 the Exxon tanker *Valdez* spilled 11.2 million gallons of crude oil into Alaska's pristine Prince William Sound, polluting not only the sea but also over 2,400 miles of shoreline.[8] A study of the nearby communities of Valdez and Cordova after the spill found that most of the 117 randomly selected subjects had suffered as a result of the spill, particularly from depression and post-traumatic shock.[9] The ecological Hoop had been wounded.

Lakota (Sioux) medicine man Lame Deer describes how we fit into this wider Hoop:

> To our way of thinking the Indian's symbol is the circle, the hoop. Nature wants things to be round. The bodies of human beings and animals have no corners. With us the circle stands for the togetherness of people who sit with one another around the campfire, relatives and friends united in peace while the pipe passes from hand to hand. The camp in which every tipi had its place was also a ring. The tipi was a ring in which people sat in a circle and all the families in the village were in turn circles within a larger circle, part of the larger hoop which was the seven campfires of the Sioux, representing one nation. The nation was only a part of the universe, in itself circular and made of the earth, which is round, of the sun, which is round, of the stars, which are round. The moon, the horizon, the rainbow—circles within circles within circles, with no beginning and no end.
>
> To us this is beautiful and fitting, symbol and reality at the same time, expressing the harmony of life and nature. Our circle is timeless, flowing; it is new life emerging from death—life winning out over death.[10]

Spider Woman's Web

The Hopi people, among other Native American peoples, visualize our relationship with this wider Hoop through the image of a spider's web with its concentric linked Hoops. Spider Woman, the Earth Mother, weaves a Hoop-shaped web that links all of us together—humans, animals, mountains, trees, rivers—everything. Just as with a normal spider's web, if you touch any part of the web, the whole web will quiver.[11]

Similarly, Hindus and Buddhists visualize all of existence as *Indra's Net*, a great net like a fisherman's net, where every knot is a bright diamond whose facets reflect every other diamond knot. Each knot is a being. You are a knot; I am one. All beings are as surely and powerfully linked with each other as the knots in a net. The ever-so-slightest touch on one knot of a stretched net makes the whole net vibrate.[12]

Modern General Systems Theory describes the universe in almost identical terms: there is interdependence among the systems—as with points along a net, when one is displaced, all others suffer some displacement. Even our everyday language acknowledges how we are all woven together in this net or web when we speak of the "*fabric* of life."

Psychological Web, The "Field"

In all of psychology the concept that comes closest to the image of Spider Woman's Web and Indra's Net is the concept of the relationship *field*. A field is a domain where something can influence something else. We can't observe fields directly, but we know they exist because we can measure their effects. We all know the field of gravity exists, though we can't see it or touch it. The early theorists of Gestalt psychology suggested that certain emotions could be located in the field of relationship between a landscape and a person.[13] Painters such as van Gogh, with his black-green cypresses, his sulfur and lemon-gold wheat fields, amplify the emotion in this relationship and help us to see it and feel it.

Gestalt psychotherapy says that in fact there is never any isolated person or organism available to study or treat. There is only the interaction of the person or organism with its environment. We know that people behave differently depending on whom they are with and also on the environment they're in.[14] A church, a baseball stadium, an office, a forest—each evokes different sets of behavior. Every "psychological" problem occurs in a field that has social, physiological, psychological, and physical components. A key text in Gestalt therapy says, "No matter how we theorize about impulses, drives, etc., it is always to such an interacting field that we are referring, and not to an isolated animal."[15]

Experimental Evidence

> The non-human environment, far from being of
> little or no account to human personality develop-
> ment, constitutes one of the most basically impor-
> tant ingredients of human psychological existence.
>
> —Harold Searles, psychoanalyst[16]

Contemporary psychology is beginning to develop experimental evidence of our psychological interconnectedness with the earth.[17] One example is the indication that environmental damage contributes to depression, as in the case of the Exxon *Valdez*.

We know that in the United States, depression is the number one reason why people seek mental health services. We also know that with each new generation, the rate of depression is increasing and the disorder is striking earlier. There is evidence for this increase in countries around the world.[18]

When a healthy person suffers a real difficulty such as loss or bereavement in a relationship, the healthy response usually includes intense sadness or grief, and often some anger. These same feelings, when ongoing and unresolved, characterize depression. Since our relationship with the earth is being damaged at an alarming rate every day, and since this damage is unresolved, our increasing rate of depression may simply represent a healthy response to our increasing loss of relationship with the earth.

Here are two typical recent headlines: "Fishery Collapse 'Confirms Silent Spring Pesticide Prophecy,'" "Climate Discruption Is Now Locked In. The Next Moves Will Be Crucial."[19] As a friend of mine says, "If you're not depressed now, you're in denial."

While disruption of relationship with the ecological Hoop promotes illness, restoration of this relationship promotes health. Various studies have linked relationship to the ecological Hoop with lowered levels of job stress, imaginative ability in children, and quality of life.[20] One extensive study of postoperative gall bladder patients showed that patients whose rooms looked out on trees recovered faster than patients whose view was of a brick wall.[21] Psychology is also beginning to discover that when someone works to restore the environment, or simply experiences the natural world, he or she experiences some kind of personal healing.[22] Anyone who has gone for a walk along a deserted seashore, breathing the brisk salt air, hearing the thundering and scouring of the surf, the plaintive mewling of shorebirds, knows this firsthand.

The Ecological "Ring" of the Hoop: The Ecological Atom

The Hoops of the social atom can readily be extended throughout the whole field of Spider Woman's Web. This extended version is an "ecological atom": the minimum number of relationships required for you to feel in social *and* ecological equilibrium, at home in society *and* in the world. In the ecological atom the ripples widen to the furthest reaches of the universe.

The ecological atom and the social atom are actually concentric and overlapping. Perhaps the air you breathe is as close to you as your spouse, and your favorite spot in nature as necessary as your old childhood friend. If you are just beginning to think about the ecological atom, though, it may be easiest to start by drawing your "inner circle" and your "ecological circle" separately.

Nanao Sakaki praises our communion with the ecological atom in his poem "A Love Letter":[23]

> Within a circle of one meter
> You sit, pray, and sing.
>
> Within a shelter ten meters large
> You sleep well, rain sounds a lullaby.
>
> Within a field a hundred meters large
> Raise rice and goats.
>
> Within a valley a thousand meters large
> Gather firewood, water, wild vegetables and Amanitas.

Within a forest ten kilometers large
Play with raccoons, hawks,
Poison snakes and butterflies.

Mountainous country Shinano
A hundred kilometers large
Where someone lives leisurely, they say.

Within a circle ten thousand kilometers large
Go to see the southern coral reef in summer
Or winter drifting ices in the sea of Okhotsk.

Within a circle ten thousand kilometers large
Walking somewhere on the earth.

Within a circle one hundred thousand kilometers large
Swimming in the sea of shooting stars.

Within a circle a million kilometers large
Upon the spaced-out yellow mustard blossoms
The moon in the east, the sun west.

Within a circle ten billion kilometers large
Pop far out of the solar system mandala.

Within a circle ten thousand light years large
The Galaxy full blooming in spring.

Within a circle one billion light years large
Andromeda is melting away into snowing cherry flowers.

Now within a circle ten billion light years large
All thoughts of time, space are burnt away
There again you sit, pray and sing
You sit, pray and sing

Each of us is the center of set of widening hoops, like the rims of nested baskets or like widening ripples on a pond. Begin with the "inner circle" of your social atom—your spouse, significant other, best friend, parents, children. Are each of these relationships intact and in good order? Or is there some sore spot or unfinished business to attend to? Make note of what needs to be done to bring each relationship into balance. Ring by ring move outward through your social atom and through your "ecological circle."

Expand your awareness just a little bit to include the life-forms within a radius of a few feet. Perhaps there are friends nearby, perhaps some flowers or plants or a family pet. Notice your connection with these beings. You are related to them and they to you.

Now let your awareness expand a bit more. In a wider hoop around you there may be more people, other animals. If you are outdoors, there may be some small wild animals, a tree, some rocks, a body of water. Notice your connection with these beings. Let your awareness expand even wider. Be aware of birds singing, of shrubs, grass, and all that your circle encompasses. Though we are talking about hoops, the hoop is really a sphere expanding upward to include the air and downward to include the creatures under the earth— worms and microorganisms—that keep our soils healthy and allow us to grow food to eat. Notice your relatedness, your interdependence with the earth and the air and the creatures of the earth and the air. Allow yourself to feel supported by all this; take a deep breath.

Now let the radius of your awareness expand even more. You are aware of the geography surrounding you, the local watershed, river bottom, rock point, seashore, and all the green-growing, free-flying, creeping-crawling, running, stalking, nesting, breeding inhabitants. All are related to you, and you to all. Some of these you will feel more attuned to than others, but all are part of your life. Notice the rich texture and variety of life and beingness all around you.

Many wisdom traditions offer formal practices for deepening our relationship to this Hoop of all beings. Buddhism teaches a "loving kindness" meditation, a rigorous practice that expands your Hoop of relatedness eventually to include even your enemies. One of the Buddhist bodhisattva vows is to attain enlightenment not just for yourself but for all beings. In a Native American medicine-wheel practice you formally honor all the blessings you have received from all the realms of existence: mineral, vegetable, animal, human, and spirit. You might express gratitude to the mineral realm for things like the savor of salt on your food, for having your thirst quenched by water, for the silicon that makes your computer work, and for how your heart leaps at the sight of snow-covered mountain peaks.[24]

In working with the ecological atom, as with the social atom, notice how much you would miss these relationships if they were not there. Further, as with the social atom, consider whether your relationship with each is intact and in good order. Have you been reducing the pollution you contribute to the air we all breathe, to the water we all drink? Have you planted trees, tended a garden, built a compost pile, given thanks for a sunset? Here again, people often discover they want to make some changes in how they are living their lives.

There are three important things to remember in this practice: 1) Be sure to take some action whenever you realize that something is needed to heal or develop a relationship. 2) If you feel depressed or guilty that you can't heal everything right away, remember that the world is infinite and we are finite. We can do only what we can do. Pick something and make a start. 3) Be sure to appreciate the nourishment from all the relationships in your Hoop that *are* working. This is what gives you energy and heals you.

Our immersion in relationship is like the immersion of a fish in water. We move through a field of relationship, living it, breathing it. The great twelfth-century Christian theologian, physician, and artist Hildegard of Bingen wrote, "Everything that is in the heavens, on the earth, and under the earth, is penetrated with connectedness, is penetrated with relatedness."[25] Our interdependence with the earth for air, water, and food is so immediate that we may not even see it, we may take it for granted. Yet we are not only sustained as infants by our relationships, but also throughout our lives we live and breathe relationships, whether we are aware of them or not. As Zen master and psychotherapist George Bowman says, "Life is nothing but movement in relationship."[26]

In a basic way you can experience this by simply holding your breath and discovering how long you can survive without an intimate relationship with the exhalations of trees and grass.

The wisdom traditions teach that relationship with the Hoop of all things is essential not only for mere survival, but indeed for psychological and spiritual wholeness. Here is how Zen Master Dogen summarizes the path to enlightenment: "To study the buddha way is to study the self. To study the self is to forget the self. To forget the self is to be actualized [enlightened] by myriad things."[27] In the *Bhagavad Gita*, an influential Hindu scripture, Lord Krishna says that the whole person is one who sees "the Self in every creature and all creation in the Self"(6:29).[28]

All My Relations

How do you stand in relationship to Spider Woman's Web, Indra's Net, the "field," the Ecological Atom? The question "How do you stand in relation to these many realms?" is the ancient meaning of the Hopi word *hakomi*. The modern meaning is "Who are you?" In essence the ancient and modern meanings are the same question. Who are you on the Hoop dimension?

A few years ago the *Utne Reader* magazine brought a group of people of diverse backgrounds together for a series of intimate conversations about life. The first meeting began with open-ended introductions. A woman named Jeanette introduced herself by saying that "on her father's line, her family came from the mountains of northern Okanagan [British Columbia, Canada] and had been there for several thousand years. Officially their role was to protect the life of the community of animals and plants and spirits that were there, and Jeanette shared that responsibility. And her mother's line were river people, which meant Jeanette also shared responsibility to protect the river and the watershed. Then she talked about all their names, how their names were indicative of their jobs protecting or living in that place, and as part of that traditional community. So she talked about community not only as where she came from in geographic terms, but the fact that all the ancestors are still in that place, and that the ancestors are considered part of the community. They are not gone; they are still there and they are still part of the community, and they all have names and identities. She talked for 45 minutes in answer to the question of who am I, and she didn't even get to her own work as an artist and writer and community organizer until about 40 minutes into it."[29]

For Jeanette to feel fully healthy and in balance, her whole Hoop of relationships—both her "inner circle" and her "ecological circle"—has to be intact. Otherwise she would feel as out of sorts as she would if a dear friend had died or left her.

This is what it is like to live with full consciousness of the field, the Web, the Hoop: to live as companions to the whole of creation. This includes companionship with the diversity of humankind—of race, gender, culture, and lifeways—and with the diversity of all the other realms—mineral, vegetable, animal, and spirit. The ecological atom includes a circle or a place in the Hoop for each. This is what is acknowledged and honored in a Lakota prayer that is said whenever crossing a threshold to enter into the world, as when leaving one's home for the first time in the morning or when exiting a sweat lodge. The prayer is, in its entirety, "All my relations."

Building and Maintaining Relationships

> He drew a circle that shut me out—
> Heretic, rebel, a thing to flout.
> Ah, but Love and I had the wit to win:
> We drew a circle that took him in!
>
> —Edwin Markham, "Outwitted"[30]

How do we nurture our relationship with all our relations? Since we are already all related through Spider Woman's Web / Indra's Net, nurturing a relationship is not a question of creating something anew, but rather of manifesting and honoring what is latently present.

We know from psychology how important it is to develop relationships with those areas in our own psyche that we have neglected or abandoned. We also know from psychology a fair amount about how to develop and maintain healthy relationships with other people. We know less, however, about relationships with the nonhuman realms of the Hoop. But we *do* know that too often these relationships are neglected or abandoned. We also know that the dominant industrial/commercial culture generally ignores the Divine immanent in Spider Woman's Web. So we have work to do in rebuilding right relationship.

Psychology teaches that if we take any relationship for granted and don't work at it, the relationship usually decays. But relationships don't have to decay; they can grow. Instead of being depressed or feeling guilty about the ecological crisis, for example, we can transform our guilt by working on our relationship with the ecosystem. Instead of just worrying about wars or violent crime, we can work on building relationships with those who seem different from ourselves. At any ring of the social atom or the ecological atom we can actively work on developing relationship.

How does one build a relationship? We know that having good relationships with others and having a good relationship with oneself go hand in hand. We also know that to build any relationship it takes four things. The first two are:

1) Attention to the other, true listening, which requires:
2) Stilling of the self (i.e., quieting the ego, relaxing and letting go of the need to talk, to press one's point of view)

Attention is the core practice of relationship. You can't relate even to yourself if you are not aware of yourself. One of the joys of being in the first stage of a romantic relationship is that someone else is finally and truly paying attention to you and who you are. Attention is also the way to begin a relationship with all the rings of the Hoop. Simone Weil, the modern French mystic, tells us that prayer itself consists of attention: "It is the orientation of all the attention of which the soul is capable toward God."[31]

Before an orchestra begins a performance, the concertmaster sounds an A on the violin, and all the other musicians listen and tune their instruments to that note. When you tune a guitar, you sound the same note on two strings, and adjust the tuning peg of one string as you listen for the notes of the two strings to stop "beating" and come into perfect resonance. Building and maintaining a relationship is something like this. You quiet yourself and listen carefully to the other so you can discover some place inside where you resonate with the emotion of the other. This doesn't mean that you feel angry when the other person is angry, but that you know how it feels to be angry. The relationship can be exquisite when you can tell precisely the color and taste and weight of that anger. You are in tune.

Building and maintaining relationship also takes:

3) Gifts of time and energy (cultivating generosity of the heart), and

4) Risk-taking (in the sense of being open and emotionally vulnerable to the other or for the sake of the other)

Gifts to the human ring of the Hoop include the gifts of forgiveness, of spending time listening to a friend, volunteering to work at a homeless shelter or with adolescents needing role models, or even simple acts of kindness to strangers. Gifts of time and energy to other rings of the Hoop include such activities as cleaning up a watershed or planting trees. They also include doing the work of learning. Where does your drinking water come from? What forest or plantation or oil field does your clothing come from? Was the clothing made by people who are oppressed or by people who are treated well? What about your food, your shelter, the energy you use? Where does your sewage and garbage go? How much is recycled? Into what? You don't have to learn everything, or learn everything overnight. Relationships are ongoing. Just make an overture.

In a true relationship one is open to the "ten-thousand joys and ten-thousand sorrows," all the pain, suffering, *and* joy of life. In interpersonal relationships, this means taking the risk of being willing to disclose your own weaknesses, doubts, and neediness. It means loving someone and risking suffering or loss of relationship. It means taking the risk to be truly alive.

These four principles of relationship hold true for relationships with oneself, with other humans, with the world of nature, and with realms of the spirit. Learning how to do these things with his social atom was what helped the engineer Mark restore himself to success in the human realm. The Hoop wisdom traditions teach that knowing how to do these things with the more-than-human world lets us feel at home in the universe.

A Hoop of Many Hoops

> The Hoop blooms like a flower, spreading its pet-
> als in every direction. The spirits of all things, like
> bees, come to feed at this Hoop as to a sweet flower;
> and the spirits of all things go to feed at the flowers
> of all things, for the one Hoop is made of many
> Hoops.
>
> —from "Mending the Hoop," C. H.

Once we are immersed in the Hoop view, we begin to feel our interdependence in an infinite web of relationship, a great "Hoop of many Hoops." We begin to appreciate the cycles of life, and the cycles of energy within life. We feel the flow of things and are able to be receptive. We are able to grow toward wholeness on the Hoop dimension. The following are several of countless ways to "enter the flow" and reconnect with the Hoop dimension of wholeness.

Hoop of Allies

> Tell me the landscape in which you live and I will
> tell you who you are.
>
> —Jose Ortega Y Gasset (1883–1955)
> Spanish philosopher[32]

One way to begin to relate to the landscape, and to the more-than-human world in general, is to think of each of the four cardinal directions and what they represent, what happens there, and what gifts and challenges each brings us. Most Hoop traditions have developed a mandala of what could be called "allies" of the four cardinal directions. The allies of the four directions serve as mediators between the finite human *I am* and the infinite terror and wonder of the universe. Black Elk's allies in his vision were horses of the four directions who led him to meet the Divine in the form of the Grandfathers. Allies are a skillful means of creating relationship.

You might think of such allies as intermediate forms. They are not human, but they are typically closer to human than rocks, trees, cliffs, weather, the sun, and all the other forms that the great mysterious life assumes around us. They come from this great mysterious, or immanent Divine, and approach the human realm halfway, so to speak. They are ways through which the infinite can manifest so as to be apprehended by finite human consciousness. Since there are usually just four of them, they save us the infinite work of developing relationships with every single blade of grass. Sometimes there are six of them, adding the above and below to the four cardinal directions and making the Hoop a sphere; the function is the same. They are graciously sympathetic to humans. All we have to do on our part is reach halfway toward them. Then we find ourselves appropriately in relationship with the more-than-human world. We find ourselves at home, centered in the living mandala of our spiritual and physical environment.

It was one of the times in my life when I was feeling less than centered that I first tried a medicine-wheel meditation. This practice, from the Native American Paiute tradition, is a way of relating to all the realms of the Hoop—mineral, vegetable, animal, human, and spirit—to give thanks and ask for guidance.

I made my medicine wheel on a beautiful moraine in Rocky Mountain National Park, in a surround of snow-capped peaks, just as the sun was setting. The medicine wheel itself was quite modest. I made it of pebbles, carefully gathered; the whole diameter fit between my knees as I knelt on the ground. I had no expectations that anything would happen. I probably even felt a little foolish. But I was following an inner prompting I could not deny.

When I had entered the deepest part of the meditation, there appeared in the sky above me a nighthawk, darting and swooping. By now the sun had dropped so far behind the mountains that black night enveloped everything at ground level. But the sky above was still luminous blue. While time seemed to stand still, brother

nighthawk circled directly above me, making his characteristic boom-
ing dives that sound like the silk taffeta of the sky is being ripped.

After I don't know how long, nighthawk made one last circle above me and flew off directly west. The direction he took
answered a specific question that was in my heart at the time. From
that moment on I have never doubted the power of the medicine
wheel. And I honor the nighthawk as an ally of the West.

The Zuni people place sacred ceremony at the center of a mandala through an invocation of these allies. They associate the North
with mountain lion, West with bear, South with badger, and East with
wolf. These animals, who are also spiritual powers, bring the ecosystem into the whole psyche. Here is one of their beautiful invocations:

> Yonder in the north,
> You who are my father, Mountain lion,
> You are life-giving society chief;
> Bringing your medicine,
> You will make your road come hither.
> Where lies my white shell bowl,
> Four times making your road come in,
> Watch over my spring.
> When you sit down quietly
> We shall be one person.[33]

After all the allies of the four directions arrive, the Hoop is
whole and the petitioner is made whole. "We shall be one person."

The Hoop of Allies, or mandala of four allies, appears in many
other Hoop traditions around the world. Far from the Zuni pueblo,
up around Lakes Huron and Superior, the Midewewin healing society of the Ojibway also petition the energies of the four directions
in their ceremonies.[34] The Celtic tradition associates geographical
regions, otherworldly cities, and mystical gifts (stone, spear/staff,
sword, and cauldron) as well as animals with each direction.[35] Contemporary Wiccan practice invokes Guardians of the Watchtowers
of the four directions.[36] The Kabbalistic tradition honors the allies
as the four Archangels.[37]

Traditional Hoop wisdom teaches that one should work with the allies of the four directions as one would work to maintain any important relationship. The Zuni, for example, have little stone carvings, called fetishes, which represent the allies. They honor these by "feeding" them sacred cornmeal at regular times and through prayer. They are not worshipping the stone carvings, of course, but feeding the relationship with their intention and devotion.

The idea of the allies of the four directions is typically not a familiar concept to those in modern commercial/industrial culture. Yet the reality of the allies is often right below the surface of our consciousness. One way to begin to discover your allies is to imagine that you are a place in nature, and to consider what that place might be. What is one of the most beautiful or powerful places you've visited in nature? What were the sounds and smells? How did you feel? What aspect—light, trees, water, distant view, wind, sound—did you notice most acutely?

I once asked a bright, accomplished professional woman what place she would be if she were a place in nature. Up until the moment I asked her, she had never considered this question nor had she heard of the idea of the four allies. Yet she was able to describe herself as a place in nature by thinking of the place she likes to visit: a valley in northern New Mexico, with old, solid cliffs and unique colors and formations.

With this warm-up, I then asked her to name her allies of the four directions. After only a little hesitation she named: owl, wise old woman, snake, and a clear sufficient stream. Even at this early point in her relationship with allies, she could tell that the owl brings her wisdom, the snake brings ability to survive in harsh conditions, and so on. She mentioned that she identified with the particular valley because it had a feeling of being "central." This of course is one of the functions of finding your Hoop of allies: the allies center you in physical, psychological, and spiritual landscapes.

Most Hoop traditions similarly associate each ally in the Hoop with elements of the ecosystem—animals, plants, and geographic features, though specific associations with specific directions vary from culture to culture, depending on the local ecosystem. In other words, the ecosystem occurs not only "out there," but also "in here" where we experience psyche and spirit.

The Hoop of Allies is a form of "medicine wheel" mandala. It links the inner and outer, spiritual and physical, psyche and ecosystem. The unifying theme in all this traditional wisdom is that *nature is a living mandala within which the healthy psyche orients itself.* Healing occurs when one establishes right relationship with this Hoop.

Anyone who has worked with allies will be able to tell you something wonderful. Whether your ally is medicine bear or Saint Luke, your ally will come to you in times of need.

Hoop of Development

In the Hoop view, one comes to be psycho-spiritually mature and whole by integrating the wisdom represented by the four directions on the medicine-wheel mandala.

Soon after the Hopi People emerged into this world, Ma'saw, the caretaker, gave them an assignment. "He explained that every clan must make four directional migrations before they all arrived at their common, permanent home. They must go to the ends of the land—west, south, east, and north—to the farthest *pa'so* (where the land meets the sea) in each direction. Only when the clans had completed these four movements, rounds, or steps of their migration could they come together again, forming the pattern of the Creator's universal plan."[38] These migrations show an entire people orienting themselves to nature's mandala in order to "come home."

A similar Hoop of development appears in Carl Jung's concept of "the four functions." Jung says that consciousness has four primary functions: two of them have to do with how we perceive, or take in data about, the world; two of them have to do with how we act on that data—how we make decisions. Jung's terms for these four functions are: *sensing, intuition, feeling* (values), and *thinking* (logic). When Carl Jung introduced the four functions, he drew them as a mandala: a simple equilateral cross with each arm of the cross representing one function.[39]

These four functions are, in a sense, four allies of consciousness. They are ways that the conscious ego relates to the great

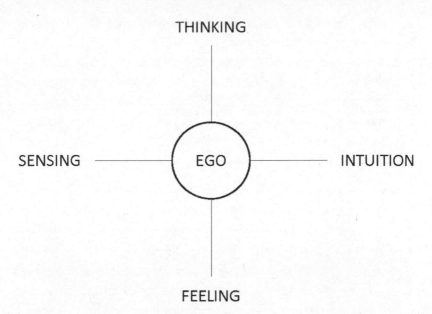

infinite world all around. Jung's concept forms the theoretical basis for a psychological instrument called the Myers-Briggs Type Indicator (MBTI), widely used in team development, conflict resolution, and marital, individual, and career counseling.

Jung said that early in life only one of the four functions is consciously accessible. For some people the most accessible (the "dominant") function is the sensing function. For others, it is intuition or thinking or feeling. According to Jung, personal growth or *individuation* involves developing not just the dominant function, but all of them. Wholeness requires the full mandala.

Jung's idea about growth around the mandala of the four functions exactly parallels the Native American teaching that says that "at birth, each of us is given a particular Beginning Place within these Four Great Directions on the Medicine Wheel. This Starting Place gives us our first way of perceiving things, which will then be our easiest and most natural way throughout our lives. . . . After each of us has learned of our Beginning Gift, our First Place on the Medicine Wheel, we must Grow by Seeking Understanding in each of the Four Great Ways. Only in this way can we become Full, capable of Balance and Decision in what we do."[40]

Our dominant function, like this Beginning Place, will usually be our easiest and most natural way throughout our lives. But any person who uses only one of these four functions will remain just a partial person. Each of us must grow by learning how to use the four functions, the Four Great Ways. Only in this way can we become full, capable of balance and decision in what we do.

Another Modern Hoop Story

A few years ago on a train trip from Boston to New York City I happened to be sitting next to a young woman from India. After some preliminary conversation, she told me a story about her grandmother. It seems her grandmother had died and, as was the Hindu custom, her family was preparing to cremate her. Lovingly they had placed her body on the top of the pile of wood and incense. Just as the pyre was about to be lit, the grandmother sat up, fully alive.

The grandmother told her astounded family what she had experienced. After she had died, she had been greeted by a pair of devas (good spirits) who had guided her on a long journey by foot. After a while they came to a desert of burning sands. The grandmother, who was barefoot, was unable to cross the sands because they were too hot. The devas asked her, "Have you ever helped the poor?" The grandmother remembered that once she had given a fine pair of her own shoes to a beggar. No sooner had she remembered this than that very same pair of shoes appeared before her feet. She was able to put them on and cross the hot sands without difficulty. A little while later they came to a stream, a stream far too swift and deep for the aged woman to cross. The devas asked her, "In your life, have you venerated the cow?" The grandmother recalled that as a good Hindu she had always honored the cow. No sooner had she remembered this than a strong and kindly cow appeared and carried the grandmother on its back across the raging stream.

Eventually the devas led the grandmother into the presence of a deity, who told her that it was not yet time for her to die. She was to live for seven more years. The next thing the grandmother knew she was awakening on top of a funeral pyre. My train companion told me that it had been fewer than seven years since this had happened, and that her grandmother was still alive and healthy, and that everyone who met her felt blessed in some way. The grandmother's practice of goodness in this life returned, Hoop-like, to help her in her near-death experience.

This story illustrates many Hoop qualities. For one, it points out the importance of what the Hindus call *ahimsa*, or respect and consideration for all life, and fellow feeling with all living beings.

Hindus (as well as many other traditions) consider life to consist of cycles within cycles, Hoops within Hoops. In this view, living beings die from one life only to be reborn in the next. In the Hindu *Bhagavad Gita*, Lord Krishna teaches: "As a person abandons worn-out clothes and acquires new ones, so when the body is worn out a new one is acquired by the Self, who lives within" (2:12–13, 22).[41] It is a rare person who can become free of this endless birth-rebirth cycle of *samsara*. In this view, ahimsa is quite practical when you consider that there is no telling where you might land in your next rebirth, or whose reincarnated relative is nearby.

The "Hoop of Rebirth"

Regardless of whether reincarnation occurs or not, the Wheel of Rebirth is a powerful metaphor for our interrelationship in the Hoop. The Hoop of Rebirth is simply the Hoop of Relationship as viewed through time: I am related to you not just because we are brothers or sisters in this life, but because you may have been my great-grandfather in a previous incarnation and you may be my great-granddaughter in a future incarnation. Several traditions of the Hoop of Rebirth go so far as to say that I may once have even lived in the form of this very water buffalo that pulls my plow today. Every created being is a comrade in the great round of life and death. All are related to all. Therefore: practice ahimsa.

Hinduism is not the only Hoop tradition to teach about the Hoop of Rebirth. The Celtic Druid and Wiccan traditions hold that after death your soul is reborn in a new human body, so that you may have an opportunity to learn from mistakes in previous lives (mistakes that are not "sins" in the Christian sense) and finally come into harmony.[42] Celtic tradition also gives us the image of the "king's wheel," which is a Hoop-shaped brooch worn by the king to remind him of the cycle of death and rebirth.[43] The Hoop of Rebirth appears in the Jewish Kabbalistic teachings about *Gilgulim* (Hebrew for "the Turnings").[44] According to this tradition, each of us is sent down to accomplish a certain task that is related to the whole scheme of creation. Since accomplishing such a task may not be possible in one lifetime, rebirth may be necessary.

The Taoist Chuang Tsu says, "You were born in a human form, and you find joy in it. Yet there are ten thousand other forms endlessly transforming that are equally good, and the joy in these is untold. The sage dwells among those things which can never be lost, and so he lives forever."[45] The Buddhists teach: If you want to know what your past life *was*, look at your *circumstances* right now. Are they favorable? Unfavorable? Easy? Difficult? If you want to know what your future life *will be*, look at your *behavior* right now. Is it selfish? Selfless? Base? Noble?

One of the most impressive images of the Hoop of Rebirth is the Tibetan Buddhist teaching mandala *The Wheel of Life*. The Wheel of Life depicts six realms into which a human being may be "reborn." These realms can be interpreted as actual physical realms of incarnation or as psychological states. So even if reincarnation does not occur, we can learn from the "Hoop of Rebirth" as a psychological and spiritual metaphor. For example, we all know the state of craving something but never feeling satisfied. This is the realm of "Hungry Ghosts," who are depicted as miserable beings with bloated hungry bellies and straw-thin necks, necks so thin that nothing can pass down the throat to satisfy the belly. The Wheel of Life reminds us to "stay related" psychologically and not forget about this potential within ourselves.

Hoop of Interdependence

Around the circumference of the Wheel of Life, surrounding the six realms, are pictures that show another aspect of the Hoop: the twelve links in the Hoop-shaped chain of *dependent-arising*.[46] Simply put, dependent-arising means that nothing exists in and of itself. Whatever exists, exists because of other things or other conditions. Aging and death only arise because of birth, grasping at things only arises because of wanting things, and so on. Furthermore, everything that exists has parts on which it depends, and these parts have parts, and so on. Ultimately, when we probe and probe to find the answer to the question "Who am I?," we cannot find any solid thing. Every object is as ultimately unfindable as this "I." Objects do not *not* exist. But everything depends on everything else, and it all arises together. Life is a Hoop—of Relationship and of Rebirth. The Vietnamese Zen master Thich Nhat Hanh called it "interbeing."[47]

Interbeing is why traditional Hoop cultures teach us to consider the effects of our decisions on the seventh generation of our descendants. Interbeing is also why maturity on the Hoop dimension calls us to act in an ecologically responsible manner. We can't give in to our temptations to consume recklessly without throwing our relationships with the air, the water, the earth, and all other living things out of balance. Interbeing is also why environmental protection is inseparable from social justice. They are just two aspects of the same dimension.

The story about the grandmother also teaches about our Hoop interdependence with nonhuman beings, and how the Hoop swirls with cycles of energy.

The grandmother was helped by a cow. Hoop wisdom traditions tell many stories of humans being given wisdom by animals or being aided by animals. Several of the Navajo healing ceremonials, for example, are based on wisdom given to humans by animals. In the healing story of Flint Way, when the hero, (the original "patient") has been dismembered, "shattered beyond recognition," his shattered being (psyche) is pulled together into a new wholeness by Gila Monster, aided by several other members of the ecological Hoop:

The hero's . . . blood is gathered by ants, his nerves replaced by spiders, his eyes and ears by Sun, his body and hair by Moon and Darkness People, his face by Dawn People, his mind by Talking God and Pollen Boy and his "traveling means" by Cornbeetle Girl. Then Thunder's participation is necessary, and after receiving his proper offerings he creates a lightning storm similar to the one that originally destroyed the hero. This time the hero comes back to life. Finally Sun restores the hero's tears and replaces his eye nerves. The Wind People cause his nerves to move and he is carried home on a stretcher prepared by Spider and Bird People.[48]

This story reminds us that the more-than-human beings in the universe have healing power, if one stands in right relationship to them. It also forms the narrative for a Navajo sand painting mandala or Hoop of Healing.

Many traditions emphasize our interdependence by telling stories of humans shape-shifting into animals or marrying animals.[49] Walt Whitman honors this same interdependence in "Song of Myself" when he says:

> I find I incorporate gneiss, coal, long-threaded moss, fruits,
> grains, esculent roots,
> And am stucco'd with quadrupeds and birds all over, . . .
> I am large, I contain multitudes.

In physical terms, the Hoop of Interdependence is undeniable. For decades most of the electricity used in Colorado was generated on generators made by workers in Pennsylvania, with coal mined in Wyoming—the coal itself a legacy of trees that lived millions of years ago—and with steam made from water combed from the clouds by the Rocky Mountains, the water itself a gift of the sparkling Pacific Ocean evaporated by the sun.

For much of the food we eat we are dependent on the services of wild and semi-wild pollinators—mostly insects, bats, and birds. Eighty percent of all cultivated crop species, representing some 1,330 varieties, including fruits, vegetables, beans, coffee, and tea, are pollinated by the 120,000 to 200,000 pollinating species. The economic value of wild blueberry bees alone is so great that farmers view the bees as "flying $50 bills." Tragically for the honeybees and for us, more that half the honeybee colonies in the United States have been lost in the last fifty years, with 25 percent lost within the last five years alone, due to exposure to pesticides and loss of habitat.[50] Most wild pollinators are suffering similar declines.[51]*

As part of a Hoop of many Hoops, we depend on each other for our very lives.

Hoops of Energy and Flow

> Whoever degrades another degrades me,
> And whatever is done or said returns at last to me.
>
> —Walt Whitman, "Song of Myself"

> From thee I receive.
> To thee I give.
> Together we share.
> By this, we live.
>
> —Nathan Segal

In the story of the grandmother, the gifts she gave in one realm returned miraculously to help her in another realm. This is another quality of the Hoop: the Hoop of Cycles of Energy that bonds relationships and affects healing. The energy can be in the form of a physical gift, which is a type of stored or potential energy, or in the form of an action—a type of kinetic energy.

---

* One way to learn more about how we are interconnected is to take any object of everyday life and trace it back through the economy to the ecosystem. John Ryan and Alan Durning do a fascinating job of this with coffee, newspapers, and other items in their book *Stuff: The Secret Life of Everyday Things*, Seattle: Northwest Environment Watch, 1997.

In his book *The Gift*, Lewis Hyde shows that a cardinal property of gifts is that *the gift must always move*. "Whatever we have
been given is supposed to be given away again, not kept. Or, if it
is kept, something of similar value should move on in its stead,
the way a billiard ball may stop when it sends another scurrying
across the felt, its momentum transferred. You may keep your
Christmas present, but it ceases to be a gift in the true sense unless
you have given something else away. As it is passed along, the gift
may be given back to the original donor, but this is not essential.
In fact it is better if the gift is not returned but is given instead
to some new, third party . . . There are other forms of property
that stand still, that mark a boundary or resist momentum, but
the gift keeps going."[52]

In most Hoop cultures, the gift not only moves, but it moves
in a circle or Hoop. Hyde gives the example of the *Kula* ceremonial gift exchange practiced by the Massim people who live on
islands near the eastern tip of New Guinea. Here the gifts move in
two great circles, both clockwise and counterclockwise around the
archipelago in a flow that may take up to ten years for a complete
cycle. At each Kula transaction along the way, the exchange is different from economic trade by virtue of two key qualities. First,
the gift is given in silence. There is no haggling, no barter. Second,
the equivalence of the counter-gift is left to the giver and cannot be
enforced by any kind of coercion.[53] The gift comes "round the cor-
ner," as Hyde says, from out of sight. The Hoop of the circulation
of gift energy weaves together an emotional network of gratitude,
caring, and obligation that produces community.

The kinetic energy of our actions also flows in a Hoop. Your
actions, whether for good or ill, have consequences that sooner or
later will come back to affect your own life. Good actions eventually
bring good consequences, in this lifetime or the next; bad actions,
bad consequences. The grandmother's compassionate actions
returned to her as help in time of need. The Hindu tradition calls
this the law of *karma*. The European Wicca tradition holds a similar belief. They say that whatever spell you cast on another, whether
for good or ill, eventually returns threefold to yourself.

Of course this is true not just for Hindus or Wiccans, but for all of us. We are all embedded in Spider Woman's Web, Indra's Net, psychology's field. Whatever vibrations we send out along the web eventually work their way back to us. We acknowledge this fact, and the circular, Hoop quality of it, in the common expression "Whatever goes around, comes around."

The Hoop of Energy also manifests in the food cycle, where the gift of life-giving energy flows from vegetation to herbivore to decay bacteria to humus to vegetation and around again, sometimes also passing through carnivore on the way. It also manifests in the ecological realization that there is no "away," as in "I'm going to throw this away."

The Hoop of Gifts and Energy can cycle through the Divine realm as well as through the human realm. There are traditions throughout the world of holding special ceremonies to feast and entertain a particular bear or a particular salmon as a representative of the divine Keeper of the Animals. The Keeper of the Animals gives of the gift of game to the people. The people complete the Hoop of the Gift by giving songs and feasts to honor the Keeper of the Animals.[54] Any energy we expend in prayers or ceremonies of thanksgiving serves the same function.

Cycles of energy flow not only in the outer world but within us as well. In India this vital energy is called *prana*; in Japan it is called *ki*; in China, *chi*. Traditional Chinese medicine promotes healing by tuning the cycles of chi in the body with acupuncture needles.[55] Chinese *t'ai-chi ch'uan* and Japanese *aikido* bring balance and vitality to the body and spirit through martial arts practices that work with this vital energy. T'ai-chi master Bob Klein reminds us that "this energy is part of the energy system of the planet. So not only must the body be free of energy blockages within itself, it must also be free of any blockages to energy between the body and the environment."[56]

The flow of energy in the universe is a principal implication of one of the world's most widely recognized Hoop images: the yin-yang *t'ai chi* symbol of Taoism. This is a circle half-filled with dark, half-filled with light, the light and dark forever circling each other.

The fullness of the dark or *yin* contains within it the seed of light; the fullness of the light or *yang* contains within it the seed of dark. This is an image of the Tao, the flow, the path, the "supreme ultimate" principle of creation. It symbolizes the understanding that all opposites always transform into each other. There is flow around the Hoop, from yin to yang to yin to yang and on and on.

In order to enhance your own Hoop, Taoism teaches that you should practice *tzu-jan* and *wu-wei*. Tzu-jan means to follow nature, be spontaneous, and take no forced or unnatural action. This is to be one with the Tao, the unique source of the universe that determines all things. This is to be *organic*, in the sense of coming into existence by the inherent life force of the organism. All unnatural efforts are ultimately doomed to frustration or failure.

Wu-wei literally means "nonaction" or "doing nothing." Its full expression is wei-wu-wei: action without action. By this the Taoists do not mean doing absolutely nothing at all. Wu-wei suggests instead the absence of human willfulness in any action, and taking as little action as necessary, simply working with the spontaneously arising transformations in the universe. It suggests going with the grain of things, going with the flow. The ancient Taoist master Chuang Tsu says, "Flow with whatever may happen and let your mind be free; stay centered by accepting whatever you are doing. This is the ultimate."[57] It might be likened to the effortless skill of a surfboard rider who needs only one or two strokes to catch a great wave.

The Hoop of Relationship and the Hoop of Flow are not different Hoops. If you are fully related to yourself and to the surge of the ocean, you are in the flow. You don't create the wave, but you have enough intimate relationship with yourself and waves to be in the right place at the right time with the right awareness to make the few strokes that will let you ride the wave all the way in.

The Hoop of Flow has a psychological counterpart in the principle of *spontaneity*. Spontaneity is behavior somewhere in the middle between rigid conformity and chaotic unpredictability. The behavior is just right, not overly forced yet not passive.

Psychologist Jacob L. Moreno says that psychopathology is often caused by not enough Hoop of Flow.[58] The Hoop of Flow also corresponds to what athletes call "the zone."

If you've ever been "in the right place at the right time," you've been in the flow. If you've ever been making music with others and had the music itself carry your own playing to a level you never thought possible, you've been in the flow. If you've ever lost all sense of time and self when doing any activity, you've been in the flow.

The essence of flow is in not clinging to any particle of matter or to any instant of experience as they swirl in the great round of existence. It is as free and unencumbered as natural breathing. Inhale: OK. Exhale: OK. Cling to your breath, hold on to it: soon die. All living flows in cycles of relationship.

Hoop of Receptivity

To be in the flow you need to be able to be receptive. You need to "listen" to the water in order to catch the great wave. You need to listen to your partner in order to foster relationship. To listen you need to be "empty" of yourself. The Taoist classic *Tao Te Ching* says that the ideal human is "receptive as a valley," and is "available to all people and doesn't reject anyone. If you receive the world, the Tao will never leave you. If you want to become full, let yourself be empty."[59] Similarly, Buddhism teaches the importance of *shunyata* or being empty of yourself.[60] Kabbalah teaches that every being in creation is a vessel that can receive and contain the pure light of awareness. All spiritual work in Kabbalah is directed toward increasing our receptive capacity for this light.[61]

Hoop of the Cycles of Life

When we look at life we see that it flows in cycles. The earth cycles around the sun, giving us cycles of weather and seasons, plantings and harvests. In our own lives we cycle through emotional ups and downs; we cycle through projects started and completed; we cycle through youth, courtship, adulthood, old age, and death;

we cycle through sickness and health 'til death do us part. And even then we ask that the "circle be unbroken." Hoop wisdom and Hoop festivals celebrating recurring events in these cycles help to put us in accord with the natural ways of life.

The Hoop understanding of the cycles of life is also the basis for the ancient Chinese wisdom tradition contained in the Classic of Changes, or *I Ching*. Perhaps the oldest book on the planet, the *I Ching* is still widely used today as a source of inspiration and guidance.[62] The *I Ching* distills wisdom from centuries of human experience into sixty-four "hexagrams," each hexagram being a set of six horizontal short parallel lines. Each line is either straight and unbroken (yang) or broken with a gap in the middle (yin). Tradition says that the trigrams were discovered on the shell of a horse dragon (tortoise) by Fu Hsi, a legendary king of China who was supposed to have lived about 3000 BCE. Traditionally, also, it was Fu Hsi who arranged the trigrams as they are often depicted: in the form of a Hoop mandala, with each trigram across the circle from its polar opposite.[63]

Hoop of Healing

> The great ones, in their wisdom, gave us the gift of loneliness, that in seeking one another we might find, and in finding we might heal, even as we are healed.
>
> —author unknown

In terms of the Hoop dimension, psycho-spiritual imbalance results from incomplete or inappropriate relationship. Wholeness consists of being in relationship appropriately. So healing occurs within relationship, and health when one is restored to appropriate relationship.

Psychologist Carl Rogers developed an influential and effective approach to therapy that relies almost entirely on these principles. Rogers said that it is the relationship itself that is therapeutic.[64]

Over thirty years' worth of data about the effectiveness of psychotherapy tends to confirm what Rogers said. Most of the evidence suggests that a set of core factors, common to all methods of therapy, account for positive outcomes. The most important factor seems to be the quality of the client's participation in the work, over which the counselor has no control. Second in importance is the therapeutic relationship itself: the Hoop.

One widely cited review of psychotherapy outcome research estimates that 30 percent of the outcome can be attributed to relationship factors (with client participation accounting for 40 percent).[65] The "sacred space" of the therapeutic relationship creates The Hoop within which the Tree of the client's psychological core can develop.

Another Hoop-shaped container for healing is the sweat lodge constructed by the Lakota and other Native American people. To make a sweat lodge they cut some poles of willow and plant the poles in the ground in a circle, bending the poles over to make a dome and connecting the poles at the top in a square mandala to represent the four directions. Then they cover this framework with buffalo hides or tarps, blankets, or quilts. The whole structure is about as high as a person's chest. Inside the lodge is a seating area of ground surrounding a small circular pit. The pit represents the center of the whole world and also the dead who have returned to mother earth. The pit is filled with grandfather rock, brought in glowing hot from the fire outside. People sit in a circle around the circular pit to pray and receive blessings, surrounded by the circle of the sweat lodge within the circle of the universe—Hoops within a Hoop—to bring about spiritual, physical, and emotional healing.[66]

Many traditions, ancient and modern, rely on the drawing or constructing of mandalas to facilitate healing. Jungian therapists often encourage this practice.[67] Creating a mandala allows you to "pull yourself together" by visually integrating various aspects of your Self. You make yourself whole by bringing all your inner "voices," or sub-personalities and archetypes, into the council circle of the Self.

Navajo healers construct whole sequences of mandalas using sands of various colors. The ecosystem enters the mandala as images of the sacred mountains associated with each cardinal direction, mountains that are also identified as actual physical mountains, such as Mount Taylor and Mount Humphreys.[68] Many paintings also include visual reference to the sacred plants of the ecosystem—corn, beans, squash, and tobacco. In the course of the ceremony the patient is placed in the middle of each of these medicine wheel mandalas. In the midst of this sacred ecosystem the Self is symbolically reconnected to the Hoop of Relationship with all beings and is brought into balance.

Navajo sand paintings are an example of the "medicine wheel" type of mandala. These mandalas are a microcosm of spiritual and psychological truth as represented by the surrounding ecosystem. Medicine wheels also appear in many other cultures around the world. For example, Tibetan Buddhism has mandalas associated with the "place" of Shambhala, a mystical earthly paradise said to be hidden in the snowy mountains north of Tibet. Medicine-wheel practices remind us again that nature is a living mandala within which the healthy psyche orients itself.

How Is Your Hoop?

Whatever you're doing, you're always in the center of a sacred circle. You cannot survive, physically, psychologically, or spiritually without this Hoop. The question is: How do you relate to the Hoop? Are you centered in a mandala of family and social atom and ecosystem and the immanent Divine? Are you in relationship fully enough to be in the flow, in the Tao? Is your Hoop wide and inclusive? Is your Hoop whole?

For the bigot, the Hoop of Relationship is very small. It contains only one type of person. For more broad-minded people, the Hoop of Relationship holds other humans, including some of different races and different belief systems. An evolving Hoop may embrace a lot in its circumference, but perhaps not "Them": the foreigner, the enemy, the other tribe, the environmentalists, or the anti-environmentalists, or the nonhuman realms.

The broadest Hoop sees that we are all in this together; and that "we" includes the realms of mineral, vegetable, animal, spirit, and all the peoples of the earth, regardless of race, color, religion, or anything else. The symbolism of the Hoop is the symbolism of the wedding ring: we are all related.

Ultimately the Hoop is the image by which the self talks to the self about the Greater Self in whom we are all connected. It is through the Hoop that we connect with other living beings, with the rocks, the soil, the air, the green and growing things, the dying and the dead that fertilize new life, the person we once were and the person we shall be. The Hoop has to do with hearing the beat, getting with the rhythm, feeling the music of what is, and skillfully entering in with just the right amount of effort. Because in some way we are all Hoops, we admire well-rounded people, and we do wish that "the circle be unbroken." The Hoop is oneself as the process of relating.

All of us yearn to feel related and accepted, to be in harmony, to feel ourselves at home in the universe and with each other. And this is our birthright, for we are all part of the Hoop. We have only to stop, perceive, and be. If you allow yourself to connect with the Hoop, you are home.

The Fruitful Tree: The Cross as a Tree bearing fruit. Note the Hoop at the base of the Tree. (After an engraving dated 1512.)

3

The Holy Tree

Beloved, gaze in thine own heart,
The holy tree is growing there.

—W. B. Yeats, "The Two Trees"

IN THE DAYS WHEN MUSIC was sweeter, fire was hotter, and ice was colder, there lived a king of the Celts named Bran son of Febal. One day King Bran was walking alone on the shore when an enchanting melody came to his ears from some unknown place and lulled him into deepest sleep. When he awoke he found lying beside him the branch of a tree, formed of silver, with white blossoms on it. Full of wonder, he took this branch back to his royal hall and summoned his advisors for counsel.

In the midst of their considerations there appeared before them a woman of extraordinary loveliness dressed in rich clothing. She addressed King Bran with sumptuous descriptions of a land of perfection, her own land, the Land of Joy that lay westward across the sea. Her last words before vanishing were these: "King Bran," said she, "I do not make my invitation to every man, though every man may hear these words. May you both hear and understand." This experience so stirred Bran that he ordered a fine ship prepared, and with certain chosen companions embarked on his great voyage to the perfect Land of Joy.

Though our own aspirations may not be as magical as the vision of King Bran, if we "both hear and understand," we are each drawn into growth as individuals by the call of our dreams for the future. What helps us realize these dreams are our "roots." For example, Martin Luther King Jr.'s work toward his dream of civil rights probably would not have succeeded as it did were it not for his having been raised in a healthy and loving family and for his profound soul-searching during his years in training for the ministry.[1]

This axis, between our roots and our aspirations, between where we've come from and where we're headed, is the essence of the Tree. Like the Hoop, the Tree is a metaphor, intended to "carry beyond." Metaphors carry meaning beyond their literal meaning in order to carry us beyond our literal consciousness or everyday state of mind. Just as the Hoop helps us expand our sense of relationship from our inner circle outward through the far reaches of the universe, the Tree helps us establish our individuality: our uniqueness, our roots, and our central core.

The Tree is the axle of our "inner gyrocompass." It centers and complements the Hoop. The Hoop views the environment as a set of meaningful wholes, of which the person feels a part or wishes to become a part. The Tree views the environment as a chaotic collection of random and alien factors that the psyche attempts to coordinate and master with respect to itself as a governing center.[2] While the Hoop is the affiliative aspect of wholeness, the Tree is the autonomous aspect. While the Hoop is inclusive, the Tree is one-pointed or focused. Dr. King developed both his Hoop and his Tree: he became a strong individual who helped the whole Hoop of humanity.

The Tree is related to what poet Robert Bly calls "vertical longing." Bly quotes the Swedish poet Harry Martinson to describe the situation of people *without* vertical longing:

> victims of flat evil,
> with no comfort from a high place
> or support from a low place.[3]

The dimension of the self that has to do with aspiration to a high place (something "to live up to," the "highest truth," a "higher calling") and support from a low place (profundity, the "depths of the soul") is a vertical dimension that pulls us out of the plane of mediocrity and into maturity. We both deepen and ascend for individual development. How high we can go on this dimension toward our aspirations depends on how deep we can go into the roots, where the Hoop and the Tree have a hidden correspondence.

An Ancient, Widespread, and Potent Image

> Trees were temples of divinities, and in the old
> way the simple country folk to this day dedicate
> any remarkable tree to a god.
>
> —Pliny, *Natural History*, xii. 3.

In order to understand the Tree dimension of wholeness, it will help to understand a bit about the image itself.

The Tree as an image of connection with divine energy dates back thousands of years. It is one of our oldest ways to imagine the unimaginable, to talk about the ineffable. It is as widespread as it is ancient. For example, Hindus consider the Bo tree (*Ficus religiosa*) to be the dwelling place of the Hindu Trinity—Brahma, Vishnu, and Shiva.[4] Among the early British and northern European peoples the tree spirit was associated with the renewal of life; and the oldest sanctuaries were the natural woods.[5] In fact, the old Druidic word for "sanctuary," *nemeton*, is identical in origin to the Latin word for "grove," *nemus*, and it is believed that early Gothic cathedrals were designed to suggest the forest.[6] English place-names like Holyoake and Holywood recall this early reverence for groves and trees. Nathaniel Altman, in his study *Sacred Trees*, concludes that nearly every tree species is sacred to at least one human community or culture, and that nearly every culture has honored the sacred Tree.[7]

Why does the Tree have such deep resonance in the human soul? Perhaps it is because of our ancient relationship with the

Tree. Most scientific stories about the origins of the human species make us forest-dwellers from the start. As tropical biologist Donald Perry says, "Less than two million years ago our australopithecine ancestors probably spent considerable time living in treetops. Before that, our ancestors probably spent 60 million continuous years living in an arboreal environment. Tropical treetops were the womb and nursery of humankind. This arboreal phase, critical to our evolution, has left an indelible stamp on both our body design and the workings of the human mind."[8]

Our immersion in a world of trees has endured until relatively recent times. Down to the first century BCE the Hercynian forest of northern Europe stretched eastward from the Rhine to such an extent that a person could walk through it for two months without reaching its end.[9] Much of present-day England, northern Italy, and Greece were similarly forested.* Today billions of people live in dwellings made of tree products.

Because of our evolutionary history we have a long association with trees as providers of food, shelter, and sometimes clothing. We may identify with trees because both humans and trees stand upright and grow "up." We are dependent on trees for the oxygen we breathe, and thus literally for our "inspiration." We may stand in awe of them because, for the most part, trees are bigger than we are and usually live longer. In California there lives a bristlecone pine that is four thousand years old. Japan has cedars that were *already* substantial trees four thousand years ago.[10]

In a very practical and mysterious sense, we owe everything to the Tree. Sometime, a long, long, long time ago, a flash of lightning snaked out of the sky and set a tree aflame in a blast of thunder. From this burning tree some intrepid ancestor of ours stole a piece of the power that made possible all advances in human history. Electricity, hot water, cooked food, the use of metal—none of these would have been possible without fire. This gift made possible a quantum leap in human development. Myths and rituals of the

---

* Likewise, it is said that before the European settlement of North America, a squirrel could travel branch-to-branch from what is now Maine to the banks of the Mississippi without ever having to climb down from a tree.

burning tree, including the Yule log and the winter solstice tree bedecked with offerings, ancestor of the modern Christmas tree, may be as old as a thousand centuries.[11] It may well have been this primordial gift of fire from a mysterious power on high that fixed the Tree in the human psyche as a sacred image.

Whatever the reasons, the Tree does tend to evoke feelings of sacredness, or at least of mystery. If you have any doubts of this, spend an hour or two sitting in an old-growth forest. Touch the bark of one of these great trees and you will feel your palm resting against one of the pillars of time itself. If you were to listen carefully here for a hundred years you could hear the full pronunciation of a single syllable from a long conversation about God. Being here makes you humble and glad and gives you patience with your own life.

This Tree Grows Within You

> The soul in the body is like sap in a tree, and the
> soul's powers are like the form of the tree.
>
> —Hildegard of Bingen[12]

In the sacred stories of the world the quality the Tree represents most often is the "axis of the universe" or "pole of heaven." The Babylonians, Sumerians, Hindus, Aztecs, Mayans, Siberian Yakuts, and the Iroquois all had various names for this same tree-axis of the universe that the Norse knew as Yggdrasill.[13] Some traditions give this central axis quality to a Tree cognate, usually a mountain. In all these stories the Tree or Tree cognate is vertical, central to everything, and connects the above and the below.

What else is vertical and central to everything? We are, each of us. Each of us *experiences* the world as though it were happening around us, as though each of us were the axis of the cosmos. So the Tree is a double metaphor. It stands for the great central axis of the entire cosmos, around which everything revolves, and it stands for the central axis of our own psychological and spiritual being, around which our individual experience of life revolves.

It is the axis of the cosmos and the axis of the psyche. The Tree sprouts within each of us.

Since the late 1940s psychologists have used a technique known as the House-Tree-Person (HTP) Drawing to help understand a person's inner processes. Techniques such as the HTP Drawing are called "projective" techniques because the person is seen as "projecting" part of his or her inner world onto some outside object, much as a movie or slide projector projects onto a screen. In the case of the HTP, part of the inner world is projected by the drawing of three pictures: of a house, a tree, and a person. The pictures can be drawn in any way the drawer chooses. The HTP is frequently used with children, because it is nonthreatening.

Since the psyche tends to identify its life, growth, and maturation with the tree, psychologists believe that the tree drawing of the HTP represents the deepest levels of the personality.[14] Also, of all the drawings the tree drawing is least likely to change over time.[15]

The tree drawing of the HTP is modern manifestation of the ancient and widespread belief that the Tree represents the life of a person. Some wisdom traditions say that the first humans were actually made from trees.[16] The human body has a *trunk* and *limbs*. In the growth and maturation of the Tree we see our own growth and maturation. In the Jewish tradition the age of maturity is twenty-one because the fruit of the almond tree develops to its full sweetness in twenty-one days.[17] In many cultures a tree is planted at the birth of a child, and its fate and the child's fate are considered to be identical.[18]

Because of our deep psychological identification with the Tree, the Tree is an apt metaphor for the axis of the whole self, of you and of me. The ideal human, says the first Psalm, "is like a tree planted by streams of water, that yields its fruit in its season, and its leaf does not wither." The universe is a tree, says the Hindu *Katha Upanishad*, and "the pure root of the tree is Brahman, the immortal, in whom the three worlds have their being, whom none can transcend, who is verily the Self."[19]

"Comfort from a High Place"

The Tree teaches us that just as a physical tree needs to grow toward the light of the sun and to receive blessing from the sun's light in order to grow, each one of us needs to grow toward some high aspiration, and to receive blessing or comfort from that high place in order to be whole. The Tree teaches that to reach the Divine, there must be movement of the human spirit upward and of the Divine downward. The Divine has been known to descend in an act of grace to meet and elevate the aspiring soul.

In the bleakest days of the Montgomery bus boycott, when the forces of segregation and oppression seemed to be gaining the upper hand, Dr. Martin Luther King, Jr. was receiving over thirty letters and telephone calls each day threatening his life or the lives of his wife and baby daughter. Late one night he found himself pacing the floor, feeling drained, fearful, and ready to give up. Finally he began to pray. He says, "I heard the voice of Jesus saying still to fight on. He promised never to leave me alone. At that moment I experienced the presence of the Divine as I had never experienced Him before. Almost at once my fears began to go. My uncertainty disappeared. I was ready to face anything."[20]

In the Jewish tradition Moses ascended Mount Sinai (a Tree cognate) to receive, and the Lord descended in a cloud to give, the wisdom of the Ten Commandments. In the Christian tradition the vertical connection is symbolized by the descent of the Holy Spirit onto Jesus (Luke 3:21, John 1:32) and the ascent of Christ represented by the Tree of the cross. The holy book of the Islamic tradition, *Al-Qur'an* (the Koran), is a revelation "sent *down*" (*anzala*). Five times a day the faithful practice "spiritual ascent," one of the "pillars" (Tree cognates) of Islam. They model their ascent on the example of the Prophet Muhammed, the most perfect human. The supreme inner experience of the Prophet occurred when the archangel Gabriel guided him in an ascent to highest heaven (Arabic: *miraj*). This ascension is regarded as "the model for all spiritual ascent in Islam" and is the "inner reality of the daily prayers."[21]

Just like the Tree, we each grow toward the light that inspires us. What is your sun? What is the most inspiring experience you've had in the last year or so? Can you describe how or why it inspired you? What does this tell you about your own sun? Toward what is your vertical longing directed?

Your highest aspiration may be to attain some contact with Divine energy, by whatever name you know it—Christ or Buddha or Krishna or some very personal image into whose likeness you wish to shape your life.

The Tibetan Buddhist tradition includes a meditation practice (*phowa*) that involves invoking, visualizing, and being absorbed into an object of aspiration that descends from the "high place" of the sky. A practice like this can be a valuable and powerful aid in caring for the dying—or for that matter in preparing for your own death. Regardless of what image you invoke—Buddha, God, the Holy Spirit, Jesus, Virgin Mary, or any other—the important point is that you consider this being to be the embodiment of the truth, wisdom, and compassion of all the buddhas, saints, masters, and enlightened beings. Your Tree grows toward the light, whether the light is named *as-sams, taiyo, soleil,* or *sun.*

In visualizing your "sun" one important thing to remember is that regardless of what image you have of the Divine, it is not the Divine itself, but only a sort of aperture, through which the brilliant light of transcendence is reduced so as to be intelligible to you and not blind you. We finite beings cannot apprehend the infinite directly. Our images of the Divine act like transformers that reduce a dangerously high voltage to a voltage that we can handle safely. Ultimately any image of the Divine is just a door through which we may step to transcendence.

For some people the aspiration may not appear as an image that is explicitly spiritual. Psychologist Abraham Maslow named our experiences of highest happiness and fulfillment "peak experiences," a term that has become part of our general vocabulary.[22] At the "peak," the top of a Tree cognate, people feel they are embodying their full potential. Studies such as that of Fred Polak, mentioned in the first chapter, tell us how essential it is for societies and individuals to have some aspiration "to live up to." Your own highest aspiration may be toward "peak experiences." What are peak experiences for you? How would you describe them? Why do you seek them? What do they give you? What ideal do you wish to live up to?

By pointing us upward toward an aspiration, the Tree dimension gives our lives a sense of direction or purpose. The Tree allows us the possibility of accomplishment. What qualities does your object of aspiration demonstrate (e.g., love, mercy, generosity, creativity, insight, profound peace)? How is your ideal helping you manifest these qualities in your daily life?

A Means of Ascent

> All the companions [the initiated] liken it [the Tree
> of Life] to a man who has a ladder in the midst
> of his house whereby he can ascend and descend
> without anyone to prevent him.
>
> —sixth-century Babylonian Kabbalist[23]

This Tree, which is the axis of the universe and grows vertically through the core of our being, has the qualities of a ladder. It enables both ascent and descent. An eloquent sermon once attributed to St. Chrysostom calls the Tree of the cross "the stairway of Jacob."[24] The rule of St. Benedict says that we must make our lives like a ladder going up to God.[25]

The "rungs" or levels on the Tree axis correspond to various stages of opening or psycho-spiritual development. The Catalan mystic Ramon Lull (thirteenth century) says of his illustration of the ladder: "We begin at the imperfect, so that we might ascend to the perfect; and conversely, we may descend from the perfect to the imperfect." Lull also says that it is through climbing such a ladder that one reaches the ultimate knowledge.[26]

Various wisdom traditions have given different names to the "rungs" on the ladder, but there is consensus that levels do exist. Most traditions say that a fully developed human is one who has appropriate access to all levels as circumstances require. These levels can also help us to see how far we have developed, and how far we have yet to go. There are ancient systems and modern systems. In tantric Hinduism the levels are called "chakras," in Jewish Kabbalism, "sefirot," and in the western psychological tradition Erik Erikson has called them the "eight ages of man."

The Hindu tantric system of Kundalini yoga is perhaps the most thoroughly developed system of levels on the Tree. Kundalini identifies various energy centers in the body that are Hoops (*chakras* = "wheels") aligned along the spine, which is an inner Tree cognate (sometimes called Mount Meru).

Physically, the Hoops of the chakras are located on this Tree axis at: (1) the base of your spine, (2) the sexual center (sacrum), (3) the solar plexus, (4) the heart, (5) the throat, (6) the center of your forehead, and (7) the very crown of your head. As you might expect by now, the name for the base chakra comes from the word for "root" (*mula*).

Each chakra corresponds to certain physical systems and organs. The base chakra, for example, is related to the adrenals; the sacral chakra to the ovaries or testes. The chakras also serve as the bridging mechanism between the physical realm and more subtle realms. Kundalini also teaches that the body has a network of energy channels called meridians or *nadis* (from *nad*, "to flow"). The central nadi, the *sushumna*, rises from the base chakra to the crown chakra, following the spine. The sushumna/spine is the Tree. The chakras, the Hoops, are strung on the inner column of sushumna "like jewels on a necklace."[27]

In each of us a latent energy, known as Kundalini Shakti, often visualized as a female serpent, lies coiled and drowsing at the base chakra. Shakti refers to the feminine aspect at all levels of creation. When Shakti is awakened from her slumber she can rise up from the base chakra through the central energy channel and stimulate all the higher chakras. At each chakra level, a Shakti power becomes an active partner with the male energy at that level.

The highest aspiration of the Kundalini system is the unification of divine Shakti and Shiva (male) energy in the highest chakra.

This "is the place of union where the marriage is celebrated. Shakti, mother of form, rises to meet Shiva, consciousness. Two opposite yet mutually attractive powers meet and coalesce."[28]

This embrace is similar to Dante's mysterious conjunction of "instinct and intellect balanced equally." The divine union of Shiva and Shakti brings wholeness and final liberation from the wheel of rebirth. It represents the ultimate integration of the Hoop and the Tree.

To bring about the union of Shiva and Shakti you must carefully open all the lower chakras in proper succession and allow Kundalini to rise. Opening a chakra involves learning and integrating the spiritual life lesson represented by that chakra. When the chakras are open, Kundalini energy can circulate in the body. In other words: growth is possible along the Tree dimension by opening the Hoops, and wholeness is well-modeled by the Hoops (chakras) on the Tree (spine/sushumna).

In psychological terms, the "root support," *muladhara*, of Kundalini's Tree represents the will to survive.[29] The second chakra (*svadisthana*) governs sexuality and procreation. The third chakra (*manipura*), the one at the solar plexus, is associated with power and will. If this "wheel" is out of alignment, a person will be either weak-willed and wishy-washy (too little will) or else willful, exercising power without regard to others (too much will).[30]

At these lower levels the Tree expresses itself in the drive to do things, to make things happen, sometimes without any ultimate purpose but for the mere joy of action, for the sake of experiencing oneself as the cause of changes. This tendency also appears in the desire to "conquer" the environment for the sake of conquest and to achieve greater efficiency at doing so. The Tree also expresses itself in the drive toward superiority and the drive toward acquisition. At the lower levels we perceive that the more we own the more of the universe we can subjugate to our own will. We can also see these qualities of the Tree in our more positive traits, such as curiosity and eagerness to explore and to know the world. That which we know is in a certain sense conquered.[31]

The heart chakra (number four, *anahata*) is associated with loving, nurturing, caring, supporting, and protecting. The throat chakra (five, *vishuddi*) has to do with communication and creativity. The brow chakra (six, *ajna*) is associated with direct perception and self-mastery. This is a higher manifestation of the urge to "know." The crown chakra (seven, *sahasrara*), which is often visualized as a multilayered lotus of a thousand white petals, has to do with union with the divine, and bliss.[32]

In addition to the central nadi or channel, the Kundalini system describes two other important channels related to the spinal Tree. These channels emerge from either side of the base chakra and travel up the body in a series of loops spiraling around the central channel. Each channel makes the shape of a Hoop extended on a Tree axis into a helix. The pattern they make has been likened to a pair of intertwined serpents.[33]

This pattern of intertwined serpents is virtually identical to the image of the caduceus, a winged staff with a pair of snakes twined around it. Historian Heinrich Zimmer traces this caduceus image as far back as at least ancient Mesopotamia (2600 BCE) as a symbol of wholeness and healing.[34] The Greek god Hermes carries this staff as he guides souls during transformation or after death to the upper or lower worlds. The Greek god of medicine and healing, Asclepius (Latin: Aesculapius), carries a similar staff. This same symbol lives today on medical stationery and hospital uniforms. In the helical snakes-on-the-staff we have another very ancient confirmation of the Hoop on the Tree as a pattern of healing or wholeness.

Many other wisdom traditions describe a similar Kundalini pattern of levels of Hoops on the Tree.[35] Since the Tree is a double metaphor, as axis of both the universe and the self, many of these Hoops-on-Tree systems show the Hoop-and-Tree pattern to be a fractal. Its shape at one size or scale is similar to its shape at another size or scale. Thus it is a pattern of wholeness both in the universe and in the individual psyche. For example, the Tibetan Buddhist Kalachakra mandala displays a series of levels of Hoops on a Tree axis to depict both individual and cosmic wholeness.

Another way to understand the levels on the Tree, especially the lower levels, is though psychology. Erik Erikson, building on Freud's work, created a hierarchical model of human development, which Erikson called the "eight ages of man." Erikson says that at each developmental stage a person confronts a "crisis" or struggle between a pull toward growth and a possibility of regression. In the first stage the struggle is between what Erikson calls Basic Trust in the universe and Mistrust. Normally a person resolves this issue during the first year or two of life. "The infant's first social achievement," says Erikson, "is his willingness to let the mother out of sight without undue anxiety or rage, because she has become an inner certainty as well as an outer predictability."[36] Later on, the struggles we confront are: Autonomy versus Shame and Doubt, Initiative versus Guilt, Industry versus Inferiority, Identity versus Role Confusion, Intimacy versus Isolation, Generativity versus Stagnation, and Ego Integrity versus Despair.

Erikson's modern psychological "chakras" bear a striking correspondence to the chakras of the Kundalini system. Kundalini chakra six, the brow chakra, is associated with direct perception and self-mastery. Self-mastery occurs when all parts of the self are integrated in a harmonious whole. So the function of the sixth chakra corresponds quite nicely with the ultimate stage of Erikson's eight ages: Ego Integrity and its fruit, wisdom. Generativity, Erikson's seventh age, is clearly related to Creativity of the fifth chakra. Intimacy, Erikson's sixth age, corresponds to Loving of the fourth chakra. Initiative and Industry, with their fruits of willpower and purpose, correspond to Power and Will. So Erikson's third and fourth ages map to the third chakra. The sense of basic trust established in Erikson's first age is equivalent to a firm sense of grounding and support in one's survival. So Erikson's first age corresponds to the first chakra.

The work at each of Erikson's "ages" is for the individual to achieve and integrate a *favorable ratio* of the tendency toward growth over the tendency toward regression. Total elimination of the regressive tendency is not the goal. Total elimination of Mistrust, for example would leave a person immaturely naive. What

Levels on the Tree

Kundalini Chakras   Erikson's Eight Ages

Kundalini Chakras		Erikson's Eight Ages
Divine Union	◯	
Self-Mastery	◯	◯ *8 Ego-Integrity (Wisdom)*
Creativity	◯	◯ *7 Generativity*
Loving	◯	◯ *6 Intimacy*
		5 Identity
Power, Will	◯	◯ *3,4 Initiative, Industry (Willpower, Purpose)*
Sexuality	◯	◯ *2 Autonomy*
Root Support	◯	◯ *1 Basic Trust*

is necessary at each stage is an appropriate resolution of the crisis. Erikson says that by achieving favorable ratios at each stage one attains essential human strengths: hope, willpower, purpose, competence, fidelity, love, care, and wisdom. The stages tend to follow each other in sequence, and success at a later stage depends on success at an earlier stage. Using a Tree metaphor, Erikson calls Ego Integrity, the positive aspect of the last stage, the "fruit" of the seven preceding stages.[37]

Erikson's developmental theory is not the only psychological counterpart to the Kundalini chakra system. Abraham Maslow identified five sets of needs that motivate us. Maslow ranked these needs in hierarchical order and said that we try to satisfy lower level needs before we try to satisfy higher level needs.[38] His "hier-archy of needs" also maps quite closely to the chakra system.

To investigate the Tree's levels fully takes years of study, but simply put: We all know that there are major lessons to learn or obstacles to overcome in the course of psycho-spiritual develop-ment. From all the various "chakra" systems, ancient and modern, we can say that our major lessons of individual development include those having to do with: (1) bodily survival, (2) bodily sexuality, (3) power/will, (4) heart/love, (5) communication/creativity, (6) self-mastery, and (7) divine union. All systems agree in associating health and well-being with the balanced opening of all the levels, all the "chakras" or Hoops, on the Tree of growth. All the systems also tell us that development generally takes place in ascending order, that it can be dangerous to try to ignore or "skip" levels on the way up, that greater maturity corresponds to higher functioning on the Tree axis, and that full maturity or health consists of being able to access the appropriate level at the appropriate moment.

Consider for a moment your own level of development on the Tree. Although there is not space here to go into great detail about the opening of each level on the Tree, you can gather a sense of your level of development by considering what life would be like if all the levels were open and available to you.*

If all the "chakras" were open and accessible, you would: feel yourself rooted in the living universe (chakra 1), be able to joy-fully consummate sexual union (chakra 2), be able to make deci-sions and use power appropriately (chakra 3), feel compassion for all living beings (chakra 4), be creative and express your deepest thoughts and feelings with clarity (chakra 5), master yourself and be in tune with an infinite source of guidance (chakra 6), and achieve a connection with the Divine, or ultimate being, which is beyond words (chakra 7).

---

* A few of the many books on chakra development include: Naiomi Ozaniec, *The Elements of the Chakra* (Rockport, MA: Element, 1990); Charles Breaux, *Journey into Consciousness* (York Beach, ME: Nicolas-Hays, 1989); Caroline Myss, *Anatomy of the Spirit* (New York: Three Rivers, 1996); Harish Johari, *Tools for Tantra* (Rochester, VT: Destiny/Inner Traditions, 1986).

Your level of maturity on the Tree axis can be partially measured by how effectively you have resolved Erikson's eight "crises," and also partially measured by your sources of motivation on Maslow's hierarchy.

Often, the area of pain or struggle in a person's life will point to the chakra that is least open, to the lesson to be chewed and digested. For example, if you find that you are jealous of someone who has power, or if you have a tendency to bullying, the blockage may well be in the third chakra. Problems in this chakra might also be indicated if you are dependent on someone in power or, conversely, *counter-dependent* to someone in power, consistently doing the opposite of what the other person wants, just to show how "independent" you are. When a wholesome balance has been achieved between Initiative and Guilt and you are able to use your proper power appropriately, then it is likely that the third chakra of the Tree is opened.

Even after one has begun the ascent of the Tree, the journey is fraught with difficulties. The *Ladder of Virtue* drawing by the Alsatian Herrade de Landsberg (twelfth century CE) depicts a knight and his lady, a nun, a cleric, a monk, a recluse, and a hermit all climbing at various rungs of a fifteen-rung ladder toward the crown of life.[39] Many of the climbers don't make it to the top, but topple from the rungs toward the enjoyment of mundane pleasures. Demons attack the climbers and armed angels try to protect them.

We know what this is like in our own lives. We have good intentions, "high hopes," but we become distracted. We let mundane problems "devil" us and distract us from our heart's path. We focus on our car payment instead of our karmic predicament. We could not even hope to make the ascent were it not for our teachers, our "mountain guides," and the "angels" which come in the form of fortuitous encounters with the good in the universe.

The ascent of the upper reaches of the Tree axis holds danger for the immature, the unbalanced, and the wrongly motivated. The Kabbalistic tradition tells of four rabbis who were awakened one night by an angel who carried them to the Seventh Vault of the Seventh Heaven, to the top of the Tree of Life. There they beheld the sacred Wheel of Ezekiel, the Hoop at the top of the Tree. Only one of the four was properly prepared. Upon their return the first rabbi died, the second went mad, and the third became a disbeliever. Only the fourth was able to integrate what he had seen. He saw with new eyes the beauty of his wife, the innocence of his son, the miracle of each blade of grass. His heart overflowed into poems and songs of praise. And he lived his life far better than before.

The Fruitful Tree

As you mature on the Tree axis you begin to yield fruit. Rumi reminds us that though it appears the tree *causes* the fruit, in reality the tree comes into existence *because of* the fruit.[40] This is the purpose for which your Tree grows. Saint Matthew says that Jesus once caused a fig tree to wither because it bore no fruit (Matthew 21:19). Denise Levertov, in her poem "What the Figtree Said," tells us that the barren fig tree stands for our barren hearts. We each have an obligation to bear human fruits of compassion and comprehension. Christ, the master poet, used the fig tree as a metaphor. When he blasted it, he cursed neither the tree nor his disciples but "their dullness, that withholds gifts *unimagined*."[41]

The fruit of your lifetime can take the form of spiritual fulfillment, of "gifts unimagined," or of attaining your highest aspiration. It can also take the form of wisdom, knowledge, creativity, skill, or power. Each of these "fruits" is related to a level on the Tree axis.

The fruit of Wisdom or Profound Knowledge is associated with Kundalini chakra six (the brow chakra). Language itself associates the Tree with wisdom. The words for wood and wisdom are very close: Irish *fid* and *fios* mean *trees* and *knowledge*; Welsh *gwydd* and *gwyddon* mean *trees* and *knowledgeable one*.[42] *Gwydd* is also related to the English word *wood*. The word *truth* as well as the word *Druid* and the word *tree*, all come from the same old Indo-European base *dru-*, which itself means tree.

Other fruit include the fruit of creativity (associated with chakra five, the throat chakra), the fruit of loving relationships (associated with chakra four, the heart chakra, which is the principle intersection of the Hoop and the Tree), and the fruit of skill and power (third chakra, at the solar plexus).

There are many ways to be fruitful. One can connect with the Divine and conduct healing energy into the Hoop of the world, as Christ does from the Tree of the Cross, as Kabbalist masters do through the Tree of Life. One can develop wisdom, create works that are beautiful and helpful, use one's skill and power for the good of the Hoop, raise children—the "fruit" of one's loins—to be fine adults. In a lifetime we can do some or many of these things. Jesus reminds us that we will be known by our fruit (Matthew 7:17, 20). By what fruit would you wish to be known?

One exceptionally powerful way to discover the answer to this question is to write your own obituary. For what do you most want to be remembered? How do you want people to feel when they remember you? What legacy do you want to leave? What would you like to have said about you after you are dead? "So-and-so was best known for . . ."

The Tree-and-Hoop Process of Development

> Human nature is not a machine to be built after
> a model and set to do exactly the work prescribed
> for it, but a tree, which [must] grow and develop
> itself on all sides.
>
> —John Stuart Mill, "Individuality"

The transpersonal psychologist Ken Wilber points out that the world's great wisdom traditions, including modern psychology, evolutionary theory, and systems theory, use Tree hierarchy in a multidimensional sense.[43] In other words, a hierarchy is not a simple ranking of one thing over another. It is a ranking of levels of wholeness. A silicon atom is a whole silicon atom, but it is only part of a grain of sand, which itself is a whole grain of sand but only a part of a beach. Arthur Koestler coined the term *holon*, "to designate these nodes on the hierarchic tree which behave partly as wholes or wholly as parts, according to the way you look at them."[44]

Any given stage, or holon, is higher than another because it *includes* the capacities, patterns, and functions of the lower stage and *adds* its own unique and more encompassing capacities. So the Tree hierarchy is actually not so much like a succession of geological strata or rungs on a ladder, but more like a nested set of Chinese boxes or Hoops on a Tree.

This same shape is evident in the evolution of consciousness itself, where the general pattern is *transcend and include*. Wilber says: "As the higher stages of consciousness emerge and develop, they themselves include the basic components of the earlier world-view, then add their own new and more differentiated perceptions. They transcend and include. Because they are more inclusive, they are more adequate. So, it's not that the earlier worldview is totally wrong and the new worldview is totally right. The earlier one was adequate, the new one is more adequate."[45]

Wilber emphasizes that it is only by rising up the Tree to higher levels of consciousness that one is able to embrace the wider rings of the Hoop. Each higher level on the Tree has a new and more inclusive worldview. The oak is categorically different from the acorn, though related to it. To move from the self-centeredness of the young child to the wider but still limited view of tribalism or ethnocentricity to the widest "worldcentric" morality requires growth up the Tree axis. Ultimately, from a high perspective, you begin to see the Divine in all. Wilber says, "To reach this higher and relatively rare stance of universal care, I must rise above my natural *biocentric* impulses (sex and survival), my *egocentric* wishes, and my *ethnocentric* proclivities—and stand instead as a relatively *worldcentric* locus of moral awareness that insists on universal compassion."[46]

In other words, the evolution of consciousness proceeds in a Hoop-and-Tree manner. Consciousness *transcends*, or moves up, along the Tree axis; and then it *includes*, or expands its Hoop. It evolves by differentiation (Tree) and integration (Hoop).[47]

Another way of saying this is that the Tree grows within the Hoop, and Hoops are the fruit of the Tree.

One example of the Tree growing within the Hoop is the struc-ture of all successful initiation practices. Malidoma Patrice Somé is a contemporary shaman initiated in Africa, with PhDs from Brandeis and the Sorbonne. Somé says that in order for an initiation to be complete (individual growth on the Tree axis), there has to be a village (Hoop of community) to recognize, acknowledge, and welcome us back from our initiation. Without this witnessing by the community, our psyche gets the message that the initiation is not complete, so we feel we have to go out and try again. "In the absence of a village," he says, "everyone is in an initiatory jungle."[48]

The evidence of this jungle is painfully familiar in the daily news of gangs, disaffected children, and angry grown-ups, many of whom feel they have never been satisfactorily initiated into adulthood. The Hoop has not been there to support the Tree of individual growth in consciousness. Our adolescents in particular try risky behavior over and over again. Yet they never receive confirmation from the community that their risky actions have proven anything. The risks they take find no context in the wider community. There is no integration following differentiation.

A Modern Tree Story

The Tree is the valiant sprouting of each individual life force, and of each individual's urge to bear fruit. Through the Tree your unique identity matures and you are able to do in this life what you came to do.

One of my counseling clients came looking for her Tree. Jan was a newly promoted supervisor. Though successful in her previous position, in her new position she found herself feeling overwhelmed and anxious. She doubted her ability to be powerful or fruitful. One might say that Jan's elevation or promotion to a higher level had the inner meaning of calling her to a higher level of development on the Tree. In the safe Hoop of the counseling relationship we began to explore her concerns. The exploration led both downward and upward along the Tree axis.

Jan's associations to her present situation eventually led to her "roots," particularly to memories of her father. When Jan was a little girl her father had been emotionally absent; she had always felt inadequate in his presence. These roots lead up to Jan's present-day sense of inadequacy. When she tried to draw on a deep source of strength, she found little to support her. In a healthy tree the roots nourish, but here the roots were, in effect, sucking vitality out of her present life. Some of her roots were gnawed on or poisoned.

Jan's explorations in counseling eventually led also to her aspirations. Hesitatingly at first, she was able to give an image for her ideal: For the present at least, it was a warm, safe, rustic house in the woods, where she could be with her husband and also have time to be with nature and . . . to dance! Here she was reaching the level of the Tree where it starts to be creative, to bear fruit. As she allowed herself to savor this image, she began to weep with joy and relief.

Strengthened by the image of her aspirations, of who she could become, Jan was able to return to the exploration of her roots and to reach, if not peace, at least an emotional truce with her remembered father. After our period of work together Jan told me that while she still felt challenged by her new position, she was no longer overwhelmed or incapacitated by anxiety.

In my work with Jan I didn't talk with her directly about the Tree. But what she did was to develop "comfort from a high place" and "support from a low place." It was her work on the Tree axis with roots and aspiration that helped her to heal and develop.

Carl Jung says, "Healing comes only from what leads the patient beyond himself and beyond his entanglement in the ego."[49] It could be said that the Hoop approach to healing leads the patient "beyond" by leading out and in; the Tree approach leads the patient "beyond" by leading up and down, or down and up. The engineer Mark was healed by widening and connecting along the Hoop dimension. He learned how to go out and come back in to build relationship. Jan, the new supervisor, was healed by growing along the Tree dimension. She went up to her highest aspirations and down into her roots.

"Support from a Low Place"

> Just like a tree that's standing by the water, we shall
> not be moved.

> —folk song

The town may be moved, but the well cannot be
moved.

—*I Ching*, Hexagram 48

For there is hope for a tree,
if it be cut down, that it will sprout again,
and that its shoots will not cease.
Though its root grow old in the earth,
and its stump die in the ground,
yet at the scent of water it will bud
and put forth branches like a young plant.

—Job 14:7–9[50]

Who would not want to be called a person with soul?

A soulful person is someone we find it easy to be around. We have a sense that this person knows about life, with all its ups and downs, and that this person has learned something about imperfection, and might therefore even be willing to accept us just as we are, with our own imperfections. We don't have to pretend around this person. This person has been to the roots of his or her own being, roots that reach toward the water of life. This person has touched the source of moisture, the deep currents in the universe. This is a person of depth.

Traditionally "soul" is associated with water and has a downward direction, while "spirit" is associated with fire and has an upward direction. So it could be said that work on the Tree axis involves both ascending the bole toward the crown of spirit and descending the roots toward soul and toward the moisture that also fills the bottom of the well.

When the Grimm brothers traveled around Germany collecting fairy tales, they recorded the roots of modern psychological understanding. Although the stories were first written down in the early nineteenth century, they represent an oral tradition perhaps thousands of years old. Before the widespread use of a written language, oral tales were the only way we humans could pass on to the next generation our accumulated wisdom about how to cope with the trials of life. Many of these tales teach about "support from a low place" and remind us that the way down is the way up.

In the Grimm fairy tale "The Devil with the Three Golden Hairs" the hero is set a typically impossible task. He must not only find the devil himself (or in some versions a giant ogre) but also must pluck and bring back three hairs from the devil's own head. The hero is the "child of good fortune," male or female, within each of us; and the successful completion of the task will prove this child ready for the sacred marriage and worthy of "kingship," that is, capable of sovereignty in his or her own being. On his quest the youth passes through two towns. In the first town there is a well that once flowed with wine but no longer gives even water. In the second there is a tree which once bore golden apples but now does not even put forth leaves. The citizens of both towns ask the youth for help.

The youth eventually does get the three golden hairs, and from the dreams of the "devil" discovers what is wrong with both the well and the tree. There is a toad at the bottom of the well, poisoning it, and there is a mouse gnawing at the roots of the tree, killing it. The youth tells the townspeople to destroy these two creatures. When this is done the well flows again and the tree once more yields golden apples.

The doubling of the theme in this story—the poisoned well, the nibbled roots—hints at a secret correspondence between the Hoop and the Tree at some deep level. The Tree of course has its roots. The archetypal well is shaped like a Hoop at its surface level. The quality of roots is that they reach down and draw up. The quality of the well is that it wells: it fills with water from a deep source. Both of these qualities deal with moisture. In the metaphorical sense they deal with the moisture of deep mysteries not fully knowable by human consciousness, the moisture into which we all dip each night when we sleep and dream. We put forth branches at even the scent of this water.

Both the Tree's roots and the Hoop's well suggest not only reaching down to touch the water of life, but also stability and steadfastness. The Grimms' tale says that all of these qualities are essential to a healthy psyche, to a person claiming his or her "sovereignty." As the familiar proverb has it, "a tree is only as strong as its roots." And we know we've lost something profound and essential "when the well runs dry."

You'll recall that each of the three roots of the cosmic Tree Yggdrasill was watered by a spring or a well (Hoop). The descent to wisdom may allow us to get to the *source* (from the French word *sourse* meaning "a spring of water," a natural well). The descent also may allow us to get to the *root* of a problem. In the rich and mysterious underworld lies the secret correspondence between the Hoop and the Tree.

The Nibbled Roots/The Poisoned Well

In my counseling work with Jan she discovered that her psyche connected her present difficulties to childhood experiences with her father. There was a link, a thread leading from the present day to a part of her family Tree, her childhood roots. Jan's discovery confirmed what therapists find over and over again: whether conscious or unconscious, whether nourishing or draining, our roots are always with us.

In the metaphor of the Grimms' tale, Jan's roots were nibbled at, poisoned in a way that made it difficult for her Tree to bear fruit in her present life. She had her own personal dragon, just like the dragon Nidhogg who gnaws at the roots of the world Tree Yggdrasill, trying to loosen what is firm and put an end to the eternal. Jan's roots were in the underground of her unconscious until she began to look at them. Then her healing began.

Psychological Roots and Healing

Sigmund Freud was the first modern psychologist to direct attention to the depths of the Tree axis. Freud discovered the psychological underworld of the unconscious, and he looked for the causes of psychological problems in a person's "roots" in early childhood. Freud said that the task of psychoanalytic treatment is to make conscious everything that is pathogenically unconscious.[51] This work is to bring our unconscious material "up" into consciousness, to "lift" repressions, and to "sublimate" (from the Latin: *to raise*) unacceptable impulses into socially valued motivations. Freudian therapy heals along the Tree axis by delving down into the roots and then rising up again.

Freud's senior student, Carl Jung, also worked along the Tree dimension. Jung's term for the process of coming to wholeness is *individuation*. Jungian analyst Freida Fordham summarizes Jung's beliefs when she says that individuation necessitates "*the forging of a link between the conscious and the unconscious aspects of the psyche* . . . No one who really seeks wholeness can develop his intellect at the price of repression of the unconscious, nor, on the other hand, can he live in a more or less unconscious state" [emphasis added].[52] To forge this link one must travel psychologically up and down along the Tree axis between the "higher" levels of consciousness and the "lower" levels of the unconscious. This is precisely what Jan began to do.

Various Tree approaches to psychology have emphasized different parts of the Tree. It could be said that Freud and his followers were interested in the roots: the unconscious and the repressed history of early childhood. People like Erik Erikson were interested in development from the roots up through the trunk to the fruit. Alfred Adler, who developed the school called "individual psychology," focused on the motivators of social success and power. In terms of the levels on the Tree, Adler's focus is above the roots, but not far up the trunk. Skill and power can be understood as a hierarchical level on the Tree located somewhere around chakra three, below wisdom and knowledge, which in turn are below contact with the Divine. Abraham Maslow was interested in the motivational aspects near the highest level of the Tree. The highest level also provides the perspective for a school of psychotherapy known as logotherapy.

Logotherapy was developed by Viktor Frankl, a psychiatrist who survived three grim years at Auschwitz and other Nazi prisons. Through his experiences as a prisoner Frankl found that the search for meaning in life promotes psychological health. To search for meaning is to search the upper levels of the Tree, toward wisdom, understanding, and ultimately the Divine "comfort from a high place." It is an enactment of "vertical longing." Frankl says, "In logotherapy the patient is actually confronted with and reoriented toward the meaning of his life. . . . According to logotherapy, the striving to find a meaning in one's life is the primary motivational force in man."[53] Frankl speaks of a *will to meaning* in contrast to Freud's *will to pleasure* or Adler's *will to power*. Meaning, pleasure, and power are all different levels on the Tree.

To speak of different levels on the Tree is not to say that one approach to psychotherapy is better than another. There are just differing approaches that pay attention to different parts of the Tree. The individual, as a Tree, matures by reaching down into the roots and then growing up, gaining power, skill, knowledge, and wisdom, and then bearing fruit. The effectiveness of therapy will depend in part on using an approach that matches where the patient or client is on his or her journey along the Tree dimension.

The Descent to Wisdom

> The path of ascent and descent is one and the same.

> —Heraclitus

Once upon a time there was a poor woodcutter who had an only son. This woodcutter loved his son more than life itself. The man had, by scrimping, saved enough money to send the boy away to school so that he might have a better life than his father. The son did well at school and was liked by his teachers but, alas, the money ran out before the boy's education was complete. He had no choice but to return home.

Now the son strongly desired to be of help to his father, so he proposed that they borrow an ax from a neighbor and that he go with his father the next day to cut wood. This they did. After working hard all morning they stopped to rest and eat some lunch. The father sat and ate, but the boy decided he would take his meal wandering through the forest looking for birds' nests.

As he was wandering about he came upon a great danger-
ous-looking oak, certainly many hundreds of years old. In awe
he stopped and stared. Then all of a sudden he heard someone
calling in a tiny smothered voice, "Let me out! Let me out!" He
looked around but could discover nothing. He cried out, "Where
are you?" The voice answered: "I am down here, amongst the roots
of the oak tree. Let me out! Let me out!"

The boy loosened the earth around the roots of the tree and
eventually discovered a glass bottle in a little hollow. Inside the
bottle was an ugly little creature hopping up and down crying
"Let me out! Let me out!" Thinking no evil, the boy uncorked the
bottle. Immediately the creature in the bottle streamed out in a
plume of ascending smoke to become a huge and fearsome figure
towering over the boy.

"Now you shall have your reward for releasing me," said the
spirit in an angry voice. "I shall break your neck."

"Why would you do that to the person who freed you?" the
boy asked.

The spirit replied that he was the mighty Mercurius, and was
bound to break the neck of whosoever released him.

"That is all very well," said the boy, thinking quickly. "I am
ready to accept my fate, but I do not wish to meet my death at
the hands of a liar."

"What do you mean?" roared the indignant spirit.

"I do not believe that a spirit as great as you could be the same
one as fit into that tiny bottle. If you can get in again, I will believe
you. And then you may do as you please with me."

"Oh, but that is a simple matter." So saying, the spirit transformed himself again into a plume of colored smoke and withdrew
into the bottle.

No sooner was the spirit back in the bottle than the boy
rammed the cork into the bottle's neck, trapping the spirit once
more. The boy was about to put the bottle back among the roots
and return to his father, but he heard the spirit pleading piteously.
"Let me out! Let me out and I shall give you so much that you
shall have plenty all the days of your life."

Now, what would you have done?

The boy at first refused. But the spirit promised to do him no harm and to reward him richly. The boy thought: well, perhaps he will reward me, and if not, I could probably get the better of him again.

For a second time the boy uncorked the bottle. The spirit, when he emerged, was true to his word. He gave the boy a magic cloth, the one end of which when rubbed on iron would turn it into silver. The other end of the cloth would heal any wound.

With the power of silver, the boy was able to support his father in comfort for the rest of his life; and with the power of healing, the boy became the greatest physician in the world. The boy married well, and lived a long and fruitful life.

This story from the Grimm brothers' collection speaks of how our consciousness matures. At the beginning the boy is only partly mature—"half-educated" in the metaphor of the story. He still has much to learn. But he has learned enough that he can begin to approach the deep power of life. This story holds many lessons, including lessons about the potential danger of the Kundalini energy and of ascending too quickly, cautions we have heard before. But perhaps the most important lesson is that, as Jung points out, the secret of individuation, the "spirit in the bottle," is hidden not up high where the birds make their nests but in the tree's roots.[54] The secret is potentially lethal, until the boy learns how to control it—how to contain it, how to release it, and when each action is appropriate.

The descent for wisdom, worship, or boons has been a human tradition for at least ten thousand years and probably much longer. We have evidence of our ancestors' descent for blessing in the art of the great Paleolithic temple caves such as the one at Lascaux in France. Traditional mythologies throughout the world, from Arctic regions to Africa, tell stories of descent to a realm of the spirits and the dead, variously called the Lowerworld, the Netherworld, the Underworld, or Hell. Typically in these stories the descent produces some sort of wisdom or healing—either insight into the mysteries of life, or the ability to heal, or the ability to bring the dead back to life, or some object that is a talisman of wisdom.

Psychologically this deep realm is related to everything below our conscious awareness. This includes both our *personal uncon-scious*—experiences, feelings, and thoughts from our own lives of which we are unaware—and also includes what Carl Jung named the *collective unconscious*—the underground storehouse of thoughts and feelings that belongs to us simply because we are human beings. It includes our psychological *shadow*, those parts of our-selves we have succeeded in pushing out of consciousness because they are too painful or embarrassing to acknowledge.

There are many methods of descending into the roots. Yet all of these methods require a passageway. Since the goal of the descent is the unconscious, a purely conscious assault won't get you there. In many traditional stories, and in shamanic journeys from around the world, the passageway is a Tree's roots. The sha-man rappels down into the roots of the unconscious on a slender lifeline of drumming or powerful plant medicine, safeguarded by a Hoop of ceremony. The Conibo Indians in South America, for example, follow the roots of the giant catahua tree down into the ground to reach the Lowerworld.[55] In Virgil's *Aeneid*, the Tree of Persephone marks the hero's route of descent to wisdom.

The primary psychological equivalent of descending via the roots is descending via the dream. Freud calls the dream the "royal road" to the unconscious. Jungians use techniques of *ampli-fication* (making conscious associations with dream images) and *active imagination* to reenter a dream. Gestalt therapists encour-age their clients to engage in dialog with elements from their dreams and in the process to become those elements and "re-own" them. Other psychological passageways of descent include paying exquisite attention to one's inner thoughts and feelings as they arise and then following them down (as in Hakomi ther-apy) and also the non-ordinary states of consciousness used in shamanic counseling.[56]

By whatever technique, we humans need to descend from time to time because our consciousness, the part of the Tree above the ground, can dry up unless it is constantly refreshed by the mysteri-ous waters of the unconscious. In fact, it is often the darkest parts, the muck and the compost, that can be most nourishing. Marie-Louise von Franz, one of Jung's foremost students, says that the healing happens "in the underworld, it happens in the dark when there is no light shining."[57]

She also reminds us that the healing work in the depths is not always pretty. "Sometimes," she says, "one has an awkward dream which disgusts one on waking; it is either indecent or obscene, dreadfully silly or stupid and it is irritating. One wanted a wonderful archetypal dream and then this comes! But . . . it is just those dreams which are so valuable; they have an unapproachable, disgusting shell of depressing blackness but within that is the light of the unconscious. It is often in the depressing motifs of the dream that the light is to be found, and naturally it is also to be found in the shadowy impulses which are full of meaning if one can lovingly investigate them."[58]

Loving investigation means loving yourself enough to be willing to do the work of confronting the darkness or dragon that gnaws at your roots. We know from countless fairy tales that dragons guard the gold. But simply piled under the dragon's cold, scaly belly, gold is useless. Dragons just hoard; they don't know how to use the gold. To recover the riches from the depths, we must descend and deal with our own personal darkness, whose name is dragon.

Though it's all very well to know theoretically that there is some value in descending into the dark depths, we often don't want to descend. Even approaching the descent can feel like heavy work. The heaviness itself is a sign of sinking. Sometimes the descent begins involuntarily. As Robert Bly has often said, sometimes a hand will reach up and pull you down into depression. Yet there are gifts down there. No one knows exactly how these gifts come. The depths are shadowy. But proper descent into the depths may bring gifts. Hades, the Greek god of the underworld, was also known as Pluto ("wealth") and Trophonios ("nourishing").

The Darkness or Dragon at the Root, and the Gift

Once upon a time a few years ago there grew a marvelous apple tree in the king's garden. The king had such affection for this tree that he could bear no one else to touch it. In his heart the king said to himself as he said out loud, "If anyone were to pick an apple from this tree, I would wish him a hundred fathoms underground!" Now it happened that by harvesttime this tree hung heavy with succulent apples, which all were as red as blood. It also happened that the king had three daughters, the youngest of whom found herself with an overwhelming desire for one of those sweet red fruit.

"I'm sure Daddy loves us too much to wish *us* a hundred fathoms underground," said she to her sisters. "And they look so juicy. Let's have an apple." Saying this, she reached up and plucked one. No sooner had the three of them tasted that apple, than all three sank deep under the earth, "where they could hear no cock crow."

This Grimm fairy tale continues by telling of the king's grief, and of three brothers who set out to find the princesses. Eventually the youngest brother discovered where the princesses were, and descended in a bucket down a deep well to rescue them. At the bottom of the well he found them guarded by three dragons, which he proceeded to slay one after the other.

His brothers, however, betrayed him. After hauling the three princesses up through the well, the older brothers abandoned the youngest to die in those chambers deep in the earth.

The youngest brother was down there for a long time. One might say he was in a depression. He was certainly isolated from life. He had wrestled with, and defeated, some poisonous dragons. But something remained to be done. Perhaps it was a question of persevering. The story says that he wandered about in the underground chambers for such a long time that he made the surface of the ground quite smooth beneath his feet.

At last, other thoughts came to him. He had long noticed a small flute hanging on the wall in one of the chambers, but had thought nothing of it. Finally he took the flute down from the wall and played a note. Suddenly, an elf appeared. He played five notes, and five elves appeared. He played a little tune and soon the room was entirely filled. The elves asked what he desired. To be above ground and in daylight again, he replied. Each elf seized him by one of the hairs that grew on his head and quickly flew him onto the surface of the earth.

After some further adventures the story ends with this brother marrying the youngest princess, and everyone living happily ever after. But the young man also gained some gift by being underground, a creative gift, symbolized by the flute and the music.

Jazz saxophonist Sonny Rollins seemed to be at the peak of his career in the late 1950s, performing with the likes of Miles Davis, Charlie Parker, and Theloneous Monk. As a young musician he had *ascended* quickly. But he was dissatisfied with his own playing. In 1959 he made the highly unusual move of taking a sabbatical from performing. He kept to himself, living on the Lower East Side of Manhattan and practicing at night on the Williamsburg Bridge to avoid disturbing neighbors. Rollins said "I was getting very famous at the time and I felt I needed to brush up on various aspects of my craft. I felt I was getting too much, too soon, so I said, wait a minute, I'm going to do it my way."[59] Perhaps this was an underground period for him. After many months, when his constant practicing had "made the ground quite smooth under his feet," he heard inside himself a renewal of music. He noticed the flute and took it down from the wall and returned to create many exceptional performances and recordings.

Marie-Louise von Franz says, "Unless there is a latent psychosis, a depression should be encouraged and people told to go into it and *be* depressed—not try to escape . . . Listen, go deeper and deeper, until you again reach the level of the psychological energy where some creative idea can come out and suddenly, at the bottom an impulse of life and creativeness which has been overlooked may appear."[60] We all need a little "down time."

The work of wrestling, or consciously bearing the weight of the darkness, is the healing work. To "bear the weight" of something is the root meaning of the word "suffer." If we do not do our "legitimate suffering," said Jung, then we will be neurotic.[61]

It is when we do *not* wrestle the dragon, when we do *not* kill the nibbling mouse or the poisoning toad, that the poison seeps up through our roots and becomes evil in the world. Then our Tree bears evil fruit. What darkness or dragon do you wrestle with?

Many years ago I was suffering in a deadening job that was slowly killing my soul. I had tried many times to find a more suitable job, but somehow nothing had worked out. The overt part of the problem was that I had no savings and couldn't afford to quit my old job while I looked for a new one. The covert part of the problem was that I was afraid to let go and follow my heart's bliss.

I sensed that, voluntarily or involuntarily, I was going to descend. For some years previous I'd been practicing the old shamanic technique of descending into the lower world by following the roots of a tree. So one day I went high into the mountain forest and found a tree, and through the tree's roots began my voluntary descent.

In the deepest part of this waking dream I encountered a huge dragon. We began a frightful wrestling. Eventually I managed to snap off two of the dragon's front teeth. Later, walking back to my car along the forest path I passed a lightning-blasted tree that I hadn't noticed on my way in. My eyes were drawn magnetically to two balls of hardened sap that had been melted out of the tree by the lightning. Somehow I realized that these two represented the dragon's two teeth. I took them home and put them in my medicine pouch.

Less than a week later, totally unexpectedly, I received a check in the mail. It was a spontaneous loan from a friend, to be paid back whenever I could pay it. It was not a large amount, but it was enough for a couple of months' expenses if I lived frugally. And the unexpectedness of the offer and the generosity behind it gave me the courage to make the leap into the unknown. I left my job and began a difficult, sometimes painful, but ultimately successful journey to a new life.

After a period of conscious wrestling, our descent rewards us unexpectedly with some creative gift. We learn to play the flute of the elves. Deep in the cave we rub Aladdin's magic lamp. One of my clients was a man who had achieved great worldly success as senior vice president at a large corporation. Yet he was miserable to the point of tears because he was not following his heart's true aspiration. We began gently to explore some of the dark, shadowy areas of his pain, using techniques of awareness and deepening. He came at last to the image of a dark and foreboding forest. Between him and the forest was a wrought iron fence with sharp spikes. Though the gate in this fence was latched, the mechanism for opening the latch was facing my client. While he stood looking at the gate there emerged from the depths of the forest a wise old man who beckoned to my client to enter. The darkness of the forest terrified my client, but eventually he was able to open the gate and follow the wise man. The wise man became an inner companion, an image of my client's deep inner wisdom, who eventually helped my client find a new life of personal fulfillment.

Consider in your own life what unexpected gift may have come to you in a time of working in the depths. It may have been a renewal of natural creativity, or it may have been simply and profoundly the gift of being able to help others who are in despair.

One Kabbalistic tradition teaches that every descent is the predecessor of an ascent. Just as with a Tree's roots, our own reaching down to drink the water of life permits new growth upward. So the descent is always an essential part of initiation.

Once, in the time beside time, in the time beyond time, in the time beneath time, there was a young woman, both pretty and industrious, who was mistreated by her stepmother and obliged to do all the work of the household. Every day the poor girl had to sit by a well and spin and spin until her fingers bled. Now it happened that one day the spindle was stained by her blood; and so she dipped the spindle in the well to wash off the mark. But the spindle slipped out of her hand and fell to the bottom of the well. Learning of this, the cruel stepmother told the girl that she had to fetch the spindle out again. In the sorrow of her heart the girl jumped into the well and soon lost consciousness.

When she came to herself again, she was in a lovely meadow. Across this meadow she wandered until she came to a baker's oven full of bread. The bread called to her: "Oh take me out! Take me out! Or I shall burn; I have been baked a long time." The girl rescued the bread and then went on her way. Next she came to a tree full of rosy apples. The tree called to her: "O shake me! Shake me! My apples are all ripe." She shook the tree and gathered the apples into a heap.

At last she came to the dwelling of a fearsome old woman with large teeth. The old woman treated her kindly, though, and the girl entered into the old woman's service. The girl worked faithfully and had a pleasant life for some time. When the moment came for the girl to return to the upper world, the old woman led her there through a doorway that showered the girl with drops of gold like rain. The gold blessed and enriched her return to human life. This Grimm brothers' story of descent is named "Mother Holle," after the kind old woman at the bottom of the well. Mother Holle, or Mother Hel, was the chthonic or underworld form of the great goddess in northern Europe. Traditionally, wells were considered water-passages to her underground womb. Mother Holle's name is related to the words *holy* and *healing.*[62]

The rest of the Mother Holle story tells about the girl's step-sister. When our girl returned covered with gold, her stepmother was eager to obtain the same good luck for her own daughter, a girl both ugly and lazy. The stepmother bade her daughter go to the same well to sit and spin. In order that the spindle should be stained with blood, the lazy daughter pricked her finger on a thornbush. She then tossed her spindle into the well and jumped in after it.

She came, like the other, to the beautiful meadow and walked along the very same path. But the lazy and selfish girl refused the cries for help from the baking bread and the apple tree. When she came to Mother Holle's house she immediately offered to work. Although the girl worked industriously the first day, by the second her laziness began to overtake her, and by the third day she barely got out of bed. Mother Holle soon tired of this and gave the girl notice to leave. The girl was eager, expecting a rich reward of gold. But when she passed through the door of return, what showered

on her was not gold, but sticky black pitch. And the story says
that the pitch clung fast to her and could not be got off as long
as she lived.

Here the descent into the well, like the descent into the roots of
the Tree, is a descent to wisdom or healing. This story is about a
girl's coming-of-age (the bread is "baked," the apples are "ripe," the
blood on the spindle relates to menarche). It says that to become
a full adult a girl must descend and honor or "serve" the deep
feminine, who is not always pretty on first meeting.

An even fiercer story of the descent to wisdom was first
inscribed on clay tablets with a wedge-shaped reed stylus about
four thousand years ago. It is perhaps the oldest known story of
a divinity who makes a redeeming sacrifice by death and descent.
This story concerns the goddess Inanna, the Sumerian Queen of
Heaven, associated with the beautiful morning star, who was also
known to Semitic peoples by the name of Ishtar. For the Sumerians, Inanna played a greater role in myth, epic, and hymn than
any other deity, male or female.[63] She was worshipped and adored.

We know that Inanna was associated with the Tree. According
to Sumerian myth the first living thing on earth was a tree—the
huluppu-tree, which grew by the banks of the Euphrates River.
But the whirling South Wind arose and pulled at the tree and the
rising waters of the Euphrates carried it away. It was Inanna who
rescued the tree from the river and planted it in her holy garden.[64]
The wood from this tree eventually supplied Inanna with her bed
and her throne. Since one of Inanna's aspects is goddess of love,
her bed is as emblematic of her power as her throne.

As the cuneiform scriptures relate, Inanna one day "opened
her ear to the great Below," and resolved to visit her elder sister
Ereshkigal, Queen of the Underworld, goddess of death. Ereshkigal's husband had died and Inanna wished to descend to witness
the funeral rites. The present-day singer of Inanna's story, Diane
Wolkstein, explains: "Inanna is Queen of Heaven and Earth, but
she does not know the underworld. Until her ear opens to the
Great Below, her understanding is necessarily limited. In Sumerian,
the word for ear and wisdom is the same. . . . It is the Great Below,

and the knowledge of death and rebirth, life and stasis, that will make of Inanna an 'Honored Counselor.'"[65]

In the upper or outer world Inanna abandons her temples and her office of holy priestess. She abandons "heaven and earth" and goes to the outer gates of the underworld, where she knocks loudly. She cries out to gatekeeper in a fierce voice: "Open the door, Neti! I alone would enter."[66]

Neti carries this disrespectful demand to her mistress Ereshkigal. Ereshkigal is furious. As goddess of the Below she is just as much a goddess as Inanna, the goddess of the Above. Inanna hasn't acknowledged this. Ereshkigal therefore says, "Come, Neti, my chief gatekeeper, heed my words: Bolt the seven gates of the underworld. Then, one by one, open each gate a crack. Let Inanna enter. As she enters, remove her royal garments. Let the holy priestess of heaven enter bowed low."

Inanna enters the first gate and the crown of the steppe is removed from her head. Inanna protests, "What is this?" But she is told only that "the ways of the underworld are perfect. They may not be questioned."[67]

At each of the seven gates a symbolic garment or adornment is removed, until Inanna enters the throne room of Ereshkigal naked and bowed low. "Then Ereshkigal fastened on Inanna the eye of death. She spoke against her the word of wrath. She uttered against her the cry of guilt. She struck her. Inanna was turned into a corpse, a piece of rotting meat, and was hung from a hook on the wall."[68]

In psychological terms, in meeting Ereshkigal Inanna encounters the cool objective eye that sees death clearly, and knows that cutting asunder and dissolution are fully part of life. Ereshkigal dwells in the region of the root chakra. Jungian analyst Sylvia Brinton Perera says: "Here there is both inertia and an elemental healing source. It is the place of survival and earth and rock-solid beginnings. It is the place of the Self *in status nascendi*—the jewel hidden in matter."[69]

Before Inanna had left for the underworld, she had given instructions to her assistant Ninshubur about what to do in case she didn't return. When Inanna fails to return after three days and three nights, Ninshubur sets out to effect her rescue. In a state of mourning, Ninshubur pleads with some of the high gods for help. Two of the gods refuse her, but Enki, the god of waters and wisdom, fashions two little asexual mourners from the dirt under his fingernail. They slip unnoticed into the underworld, carrying gifts of the food and water of life. When they arrive in the deep, they find Ereshkigal moaning with the cries of a woman about to give birth. The two little mourners empathize with Ereshkigal and moan and groan with her. Ereshkigal is so moved by their empathy that she offers them a gift. The gift they ask for is the return of Inanna. Their request is granted. There is much more to the myth, but we will leave its further telling to another time.

In a psychological sense this whole drama is enacted within the psyche, and all the players represent various aspects of the same psyche. So the creation of the two mourners and their willingness to suffer with Ereshkigal represent the emergence in the psyche of something new. It is because of this new willingness to accept the lowerworld on its own terms that the part of the psyche represented by Inanna is allowed to return to the upperworld.

Inanna's descent can be seen as a description of an initiation process whereby one learns something of the mysteries of death. It can also be seen as a process of psychological balancing in which the repressed, denied, split-off, "underworld" aspects of the psyche become reintegrated with the conscious aspects, thereby forging Jung's "link between the conscious and the unconscious aspects of the psyche." The myth describes a pattern of psychological growth for the feminine principle, both in women and in men.

In this psychological view, Ereshkigal of the underworld is the neglected side of the conscious feminine represented by Inanna. None of the powers that "adorn" Inanna in the upperworld are of any avail in the underworld. In contemporary terms, these upperworld powers might be like those of being a skilled lawyer or a gracious hostess. Inanna must surrender and submit to the deep feminine. Sylvia Brinton Perera says "this openness to being acted upon is the essence of the experience of the human soul faced with the transpersonal. It is not based upon passivity, but upon an active willingness to receive."[70] She also says that by working with this myth, some modern women have been able to redeem their own potential of joyful sexuality and active assertion from the underworld of the psyche, while others have developed the capacity for appropriate receptivity and reflection.[71] In the descent, the conscious ego learns something about the deep, integral processes of life.

In her descent along the Tree axis Inanna encounters aspects of feminine energy that include cold rage and the "eye of death"—the ability to end a life process. Such qualities are the opposite of the conventional "above ground" attributes of the feminine, which are typically warm and life-giving. Certainly no one would want to live a lifetime in the dismal realm of Ereshkigal. Yet without the ability to end as well as to begin, no man or woman is capable of a true, soul-to-soul, passionate relationship with another person as an equal partner. Life is not possible without Death, and, as Clarissa Pinkola Estes says in *Women Who Run with the Wolves*, "If one wishes to be fed for life, one must face and develop a relationship with the Life/Death/Life nature."[72]

Rooted in the Universe

Descent into the roots of our psyche, burrows us into the *humus*, Latin for "earth" or "ground," and gives us *humility*. The wisdom traditions teach that it is only with proper humility that one may ascend safely. In Inanna's descent, the removal of her garments symbolizes this process of becoming humble. We each have manure of our own making, of which we feel ashamed. But when manure is composted, it fertilizes the growth of the Tree. The work of descent is the work of composting.

We are connected with our own roots through our family Tree, our ancestral Tree. The roots of this Tree can connote inescapable entanglement with the past, with family history, with the parochialism of small community. One's family history may include a lineage of negativity, silence, incest, mental illness, or alcoholism.

The work of descent is also the work of coming to terms with such entanglements, difficulties, darkness. Some shamanic traditions teach that when you heal a negativity of this sort, you heal it not only in your own life and for the benefit of your descendants, but you also heal it in your ancestors, all the way back to the original difficulty.

The roots of our past and our family history also serve to nurture, ground, and stabilize us so an overly proud, haughty, high Tree doesn't topple, and so we can indeed grow tall. Daniel Webster expressed the powerful connection between sound ancestral roots and appropriate elevation or rising up along the Tree axis when he wrote, "there is a moral and philosophical respect for our ancestors which elevates the character."[73]

Malidoma Patrice Somé, the contemporary shaman trained in the traditional practices of the Dagara people of West Africa, has some experience with roots. His own initiation into adulthood in Dagara society included a perilous shamanic descent to the underworld from which at least one of his companions did not return.[74] The underworld experience was the final initiatory mission that allowed Somé to grow into himself as an adult man. Malidoma Somé emphasizes that we cannot become fully awake, fully developed, without our roots. "This awakening is not triggered by someone in the clouds but because our feet are on the ground and the ancestors are sending heat."[75]

In our own lives we often experience a frisson of this heat when we handle an object that belonged to one of our ancestors—grandfather's watch, perhaps, or great-grandmother's brooch. One of my treasures is my grandfather Abuelo's solid black leather case that contains the remnants of the homeopathic medicines he gave his patients. Whenever I hold it I sense his presence in my life. Objects like these amplify what is happening at every moment. What kind of heat might your ancestors be sending you right now?

Another form of roots that ground us is the lineage of our craft. Isaac Newton said, "If I have seen further than others, it is because I have stood on the shoulders of giants." In any form of work we stand on the shoulders of giants. These are the foremothers and forefathers who did the work to invent the light bulb, to discover the uses of mustard seed, to figure out ways to calm a teething baby. Our lives are easier because of them. Moreover in whatever line of work we pursue, be it caring for a home or constructing a suspension bridge, we are able to solve new problems because we have been given tools and techniques by the ancestors of our craft lineage.

Dr. Martin Luther King Jr. worked in the lineage of nonviolent social change. He acknowledged and honored and was supported by his lineage ancestor Mahatma Gandhi of India. Gandhi, in turn, acknowledged his debt to the nineteenth-century American writer Henry David Thoreau. Our nourishing roots reach deep.

Ecopsychology of the Roots

Something mysterious happens down in the roots of our Tree. This is where we are healed, where the upwelling of life energy moistens us. Every conscious phenomenon wears out, and we have to be renewed through the unconscious. But what exactly happens down there is hard to say. What happens is hard to put into words precisely because the level of consciousness is so low.

Marie-Louise von Franz reminds us that "we are still faced with two unsolved mysteries which in a strange way are interdependent though we do not yet know how. They are psyche and matter. The science of physics, in the final resort, postulates matter as something unconscious, namely something of which we cannot become conscious. By definition the unconscious is the same thing: it is something psychological of which we cannot become conscious . . . We do not really know the difference between material reality and the psyche. Actually, if we look at it honestly, we are confronted with something unknown which appears sometimes as matter and sometimes as psyche, and how the two are linked we do not know."[76] She also says that Jung was inclined to think that the unconscious has a material aspect.[77]

If the distinction between psyche and matter begins to blur at such depth, then psyche must have some interior experience of matter. This experience occurs at approximately that deep and ancient level of the psyche Jung called the *collective unconscious* and Freud called the *id*. Ecopsychologist Theodore Roszak proposes that this level conserves our treasury of "ecological intelligence."[78] In other words, the psyche at its deepest level understands how to connect, and actually *does connect*, with the universe. In some mysterious way the fine root hairs of our psyche actually enter into the grains of basic matter.

All the Tree wisdom traditions confirm this connection. At its deepest level, the Tree is rooted in the universe. We all have this potential latent within us. If we ourselves can plumb the Tree to its depths, we will find ourselves rooted and supported in our own lives.

The Tree Centers the Hoop

An old riddle asks: "Where is the exact center of the world?" The traditional answer is: "Exactly where I set my foot!" When we look around we see that where we stand is the center of the Hoop of the wide horizon. From this very same spot, from precisely where each of us sets foot, grows the Cosmic Tree, because it is also a Self Tree. The Tree pierces the Hoop at the center. The word *center* came originally from the Greek word for the spiked arm of a compass that is stuck into a surface while the other arm describes a circle round it. In T. S. Eliot's famous description the center is "the still point of the turning world."[79]

Odysseus's Bedpost

At the end of the *Odyssey* the hero Odysseus has been away from home for twenty years. He has lived a life of killing, plunder, danger, and adventure, first during the war against the Trojans and then in his famous journey back home to Ithaka. In the war against Troy he led the Greeks to victory through his ruse of the Trojan horse. During his absence his wife, Penelope, has endured the taunts and parasitic debauchery of a bunch of rowdy unwanted suitors for twenty years of loneliness and single-motherhood. She has survived and remained faithful to Odysseus through great patience and subtlety, fully equal to that of her famous husband. Finally, after great trials, Odysseus arrives back in Ithaka. But he finds his house occupied and his wife held virtual prisoner by dozens of well-armed men. He has only his young son and an old swineherd to help him.

Soon, however, through great cunning and bravery Odysseus defeats the band of suitors. After the battle he bids his servants cleanse the house. Then comes the moment of reunion for Odysseus and Penelope.

Here is her situation: A strange man has come. He claims to be Odysseus. But Odysseus has been away for twenty years. If this is Odysseus, he has been living in a world not of domesticity but of exaggerated masculinity—aggression, plunder, killing. If this indeed is Odysseus he has to be restored to right relationship. Penelope is not about to let any wily fellow jump into her bed, though the wily fellow might look and act like Odysseus and be able to bend Odysseus's great bow. She tests him.

In Odysseus's presence Penelope tells her serving woman to make up their bed for him, but to move the bed outside her bedchamber. Odysseus is outraged. He knows no one could move that bed unless Penelope had betrayed him. He had built that bed with his own two hands, fashioning one of its bedposts out of a living olive tree rooted to the spot. Only he and Penelope knew the secret. By Odysseus's fierce reaction Penelope proves her true husband.

Odysseus's bedpost represents the axis of the entire relationship between this epic man and this epic woman, as it grounded their marriage bed. It was, and is, the pivot between their stories. In reclaiming the Tree of the bedpost, Odysseus reclaimed both his center and his relationship with Penelope. In John Donne's metaphor, Penelope and Odysseus are connected like the two feet of a compass used for drawing a circle. Penelope, holding the center, is

> the fixt foot, which makes no show
> To move, but doth, if th'other do.
> And though it in the center sit,
> Yet when the other far doth roam,

It leans, and harkens after it,
   And grows erect, as that comes home.
Such wilt thou be to me, who must
   Like the other foot, obliquely run;
Thy firmness makes my circle just,
   And makes me end where I begun.[80]

That Odysseus's bedpost was an olive tree is not an insignificant matter. The olive tree was sacred to the goddess Athena,
Odysseus's patron, and figured in the founding of the city of Athens. At that time Athena and the god Poseidon were competing
to be chosen patron deity of the new city. Kekrops, the first king,
judged a contest between the two. Poseidon, for his effort, struck
a rock with his trident and caused water to spring forth. Athena
planted the olive, and for this Kekrops judged her the victor.[81] In
a sense, the olive was the world Tree of Athens, and therefore the
world Tree of high Greek civilization.

At the still point where the Tree intersects the Hoop, we begin
to find ourselves. Zen master Dogen says, "When you find your
place where you are, practice occurs, actualizing the fundamental
point."[82] The Psalmist says "Be still and know that I am God"
(Psalm 46:10).

How Is Your Tree?

In hearing these Tree stories we may be tempted to think of them
as happening "out there" in some historical, prehistorical, or mythic
time and in some mythic or physical space separate from ourselves.
But if we look at them as not "out there" but "in here," in our own
being, we can see an essential dimension of the psyche: the Tree
dimension. The Tree grows within each of us. We have only to look.

This Tree centers us on the Hoop, roots us in the universe, and
gives us strength to reach our highest aspirations. It complements
the Hoop to bring us to wholeness. Where the Hoop is immanent,
the Tree is transcendent. Where the Hoop is horizontal, the Tree is
vertical. Where the Hoop tends to view time as cyclical, or moving
from an eternal present outward in all direction, the Tree tends

to view time as linear, moving from a beginning toward an end.[83] Where the Hoop is oneself as the process of relating, the Tree is oneself as the process of becoming wise.

Another way of saying this is that the Tree is one of two key images by which the self understands the self. It is the image by which the self talks to the self about its interior growing core, the core which aspires to skill, wisdom, and contact with the Divine; the core which knows where it stands in the world, and which is able to draw nourishment from its ancestry and from the deep moisture of sleep, dreams, and unconscious processes.

If we were not in some way Trees, we would not have roots, we would not expect our labor to bear fruit, nor would we call a child "the apple of my eye."

One of my favorite Tree images concerns something called the candle of the pine. At the very top of the pine tree is its growing tip, a tender green stalk feathered with needles, pointing straight to the sky. This tip is called the *candle*. If the candle is cut off, the growth of the tree is stunted. The word "candle" was introduced into the English language in the context of religion; and candles have a long association with spiritual practices. The pine tree grows by lifting its candle to the light of the heavens, and insofar as we have a Tree within us, we do the same.

The Sufi whirling dervish puts the human body into a "danced pattern of wholeness," with the whirling motion making the Hoop and the upright body and the hands passing grace from up to down making the Tree.

4

The Hoop and the Tree: The Deep Structure of the Whole Self

I live my life in growing orbits,
which move out over the things of the world.
Perhaps I can never achieve the last,
but that will be my attempt.

I am circling around God, around the ancient
tower,
and I have been circling for a thousand years.
And I still don't know if I am a falcon,
or a storm, or a great song.

—Rainer Maria Rilke
from *Book for the Hours of Prayer*
translated by Robert Bly[1]

AS WE GROW TOWARD WHOLENESS, our Hoops expand to encompass more of the world. The trunk of our Tree grows strong as we set down roots and reach toward the light. Our lives are an ongoing process of working toward wholeness as we encounter each new stage of life and grapple with the challenges life presents. Typically our journey toward wholeness begins with a lopsided emphasis on one dimension over the other, on either the Hoop or the Tree.

In the culture of the United States this imbalance is often evident in gender differences. Erik Erikson made a study of the spontaneous creations of boys and girls who were given a random selection of toys and asked to "construct on the table an exciting scene out of an imaginary moving picture." He found that the most significant difference between the girls and the boys was that the girls tended to construct enclosures or interior spaces and the boys tended to construct towers.[2] The girls made Hoops and the boys made Trees.

In communication patterns also, the immature male is often more oriented to the Tree dimension and the immature female more oriented to the Hoop dimension.

According to the studies of sociolinguist Deborah Tannen, boys in the United States tend to focus on the hierarchical social order, whereas girls tend to focus on the network of social connections, intimacy, and community.[3] It is as though boys and girls grow up in two different worlds, and communication between the two is "cross-cultural communication." This difference may result more from the socialization of gender than from innate dissimilarities.[4] Yet the difference persists as boys and girls grow into men and women, at least until they reach a certain level of development. Tannen has shown that boys and men tend to use conversation as a way to negotiate status in a group and a way to keep others from dominating them (Tree hierarchy). Girls and women tend to use conversation as a way to negotiate closeness and intimacy, and a way to gather others to them (Hoop relationship).

This difference between boys and girls begins early. Tannen cites the research of Marjorie Harness Goodwin who spent a year and a half observing interactions among city kids. Goodwin found that boys gave orders as a way of gaining social status. The high-status boys gave orders just to maintain their dominance, not because they needed anything done. In girls' play, the girls tended to be more egalitarian, with everyone making suggestions and accepting suggestions from others.

The difference in orientation between hierarchical communication and relational communication, Tree and Hoop, can cause friction and confusion in relationships. For example, a woman may begin to talk with her husband about some trouble she may be having. She talks about something important to her in order to build the relationship. From the husband's point of view of conversation as a way to negotiate status, his wife's talk about troubles is a request for a solution. Someone who doesn't have an answer (lower status) is asking help of someone who might (higher status). For their part men often feel that they are *expected* to have an answer; that if they don't have an answer they will be judged incompetent (low status). So the husband is impelled to give a solution and then considers the matter closed. He doesn't just listen and empathize, which may be what his wife wanted. And he may become frustrated when she doesn't seem to take his advice, but keeps on talking.

The difference in orientation between males and females in the United States does not mean that *fully developed* men and women are this one-sided. It was after all a man, Carl Rogers, who developed a major school of psychotherapy based on the Hoop of relationship. Yet the research Tannen summarizes shows clearly that hierarchy and relationship, Tree and Hoop, are key ways for the psyche to orient itself to the world, and that in the United States at least, undeveloped males and undeveloped females tend to be one-sided.

The Hoop-and-Tree Process of Development

The way we grow out of being one-sided has been described as a sort of spiral helix. We start out focused on one side and then lean a little bit to the other side and learn something about that perspective, and then we cycle back to our original perspective but at a greater level or degree of maturity. We develop by continuously cycling to and fro between the Hoop and the Tree perspectives, gradually gaining maturity on both dimensions.

Developmental psychologist Robert Kegan of Harvard says that each stage of human development is but a temporary resolution of the lifelong tension between these two dimensions, which he calls "the two greatest yearnings in human experience."[5]

Tensions exist because, on the one hand, our Hoop desire for connection makes us dread deviating too much from the group in any respect. Yet on the other hand we don't usually want to be just one of the masses, we want to excel, or at least to be noticed for our unique contributions. We want to rise on the Tree dimension and be known by our fruit.

Each stage of development represents our best possible (at the time) rapprochement between the Hoop and the Tree. We grow through successive approximations toward fuller Hoop-and-Tree wholeness. As we grow we are more able to tolerate the ambiguity of "both/and" rather than "either/or."

We can look at our own behavior to see whether we are emphasizing the Hoop or the Tree at the moment. Psychologist Andras Angal points out that Tree behavior (which he calls the tendency toward "autonomy") is characteristically restless and drives toward advancement, while Hoop behavior ("homonomy") has a more peaceful character and aims at permanency. Tree behavior tends to be more rationalistic, desiring proofs and certainty, while Hoop behavior is more deeply rooted in our non-rational nature, and tends to be guided by faith and intuition. As Tree, we are *stimulated* by situations and *respond* to them with some sort of self-assertive activity. As Hoop we proceed by *impressions* and *expressions*. We experience an inner impression of harmony or resonance and are moved to some form of expression of this resonance, through creative art, for example, or prayer or service.[6]

A fascinating insight into our developmental processes comes out of the work of Mihaly Csikszentmihalyi, former chair of the psychology department at the University of Chicago. This man with the wonderful name was curious about the psychology of optimal experience—those times when we are so involved in whatever we are doing that nothing else seems to matter, when the experience itself is so enjoyable that we do it for the sheer sake of doing it. Csikszentmihalyi calls this state "flow."

Over the course of many years, he and his colleagues around the world interviewed thousands of people from many different walks of life. They also used electronic pagers to remind their subjects at random intervals to stop and write down whatever they were thinking about at the time and how they were feeling. As of 1990 he had collected over a hundred thousand such cross-sections of peoples' lives.

On the basis of all his research, Csikszentmihalyi concluded that what follows an experience of flow is psychological growth, growth of the self. Growth of the self, he says, means that the organization of the self becomes more *complex*. "Complexity is the result of two broad psychological processes: *differentiation* and *integration*. Differentiation implies a movement toward uniqueness, toward separating oneself from others. Integration refers to its opposite: a union with other people, with ideas and entities beyond the self. A complex self is one that succeeds in combining these opposite tendencies."[7]

Differentiation, or movement toward uniqueness, is movement along the Tree axis. Integration, or union with other people, with ideas and entities beyond the self, is the essential quality of Hoop. So whenever we have our best experiences, we grow toward wholeness on both dimensions.

Csikszentmihalyi emphasizes that neither the Hoop alone nor the Tree alone is sufficient. "A self that is only differentiated—not integrated—may attain great individual accomplishments, but risks being mired in self-centered egotism. By the same token, a person whose self is based exclusively on integration will be connected and secure, but lack autonomous individuality. Only when a person invests equal amounts of psychic energy in these two processes and avoids both selfishness and conformity is the self likely to reflect complexity."[8]

Many experiences in our lives, not only our best experiences, work to bring us to full "complexity" or wholeness. One of the qualities of an effective human culture is that it creates experiences that support both our differentiation, or yearning to be independent, and our integration, or yearning to be included.

A few years ago the psychologist/ecologist Paul Shepard considered what the normal process of human development should look like when supported by the culture. The normal process, Shepard says, is a long process, which involves both the individual's acquisition of certain life experiences and the culture's appropriate, and appropriately timed, responsiveness to the individual.[9]

In Shepard's version of the developmental helix, the Tree perspective is called the "Autonomous phase" and the Hoop perspective is the "Symbiotic phase."[10] The Autonomous phase has to do with developing a mature sense of the separate self. Its tasks include analysis, separation, solitary trials, and other work having to do with establishing a sense of subjective oneness or autonomy. The Symbiotic phase has to do with developing a well-rounded sense of eco- and socio-kinship. Its tasks include developing relationships with the mother, with the earth matrix, and with the community.

In some cultures the father or the initiating older males guide the young person's development in the Autonomous phase, and the mother or the initiating older females guide the young person in the Symbiotic phase. Regardless of who guides the development, the key point is that a well-functioning culture supports the development of both the Hoop and the Tree.

Shepard emphasizes that full development to Hoop-and-Tree wholeness cannot take place without the natural world, the "ecological circle" of the Hoop: "The unfiltered, unpolluted air, the flicker of wild birds, real sunshine and rain, mud to be tasted and tree bark to grasp, the sounds of wind and water, the calls of animals and insects as well as human voices—all these are not vague and pleasant amenities for the infant, but the stuff out of which its second grounding, even while in its mother's arms, has begun."[11] In fact, if "there was no adequate earth matrix in the child's life between its fourth and tenth year, it can never achieve a fully satisfying philosophical rapprochement to the stellar universe or to any of the fundamental questions to which religion is always directed."[12]

Growing to Wholeness in the Ecological Hoop

> Three primary essentials of genius—
> an eye that can see nature,
> a heart that can feel nature,
> and a boldness that dares follow it.
>
> —Bardic Triads[13]

If for no other reason, we need the Hoop of relationship with the "earth matrix" or ecosystem mother because that is what evokes the full flowering of the genius latent within each of us.

The early Latin meaning of the word *genius* was "deity of generation and birth," which later broadened into "attendant spirit." The Greeks had a similar concept of "guiding spirit," which they called *daimon* (from which English gets, with negative connotations, "demon"). This daimon or genius is praised by Thoreau in *Walden*. "Follow your genius closely enough," he says, "and it will not fail to show you a fresh prospect every hour . . . No man ever followed his genius till it misled him."[14] Socrates relied on the voice of his daimon throughout his life.[15] Finding one's "genius" in this old sense of the word is what allows one to be a "genius" in the more modern sense of having exceptional or transcendent creative power. Socrates was a genius who listened to his genius.

How do you find your own genius? The Bardic tradition of the Celts instructs you to go to nature. Develop "an eye that can see nature, a heart that can feel nature, and a boldness that dares follow it."

This traditional wisdom is verified by the work of Edith Cobb. She studied the lives of some three hundred people from the Middle Ages on who were considered to be "geniuses," in the modern sense of the word. She found that "genius" almost invariably comes out of a childhood mystic experience of nature.[16]

Why is nature such a prime incubator of genius?

One's ability to be a genius in the modern sense of the word depends in part on the quality of one's thought processes. Our thought processes, and even our language, are fundamentally meta-phorical.[17] We explain one thing in terms of another. How strong is he? He's strong as an ox. We tend to understand abstract concepts in terms of other concepts that we understand more experientially. "That is a shaky argument, with no foundation" is only understood by the implied metaphor: a theory is a building. Theories do not literally have foundations. But thinking of them in this way is use-ful. Metaphors fertilize our thought processes.

Our repertoire of metaphor and simile comes from our interac-tional experience of the world. And the richest wellspring (note the metaphor) of metaphor and simile in the world is the natural envi-ronment. Here are some examples: for growth, plants, trees, and so forth; for transformation, butterfly; for hope, the greenness of nature; for spirit, birds; for purity, snow and spring water; for sta-bility or sense of belonging, roots. The list goes on and on. Nature is not only *what* we see, but *how* we see, what we see *through*.

A profound relationship with "all our relations" in the natural world maximizes the opportunities for metaphor, and therefore expands our ability to think. Edith Cobb points out that both the natural genius of the child and the cultivated inventiveness of adult genius are both in search of true metaphor. For this reason alone, it makes sense that having a childhood experience of nature would promote genius in the adult, because the experience of true meta-phor is what releases "the organizing powers of mind and nervous system into action and the making of meaning."[18]

Access to metaphor, however, is the lesser aspect of childhood mystic experiences of nature. Cobb found that what makes these experiences truly transformative is "both a momentary sense of discontinuity—an awareness of [the child's] unique separateness and identity—and a revelatory sense of continuity—an immer-sion of [the child's] whole organism in the outer world of forms, colors, and motions in unparticularized time and space . . . Inner and outer worlds are sensed as one."[19] It is an experience of both radical uniqueness (Tree) and universal relatedness (Hoop).

As a child of ten years old the poet William Wordsworth had experiences like this during his wanderings in the hills and vales of

the Lake Country of England. There, he says, "the earth and common face of Nature spoke to me . . . I held unconscious intercourse
with beauty old as creation, drinking in a pure organic pleasure
from the silver wreaths of curling mist."[20] Similarly, as a child the
founder of modern Jewish Hasidism, the Baal Shem Tov, would
run away from school to be in solitude in the forest.[21] At the age
of seventy, the noted art critic Bernard Berenson remembered his
experience as clearly as though it had just happened, although the
experience had come sixty-four years earlier:

> It was a morning in early summer. A silver haze shim-
> mered and trembled over the lime trees. The air was laden
> with their fragrance. The temperature was like a caress. I
> remember—I need not recall—that I climbed up a tree
> trunk and felt suddenly immersed in Itness. I did not call it
> by that name. I had no need for words. It and I were one.[22]

So there is some fundamental equivalence among being a
"genius," finding one's "genius," and connecting with nature. The
equivalence could be described as a resonance between two sizes
or scales of the fractal Hoop-and-Tree shape of wholeness: the
Hoop-and-Tree shape of the universe as expressed in nature and
the Hoop-and-Tree shape of the whole, healthy psyche or soul.
An experience of this resonance can alter the course of a lifetime.

Because nature so ignites the genius of the young person, many
traditional cultures encourage each young person to go on at least
one *vision quest* at an appropriate time. In the vision quest the
young person ventures into the wilderness to be alone with his or
her own soul and the powers of the universe. The quester receives
preparation beforehand, and spiritual support during this experience through the prayers of relatives and wise elders. Afterward
the community receives the quester back into the Hoop and helps
the quester integrate the experience. But the transformation happens in nature herself.

Two Forms of Intelligence

We can help ourselves along the path to Hoop-and-Tree wholeness by developing both Hoop and Tree forms of intelligence. David Wechsler, who developed one of the most influential and widely used tests of intelligence, defined intelligence as "the aggregate or global capacity of the individual to act purposefully, to think rationally, and to deal effectively with his environment."[23]

Research shows that what we commonly call "intelligence" is not a single, unitary ability.[24] Nevertheless, most intelligence ("IQ") tests, including Wechsler's own, measure a relatively restricted set of abilities. These tests often look primarily at verbal comprehension, quantitative reasoning, and other aspects of abstract thinking that, taken together, have been called "academic intelligence."

Academic intelligence has its uses. Testing for academic intelligence can help us develop certain skills and can help us make sound educational and career decisions. But academic intelligence is not the only form of intelligence.

Recent discoveries suggest that there is a wholly separate cluster of abilities related to intelligence. Like academic intelligence, these abilities also help a person "to act purposefully, to think rationally, and to deal effectively with his environment." They help us with the practicalities of life. As a cluster, these abilities have been termed "emotional intelligence."[25] Psychologist and author Daniel Goleman summarizes how the five main domains of emotional intelligence help us to thrive:

> 1. Knowing one's emotions. *Self-awareness—recognizing a feeling* as it happens—*is the keystone of emotional intelligence. . . . An inability to notice our true feelings leaves us at their mercy. People with a greater certainty about their feelings are better pilots of their lives, having a surer sense of how they really feel about personal decisions from whom to marry to what job to take.*
>
> 2. Managing emotions. *Handling feelings so they are appropriate is an ability that builds on self-awareness. . . . People*

who are poor in this ability are constantly battling feelings of distress, while those who excel in it can bounce back far more quickly from life's setbacks and upsets.

3. Motivating oneself. *Marshaling emotions in the service of a goal is essential for paying attention, for self-motivation and mastery, and for creativity. Emotional self-control— delaying gratification and stifling impulsiveness—underlies accomplishment of every sort. And being able to get into the "flow" state [Hoop of Flow] enables outstanding performance of all kinds. People who have this skill tend to be more highly productive and effective in whatever they undertake.*

4. Recognizing emotions in others. *Empathy, another ability that builds on self-awareness, is the fundamental "people skill."... People who are empathic are more attuned to the subtle social signals that indicate what others need or want. This makes them better at callings such as the caring professions, teaching, sales, and management.*

5. Handling relationships. *The art of relationships is, in large part, skill in managing emotions in others. . . . These are the abilities that undergird popularity, leadership, and interpersonal effectiveness. People who excel in these skills do well at anything that relies on interacting smoothly with others; they are social stars.*[26]

All of these are domains of Hoop intelligence. We need them in order to establish and maintain relationships.

Just as the Hoop is not the *opposite* of the Tree but is separate from and complementary to it, emotional intelligence is separate from and complementary to IQ. Emotional intelligence and IQ are clearly separate, since scientific studies show that you can be good at one without necessarily being good at the other.[27] In fact, a person can have a perfectly normal IQ and yet, because of damage to the emotion-processing parts of the brain, suffer from impulsiveness, anxiety, and disastrous life choices.[28] Yet both emotional intelligence and IQ are necessary for success in real life.

When the Hoop Is Undeveloped

Many sorts of problems may ensue when the Hoop is undeveloped. The least evolved expression of the Hoop dimension is having no boundaries. When someone has no psychological boundaries there is *nothing but* relationship: there is no perimeter and no real center. When interpersonal boundaries are missing, weak, or unstable, it is difficult for a person to maintain his or her sense of individuality. A person with weak boundaries is constantly invaded by the world and usually has an unstable self-image. They don't know where they end and where the world begins. (Psychologists call an extreme case of this a "borderline personality disorder.")

In a family system, weak or unstable interpersonal boundaries result in what is called an *enmeshed* family (Salvadore Minuchin's term) or a family where individuals are emotionally entangled, or *fused* (Murray Bowen's term) with their families. Minuchin says that enmeshment of a family can produce psychological disorders such as anorexia.[29] Bowen says that a key measure of health is the degree of personal differentiation of each person from his or her family of origin.[30] So developing some sense of Hoop boundaries is essential for psychological health in the family system and in the individual. Otherwise you'll always find people invading "your space."

I once had a client—let's call him Harry—who had Hoop boundary problems. Many people in his life saw him as "dangling carrots in front of them"—making promises which he then didn't keep. Harry seemed to be trying to please everyone but succeeding in pleasing no one. His behavior made people angry. From Harry's point of view he found himself making decisions that didn't come out of his core but which were designed to meet the needs of the person he was talking to at that given moment. He felt that other people had emotional power over him, that he had no say in the matter. He couldn't distinguish between what others wanted and what he wanted. His boundaries were too permeable: in his own words, "I throw my trust too easily."

During the course of our work together, Harry developed what he and I called his "shield muscle." This was the ability to fend off toxic invasions from other people's emotional fields, while still being able to lower the shield and be open and vulnerable for intimate relationships.

Hoop boundaries that are too rigid can be just as problematic as boundaries that are weak or unstable. Excessively rigid boundaries in a family can result in what Minuchin calls the *disengaged* family. No one in this family has any emotional intimacy with anyone else. This type of family can tend to produce antisocial behavior in children. The children of these families never develop secure attachment or bonding with anyone, so they lack empathy.

The constricted Hoop, characterized by self-centeredness, being wrapped-up in oneself, the inability to "loosen up" or to get out of oneself, is a well-recognized characteristic of many forms of personality disorder. Such persons seem to fear that opening up will bring about the loss or destruction of their identity.[31]

Overemphasis on the Hoop quality of going with the flow can lead to such problems as dreaminess, lack of creativity, and indifference to suffering. In general Hoop difficulties involve inability to form or maintain healthy relationships, as well as specific behaviors destructive to relationship such as gossip and slander. Feelings of loneliness, isolation, disconnection from life, and abandonment all hint at problems on the Hoop dimension, as do, conversely, feelings of inundation or being engulfed.

Having a well-developed Hoop of relationship, on the other hand, is a powerful support of mental health. By experiencing ourselves as a small part of a larger whole, our personal sufferings and troubles are put into perspective and proportion.

People attuned to the Hoop tend to pay attention to the inclusion variable: who is included in the circle and who is excluded—who's "in" and who's "out." Psychological studies of children on the playground show how the immature Hoop behaves: small groups of "ins" cruelly excluding the "outs." Another, equally cruel, in-out dynamic occurs when a group exerts shaming or other social pressure on a group member who tries to be a little different, someone who starts to individuate, to rise up. The attempt to individuate is the first sprouting along the Tree axis. The Hoop, when devoid of

Tree, permits no one to rise up above the plane of conformity. In fact the Hoop might then kill rather than nurture the Tree. One sure way to kill a tree is to girdle it: to cut a Hoop in its bark.

When the Tree Is Undeveloped

While the Hoop attends to who's in and who's out, the Tree attends to the ranking variable: who's up and how high, who's down and how low. Here again, the evidence from children's play shows how the Tree acts when it is not balanced by the Hoop. People who are all Tree and no Hoop are overly concerned with status and power, with little thought for how their actions might harm others in the Hoop. What is important to these people is being at the top of the pecking order. In an exclusively Tree world, the ones at the bottom of the hierarchy suffer.

When there is no integration along the Tree axis, the body, the will, the heart, the mind, and the spirit may all act independently of one another. Or worse yet, a person's consciousness may get stuck at a lower level and focus only on that level and levels below it, while ignoring development of the higher levels. You could call this a *truncated* Tree. Someone who has a truncated Tree will make decisions from the center of will and power (lower Tree levels) that have no connection with heart and spirit (higher Tree levels). (Leni Riefenstahl's famous film that glorified Nazi Germany was called *Triumph of the Will.*) We could say that dominant and oppressive people are stuck at the will/power chakra (third chakra) and haven't opened the heart chakra, which would allow them to connect with the Hoop and use their power for the benefit of others.

The Tree activity vector has to do with achievement, classification, separation, ranking, and a sense of separate identity. Overemphasis on these qualities can lead to sacrificing the juice of life for some artificial construct of "meaning," "progress," or "results." Overemphasis on the Tree can also lead to a sense of separation or isolation (no Hoop), and to rigidity (the overly stiff tree that gets blown over by the wind, instead of yielding a little).

Other symptoms of Tree problems can include an inability to "stand up" for oneself, a sense of being uncentered, a sense of being constantly thwarted, and/or feelings of rootlessness or of hopelessness.

A common consequence of overemphasis on Tree is *narcissism*. Narcissistic personalities have a grandiose sense of self-importance. They tend to exaggerate their accomplishments and talents, and expect to be noticed as superior even without commensurate achievement. They are the ones who exploit others or push to the head of the line while everyone else is waiting. They typically lack empathy.[32] Since the Tree grows within the Hoop, you could say that narcissistic types are little Trees trying to be big Trees without developing the Hoop within which Trees actually can grow big.

Narcissism is one distinguishing characteristic of the classic *puer eternus*. This "eternal youth," sometimes called a "flying boy," tries to soar toward the upper spiritual reaches of the Tree axis without being willing to be grounded or rooted in the dailiness or quotidien nature of life.[33]

The sense of having one's Tree uprooted is related to what psychologists call *dissociative* disorders, where there is a disturbance or alteration in the functions of identity, memory, or consciousness that normally give us a sense of who we are. Conscious awareness becomes separated (dissociated) from previous memories, thoughts, and feelings. Without roots and a solid core we are lost.

My client Harry suffered from Tree problems as well as Hoop problems. His roots, like Jan's, were damaged, nibbled at. Harry had suffered under a perfectionist father who constantly yelled at Harry and hit him when he didn't live up to expectations. Harry said, "In my mind I thought I couldn't do anything right. I'm a bad person." These experiences made it hard for Harry to stand up for himself as an adult. He also saw, to his great distress, that he himself was dealing with his own children in the same way his father had dealt with him. His tainted roots were poisoning his fruit.

During the course of our work together Harry discovered other roots that could support him: role models in his grandfather and in his father-in-law, both of whom were more nurturing than his father had been. Harry began to be able to see his father as his father was now: an older, retired man who had mellowed over the years and needed Harry's support. He also began to discover that his own true aspirations were different from the aspirations he had been given as a child. He began to work toward producing those fruit most dear to his own being. He began also to heal his relationship with his children. As he worked toward wholeness on both the Hoop and the Tree dimensions Harry found that he was able to be both strong (Tree) and supportive (Hoop).

We need the Tree dimension for our mental health, just as much as we need the Hoop dimension. It is through the Tree that we step into our own proper power and individuality.

In the dominant commercial-industrial culture, incompleteness on the Hoop dimension and on the Tree dimension seem to split by gender. Terrence Real, codirector of the Harvard University Gender Research Project and a senior faculty member of the Family Institute of Cambridge, summarizes the situation this way: "Healing the spectrum of disorders plaguing girls and women currently has, at its core, the renewed assertion of self [Tree]. Healing for boys and men has, at its core, the skills of reconnection [Hoop]."[34]

Addiction and Codependence

Addiction is an unbalanced relationship with a substance or with a behavior that restricts a person's ability to respond in healthy, appropriate, and authentic ways to the challenges of life. Addiction is often marked by self-deception. One way to think of addiction is as an attempt to fill the center of a damaged Hoop with a false Tree.

Addicts typically have Hoop problems of unbalanced or inauthentic relationships—with other people, with themselves, and with substances or behavior. Their Hoops are broken, incomplete, or empty. Addicts also seek some kind of "high." High is a Tree dimension. But the addictive high comes from something imported; it is not, so to speak, "home grown." Alcohol and addictive drugs can give a temporary sense of power or insight. Real power and insight require the work of establishing roots and climbing the Tree.

Addictive attempts to fill the center of the personal Hoop often have an impact on the wider Hoop. One person's addiction can disrupt a marriage, destroy a friendship, wreak havoc in a workplace or community.

A related Hoop-and-Tree difficulty is *codependence*. A codependent person is "characterized by preoccupation and extreme dependence (emotionally, socially, and sometimes physically), on a person or object. Eventually, this dependence on another person becomes a pathological condition that affects the codependent in all other relationships."[35] So a codependent person often has problems with intimacy, often suffers anxiety and confusion, and sometimes isn't even able to have fun.

Like addiction, codependence is marked by inadequate boundaries and low self-esteem, in other words: inadequate Hoop and no Tree.

A time-tested process for the healing of addiction and codependence is the Twelve-Step process pioneered by Alcoholics Anonymous.[36] It is an excellent example of a Hoop-and-Tree approach to healing. Participants in these programs work on the twelve steps in the supportive Hoop of a group of peers who are also working on their own healing. Steps two and three say: [We] "came to believe that a Power greater than ourselves could restore us to sanity. [We] made a decision to turn our will and our lives over to the care of God *as we understood Him.*" This is ascent along the Tree axis. The descent comes in step four: [We] "made a searching and fearless moral inventory of ourselves." This is going down to meet one's darkness.

Twelve-step participants then work on mending the Hoop: [We] "made a list of all persons we had harmed, and became willing to make amends to them all. [We] made direct amends to such people wherever possible, except when to do so would injure them or others." (These are steps eight and nine.) Step ten deepens the descent along the Tree axis by continuing one's moral inventory. Step eleven is ascent through prayer and meditation to improve

one's conscious contact with the Divine. The twelfth step is a classic Hoop-and-Tree integration: "Having had a spiritual awakening
[Tree] as the result of these Steps, we tried to carry this message to
others, and to practice these principles in all our affairs [Hoop]."

Currently the Twelve-Step process only deals with the human
ring of the Hoop. But globally our present ways of living constitute an addiction that harms not only ourselves but also the
wider Hoop. We suffer today not only from individual chemical
dependency, but also from global *petro*chemical dependency and
material dependency. Many people admit that they're "addicted"
to buying things. As ecopsychologist Theodore Roszak says, "They
know they are doing something compulsive; they don't want to
buy all this junk; they wish they could stop. But they say they're
trapped. That's the language of addiction."[37]

So we need to expand the Twelve Step process. We need to
make "direct amends" to the environmental ring of the Hoop.
Environmentally sound practices of Reduce / Reuse / Recycle are
not only ways to save resources, but also ways to maintain our
"sobriety." In this way we can begin to heal ourselves of our "mate-
rialistic disorder" or "affluenza."[38]

A Hoop-and-Tree problem related to the problems of addiction and codependency is the problem of cults. The Hoop and the
Tree is such a compelling pattern that people can be drawn to it
even in its weak form. Cults attract members with the combined
lures of closeness with a group (Hoop) and potential leaps of personal insight (Tree). The problem here is that the Hoop and Tree
are diminished: the Hoop is not inclusive enough and the Tree is
"capped" or limited by a reification of the Divine—people claim
they "know" the great unknowable. Cults also rarely acknowledge
the psychological depths of human beings (Tree roots), and therefore often act out the darkness instead of making it conscious.

Working Toward Psycho-Spiritual Wholeness

Every wisdom tradition in the world represents the universal human impulse to explore consciousness toward psychological and spiritual wholeness. Throughout the ages people have done this work, using the metaphors appropriate to their historical period.

During the Middle Ages alchemists employed chemicals and glassware, fire and tongs, in an endeavor that was part primitive chemistry and part metaphor for psycho-spiritual transformation. In the famous "lead into gold," the lead is both base matter and also raw psychic energy; the gold is both gold and the fully developed psyche. To bring about this transformation required both the Hoop and the Tree. The chemical retort, the alchemists' "well sealed vessel," was the Hoop. (One of its modern counterparts is the safe space or container of the therapeutic relationship.) Within this Hoop the alchemists strove to grow the *arbor philosophica*, the "philosophical Tree."[39] What they were after in the end was the fruit of this Tree, sometimes called the "elixir of life" or the "philosopher's stone." This "stone" is the mystical experience of God within one's own soul. It is the fully developed Hoop and Tree.

One of the most common metaphors throughout history for this profound mystical experience has been the ecstasy of sexual union. The historian of religion Mircea Eliade says that with the exception of the modern world, religions have always treated sexuality as a *hierophany* (manifestation of the holy), and the sexual act as an integral action and therefore also as a means to knowledge.[40] Most wisdom traditions recognize the sacred nature of sexual energy and have developed rituals for sexually charged life events such as puberty and marriage. In the language of the spirit, the image of sexual union in marriage is the image of fulfillment.

As Freud would remind us, sexual union is also the union of the Hoop and the Tree. It's clear that the Hoop is, among other things, an image of vulva/vagina/womb; and that the Tree is, among other things, a phallic image. So here again, the model for integration or wholeness is Hoop and Tree together in sacred conjunction.

In considering vulva and phallus it's important to differentiate between vulva and matriarchy and to differentiate between phallus and patriarchy. What we're talking about here is the physical organ and its psychological import, not any social system that may be associated with it.

The sexual organs carry a lot of psychic weight. Eugene Monick, who has studied the role of phallic imagery in masculine psychology, says that the phallus symbol "carries the masculine inner god-image for a male."[41] It is "the mysterious organ . . . through which a link is established between man (or animal or flower) and the creative force which is the nature of the divine."[42] It is the Tree whose roots reach toward the ancestors and which carries the seed of the future.

For a man, phallus carries the positive images of being upright, strong, creative, and purposeful. When a man integrates these values into his being he can carry them for the benefit of the whole community (Hoop). His behavior will embody these values.

Of course there is a shadow side to the phallus: rigidity, intrusiveness, and the single-eyed vision denounced by William Blake.[43] (Phallus is the god with the single eye.) To have "single vision" is to see only the physical facts of the universe, to reduce the universe to a mechanism, leaving out spirit, humans, life, and all the values that make life worth living. As the *Dragnet* detective used to say, "Just the facts, ma'am." This sort of cold, mechanistic approach to life is the danger in too much Tree rationality.

The vulva is likewise an image of the deep creative feminine. The tradition of honoring this sacred Hoop reaches back to Paleolithic times, extending across northern Europe and Asia from Spain to Siberia.[44]

In the Hindu tradition, the sacred vulva appears quite graphically as the *yoni*. The yoni, along with the male *lingam*, or phallus, is the sacred shrine at the inner sanctum of many temples. As a shrine the yoni is typically a Hoop shape of carved stone, adored with libations and offerings of flower petals. The vulva also appears as yonic images in mandalas used for spiritual meditation. Hindu and other traditions also venerate the vulva wherever it appears in the form of a spring or ever-flowing well. The seventeenth century Hindu *Shiva Samhita* says, in "the beautiful yoni . . . is the supreme goddess Kundalini . . . the creative force of the world . . . always engaged in creation."[45]

For a woman, vulva/vagina/womb carries the positive images of being receptive, abundant, and creative. When a woman integrates these values into her being, they steady and support her in developing the Tree qualities of skill, knowledge, wisdom, and spiritual attainment.

The shadow side to the vulva/vagina/womb includes the whole set of problems we have already discussed associated with immaturity or boundary problems on the Hoop dimension. This shadow side also includes restriction, confinement, conformity, and indifference. Being related to all things and events in the universe can result in a sense of equanimity. But the virtue of equanimity has what the Buddhists call a "near enemy," and that near enemy is indifference.

The Hoop and the Tree as vulva and phallus, Goddess and God, come together in yoni and lingam and in the sacrament of lovemaking, which as Eliade has noted, everywhere and always has been a manifestation of the holy. The Wiccan tradition knows this union as the Great Rite, "when sweet desire weds wild delight."[46] Here the man's roots touch the water of the woman's well.

The Hoop and the Tree as vulva and phallus also come together in the image of the hermaphrodite or androgyne. According to Mircea Eliade, the androgyne in the metaphysical rather than physical sense, represents an ideal or perfect person in numerous ancient cultures.[47] Adam Kadmon, the image of human perfection in the Kabbalistic tradition, is androgynous.[48] In the Coptic Gospel According to Thomas, Jesus says, "When you make the male and the female into a single one, so that the male will not be male and the female not be female . . . then you shall enter [the Kingdom]" (85:24–35).[49]

The goal of alchemy was precisely this hermaphrodite in the metaphysical sense, the divine original human—the psychologically and spiritually whole person.[50] This *conjunctio* is the alchemists' gold, the "philosopher's stone," the fruit of the philosophical Tree. It is the same union as that of Kalachakra and his consort Vishva-mata at the very center of the Buddhist Kalachakra mandala. It is the same as the union of Shakti with Shiva at the crown chakra of Hindu Kundalini. It is Dante's mysterious conjunction of "instinct and intellect balanced equally." It is enlightenment, knowledge in the deepest and highest sense and compassion in the widest sense. It is the harmony of the Hoop and the Tree.

We find this same androgynous balance in those people who lead the most fulfilling lives. A rigorous long-term study of adults, led by researcher Douglas Heath, investigated the psychological character-istics of successful and fulfilled people. The study followed a group of men, and subsequently their life partner (sixty-five men and forty women), from the time the men were in their junior and senior years of college until the men were in their mid-forties. The study involved extensive interviews, ratings by intimate others (closest friend, spouse), and batteries of some of psychology's most respected tests. The study identified the core strengths necessary for adult success in the roles of citizen, marital and sexual partner, parent, friend, and worker. A key finding of the study is that one of the two most consistent predictors of successful and fulfilled lives is androgyny.[51]

By androgyny the researchers mean having many of the strengths associated with *both* masculinity and femininity: "Some stereotypic masculine strengths are self-reliance, independence, and ambition; some typical feminine strengths are sensitivity to the needs of others, loyalty, and compassion. Among other things, androgynous men and women feel fulfilled and make good marital partners, vocational colleagues, close friends, and responsible com-munity members."[52] In the study's subjects, mature androgyny did *not* result in a diffuse sense of self, ambiguous sexual identity, or paralyzing emotional conflicts. The subjects were typically vigor-ous, clear about who they were, and had energy available for a zestful life.

This finding about androgyny is totally consistent with the alchemical image of the hermaphrodite as the goal of the work, and with the image of the embrace of Shiva and Shakti at the crown of Kundalini's ascent. This finding says that the whole self has both Hoop and Tree elements, and both are in balance.

So a developmental question to ask yourself is: How balanced are you? Can you, as the situation requires, be assertive *and* sensitive to the needs of others, independent *and* loyal, ambitious *and* compassionate, and so forth?

This study also found that the course of healthy development involves widening the Hoop, from self-centeredness to other-centeredness. Many of the core strengths necessary for adult fulfillment are Hoop qualities: caring, compassion, openness, and undefensiveness about sharing one's feelings, tolerance and acceptance of others' quirks and failings, and understanding, respecting, and empathizing with others.[53]

The Fully Developed Self *Is* Ecological

Many years ago in Sung Dynasty China, a man named Su Tung-p'o was riding his horse in the mountains, absorbed in a teaching his Zen master had just given him. "How dare you come to me seeking the dead words of men!" his master had shouted. "Why don't you open your ears to the living words of nature? Go away!" While pondering this teaching Su Tung-p'o had let his horse wander wherever the horse willed to go. At one point the horse carried him by a waterfall in the mountains. The sound suddenly awoke Su Tung-p'o into enlightenment. In this moment he perceived the roaring waterfall as the Buddha's golden mouth and the distant mountains as his pure luminous body.[54]

The fully developed self not only balances male and female, the Tree and the Hoop, but also extends the Hoop of relationship beyond the human circle to the ecological circle.

Psychologist Abraham Maslow studied *self-actualizing* people, people who have reached high levels of maturation, health, and self-fulfillment. Compared to others, self-actualizing people are characterized by:

- Clearer, more efficient perception of reality
- More openness to experience
- Increased integration, wholeness, and unity of the person
- Increased spontaneity, expressiveness; full functioning; aliveness
- A real self; a firm identity; autonomy; uniqueness
- Increased objectivity, detachment, transcendence of self
- Recovery of creativeness
- Ability to fuse concreteness and abstractness, primary and secondary process cognition
- Democratic character structure
- Ability to love

These are the more measurable characteristics. Less measurable are the subjective feelings of zest in living, happiness, serenity, joy, calm, responsibility, and confidence in one's ability to handle stresses, anxieties, and problems.[55]

Maslow found that these mature, self-actualizing people "look upon nature as if it were there in itself and for itself, and not simply as if it were . . . put there for human purposes." A self-actualizing person sees nature "in its own Being . . . rather than as something to be used, or something to be afraid of, or to be reacted to in some other human way."[56] In other words, *part of what health means is having this sort of relationship to nature.* According to Maslow's research, people who are most fully developed have this ecological orientation.

Maslow's research also suggests that growth toward self-actualization takes the form of Tree within Hoop. Maslow says, "Human beings demonstrate *in their own nature* a pressure toward fuller and fuller Being, more and more perfect actualization of humanness in exactly the same naturalistic, scientific sense that an acorn may be said to be 'pressing toward' being an oak tree. . . ." Here is the Tree. Where does it grow? Within the Hoop: "Living in a family and in a culture are absolutely necessary to *actualize* these psychological potentials that define humanness."[57]

We know from Cobb's work on genius and from the wisdom practices of the vision quest that the wider Hoop of the

environment is also absolutely necessary to the full development of human potential. Experience in the natural world trans-
forms the developing psyche as a caterpillar is transformed in
its cocoon. Because of this, and because a respectful relationship
with the Hoop of the environment characterizes self-actualizing
people, we can say that the psychology of health is ecopsychology. It is the psychology of the individual Tree in the Hoop of
all our relations.

The lives of self-actualizing people confirm this in their Hoop-
and-Tree stories. Before Morihei Uyeshiba (1883–1969) founded
the Japanese martial art of aikido, he had already mastered many
of the traditional martial arts, including sword, spear, staff, and
various schools of jujitsu. But he wasn't satisfied with mere physical strength and the perfection of technique. One day, after a duel
that he won easily, Uyeshiba had a vision that revealed to him the
secret of how to transform aggression and cultivate harmony. "At
that moment," he says, "I was enlightened: the source of *budo* [the
way of the warrior] is God's love—the spirit of loving protection
for all beings. Budo is not felling the opponent by our force; nor is
it a tool to lead the world into destruction with arms. The training
of Budo is to take God's love, which correctly produces, protects,
and cultivates all things in Nature, and assimilate and utilize it in
our own mind and body."[58]

His was a classic Hoop and Tree realization: ascend the Tree
("take God's love") and assimilate it for the "loving protection for
all beings" (Hoop).

Albert Einstein certainly was a genius in the modern sense
of the word. Einstein's intellectual power puts him at a high
stage of development on the Tree axis. Now listen to what Einstein has to say about the Hoop's "circles of compassion" and
nature:

> *A human being is part of a whole, called by us the "Uni-*
> *verse," a part limited in time and space. He experiences*
> *himself, his thoughts and feelings, as something separated*
> *from the rest—a kind of optical delusion of his consciousness.*

This delusion is a kind of prison for us, restricting us to our
personal desires and to affection for a few persons nearest
us. Our task must be to free ourselves from this prison by
widening our circles of compassion to embrace all living
creatures and the whole of nature *in its beauty.* [emphasis
added][59]

We know from all our mythological and psychological evidence that with your Hoop fully developed you would have this
wide circle of compassion. You would be able to draw an ecological atom that includes representatives from the mineral realm,
the animal realm, the plant realm, and the spirit realm (including ancestral spirits) as well as the human realm including the
diversity of humankind—of race, gender, culture, and so forth.
These relationships would not be psychologically enmeshed, but
would have appropriate boundaries. For you all of nature would
be a medicine wheel within which to orient your being. You
would act from a sense of *ahimsa*—respect and consideration
for all life, and fellow feeling with all living beings. You would
believe, like the true follower of Islam, that "the earth itself is
the primordial mosque."[60] You would say with the great Christian mystic Meister Eckhart, "Apprehend God in all things, for
God is in all things."[61] You would practice relationship with the
immanent Divine.

With your Tree dimension fully developed you would recognize that the axis of the universe runs mystically through the center
of your own body. You would instinctively honor trees and mountains as images of the Tree (mountain) at the center your being.
You would not get "stuck" or "hung up" or fixated at any level
of the Tree—not at sexuality, not at power, not at skill, not even
at knowledge or wisdom. You would recognize all these psycho-
spiritual levels as just rungs on the ladder, chakras to open at
their appropriate time. You would take responsibility for being
upright, for honoring your roots, and for being fruitful. You would
be grounded and would have some practice of aspiration toward
the transcendent Divine.

Such degrees of Hoop-and-Tree development are the ideal of wholeness toward which we all work, through all the lessons, joys, and sorrows of life. We endeavor to be fully developed Hoop-and-Tree persons who are ecological, rooted in the universe, growing toward the light, and centered in relationship with all beings.

One of many Hoop-and-Tree images of wholeness from the world's wisdom traditions: The Haudenosaunee (Iroquois) Tree of the Great Peace, whose roots take the shape of a Hoop mandala.

5

Go in Beauty

The Self has only become real when it is expressed
in one's actions in space and time.

—Marie-Louise von Franz[1]

ONCE UPON A TIME THERE was a marvelous chicken who always
laid a single golden egg every year. This chicken had lived forever
and had belonged to a simple farming family for generations. The
chicken's annual golden egg was always enough to pay for anything
the family needed beyond what they could raise on their farm. For
generations the family tended the earth, sang songs of thanksgiving
together, and through all the cycles of life lived well and happily with
their neighbors, for every other family also possessed a marvelous
chicken. The air was pure, food was plentiful, and the streams were
clear and sweet to drink from.

One day, one year, in a certain generation, a peculiar little man
knocked on the farmhouse door. "This isn't enough!" the man told
the family. "What you need are cell phones, sport-utility vehicles, a
much larger house, four televisions, and many other things besides."
The little man was so persuasive that the family soon agreed with him.

"Of course you will need more gold to purchase these things,"
said the man. "But fear not, I can sell you some special feed for
your chicken that will make it lay more eggs."

Sure enough, the special feed, which looked like dry bone dust, had the chicken laying two golden eggs the very next morning. With the extra gold the family bought many of the attractive things the little man offered for sale. That night the moon disappeared from the sky and was never seen again.

Evidently the peculiar little man visited all the neighbors too, for soon the valley was filled with the sounds and smells of machines, while large chunks of the forest were cut down to make way for many fine new houses.

Every year the peculiar little man visited the farmhouse with tempting new products, and newly improved chicken feed. In what seemed like no time at all the chicken, now looking rather pale, was laying ten eggs per year. Of course this was fortunate, because the prices of things were rising. The stream was no longer sweet to drink from, but foul and bitter, so the family had to buy bottled water imported from far away. The family stopped singing and dancing together so they could have more time to use and maintain their new possessions.

One day the family heard the distressing news that their neighbor's marvelous chicken had died. The family realized that they themselves should start having more children, so that if they ever needed to protect their marvelous chicken from theft, they would have enough soldiers to do the job. Of course once the family began having more children it also began needing more golden eggs to provide basic necessities. When the little man visited later that same year he told the family that for a few extra golden eggs he would sell them some weapons.

Soon the family was buying more weapons than food. Sometimes a sick child had to go without seeing a doctor because the golden eggs had all been spent on bullets and teargas. The family noticed, to their concern, that after every visit of the little man, hurricanes and earthquakes often followed, and the sky grew darker. Also, there were fewer fish in the sea, and fewer birds singing each springtime.

Eventually the marvelous chickens of all the neighbors died from overexertion. This family's chicken was the only one left, and this chicken itself no more than a feeble feathered twig, though producing fifty eggs a year for the bottom line. Well-armed and desperate militias made up of the family's former friends were massing at the edges of the farm. War seemed inevitable.

The little man came once more. "I can help you, with a new genetically altered chicken feed, that will give you the gold to buy the weapons to kill your neighbors," he said. "But I am running low on certain materials. I'd like your children to accompany me to my factory to help."

The parents agreed, with some misgivings, for the sky by now was a filthy yellow. Shortly after the children left with the peculiar little man, the parents came to their senses. They ran after the little man, but he was far ahead of them by now. They pounded on the factory door. It was locked. They climbed up to a bleary window, rubbed the pollution away with their sleeves and looked inside.

They saw their beloved children walking one by one into a door at one end of a machine. From the other end emerged spurts of dusty bone-dry chicken feed.

Hearing a sudden commotion behind them, the horrified parents turned around. It was their neighbors, warring over the last marvelous chicken. Many frantic hands grabbed at the chicken, and in the fear and fury, the greed and confusion, the last marvelous chicken was ripped to death.

Our Current Situation

The modern world's dominant commercial-industrial culture shrivels the Hoop. It reinforces the illusions of separateness and self while undermining community. The Hoop of Relationship with non-human species and with the earth herself is out of balance. Those who speak for the Hoop, such as the many Native Americans who try to preserve portions of the natural world as undeveloped sacred sites, are usually overridden.

Ancient Norse myth tells us metaphorically how dangerous it is for the Hoop dimension to be missing or broken. As you recall, the Norse image for the deep structure of wholeness is the great world axis Tree encircled by the Hoop of an enormous serpent, biting its own tail. In the catastrophe at the end of time this serpent will release its grip on its tail, breaking the Hoop. Then like an uncontrolled fire hose it will thrash about, spewing venom and death all around.[2]

Psychologist Andras Angyal saw clearly how this devastation could come about. When I first read his explanation it sent a shudder through my body:

> It has frequently been said that people go to war because they are forced to do so, or because they have an opportunity for a release of their aggressive tendencies. If one has occasion to observe the behavior of people in mass demonstrations, as, for instance, at the beginning of a great war, one is impressed by still another fact. Such mass demonstrations give people the opportunity to experience that they belong to a group. This is probably the most important factor. It is quite possible that "extraverted" Western culture which places the main emphasis on power and achievement does not offer sufficient opportunity for the expression of the basic human need for "belonging"; hence the drive for its expression readily flows into whatever channel is opened for it. Paradoxically people may go to war because they are starved for love, for longing, in brief, for homonomy [the Hoop].[3]

Though the dominant culture emphasizes Tree, it is a diseased and stunted Tree. Economic pressures, easy mobility for many, wars and genocide around the world have all wrenched peoples from their roots. Robert Bly points out that we have collapsed the useful aspects of hierarchy and live in a flat society of "siblings."[4] We ignore our elders and those who have done the work of ascending the Tree toward spiritual greatness; we give less and less time and attention to those below us—our children. Mass culture undermines our longing for the highest good. It focuses on the lower levels of the Tree—sexuality, power, and technical knowledge, rather than the higher levels of wisdom or transcendence. It discourages a deep exploration of evil.

We are living in an age almost entirely without Hoop, having at best a truncated Tree with rapidly withering roots. One might even say we are "stumped."

The Deep Structure of the Healthy Society

As a deep structure of the universe, the Hoop and the Tree provides a model for how our society can develop out of this mess. Our own story doesn't have to end with the "marvelous chicken" being ripped apart. We can replace greed and fear and confusion with the Hoop and Tree of compassion and wisdom.

Sociologists have long distinguished two organizing principles for society. There are egalitarian, kin-based societies (Hoop-orientation) and chiefdom, or hierarchical societies (Tree-orientation).[5]

Cultural historian Riane Eisler suggests that this distinction between the horizontal, egalitarian emphasis and the vertical, hierarchical emphasis is the fundamental distinction underlying the great surface diversity of human culture. She calls these two basic patterns of society the "Chalice" model and the "Blade" model.[6]

The model symbolized by the Chalice, which Eisler also calls the *partnership* model, is characterized by relatively egalitarian relationships, particularly between the sexes, as well as by worship of the Goddess and a predilection for peace. Our Neolithic agrarian ancestors maintained such a partnership society. Between about 7000 and 5000 BCE, these inhabitants of southeastern Europe developed a complex economy that included the cultivation of wheat, barley, vetch, peas, and other legumes, as well as the raising of domesticated animals, the working of bone and stone, copper metallurgy, techniques of boatbuilding and sailing, and complex religious and governmental institutions. There is evidence of equality between the sexes and a marked lack of warfare. The ancient cities "Catal Huyuk and Hacilar . . . show no signs of damage through warfare for a time span of over fifteen hundred years."[7] Minoan Crete, another partnership culture, produced no known statue or relief of any ruler.[8]

The Blade model of society Eisler also calls the *dominator* model. Authoritarianism and hierarchy, particularly by the ranking

of men over women, characterize Dominator societies. These societies also have a predilection for warfare. Eisler describes the physical and cultural disruption that occurred beginning around the
fifth millennium BCE when waves of steppe pastoralists or *Kur-
gan* people invaded the partnership societies of prehistoric Europe.
In the traces of art remaining from this period we begin to see
increased representation of weapons. There is also evidence from
burial practices of a ranking of adult males over women and male
children.[9]

As the partnership model is based on the principle of *linking*,
it resembles the Hoop. As the dominator model is based on the
principle of *ranking*, it resembles the Tree—an immature Tree.
One may argue with some of Eisler's specifics, but it is clear that
historically some societies have been more egalitarian, built around
the linking principle, and some societies have been more hierarchical, built upon ranking.

Eisler says that we face a choice between the "good" partnership society and the "bad" dominator society. But this is not our
only option. We could learn to integrate both relationship *and*
hierarchy as they are fully expressed in the Hoop and the Tree.
Eisler's evaluation of "the Blade" and "the Chalice" is not a com-
parison of equivalent factors. Eisler's historical material can be seen
as the intrusion of an *unevolved* Tree culture on a *more evolved*
Hoop culture. The Blade is unevolved Tree; the Chalice is more
evolved Hoop. Instead of *either/or*, with one being good and one
being bad, an alternate possibility is *both/and*, with *conjunctio*,
integration, harmony as the goal when both are fully developed
and in balance.

One culture that began to bring the Hoop and the Tree into
balance was the Five Nations (later Six Nations) of the Haudenosaunee ("hoh-DEE-no-show-nee," also known as Iroquois) people.
This same civilization provided the model for the fundamental
political structure of the United States of America. At the time of
the founding of the United States, the league was the greatest native
power on the North American continent. From their homeland
in northern New York between the Hudson and Niagara Rivers,

the Six Nations maintained a *pax iroquoia* that at one time had extended from what is now New England to the Illinois region and from the Ottawa River to Chesapeake Bay.[10]

The story of the Iroquois League begins in a time of great terror and sorrow. As historian Paul Wallace tells the story:

> All order and safety had broken down completely and the rule of the headhunter dominated the culture. When a man or woman died, whether of accident or natural causes, their relatives hired a soothsayer who then interpreted the death as the result of the magical charms of a specific other. The aggrieved family then sought vengeance and a member set forth with the purpose of finding the unsuspecting and arguably innocent offender and exacting revenge. That killing sparked a spiral of vengeance and reprisal which found assassins stalking the Northeastern woodlands in a never-ending senseless bloodletting.[11]

Into this situation came the culture hero Deganawidah, known as the Peacemaker. Deganawidah brought a message of peace and power, whose central image is the Tree of the Great Peace. Obviously this is a Tree image. This Tree is the Tree of aspiration that pierces the sky and reaches the sun. It is also the Tree of Justice; the Iroquois used the same word for both peace and law. This word is also used for "noble" and for "the Lord" in Iroquois translations of the Bible. "Peace" for the Haudenosaunee was not a just a negative thing, not simply the absence of war: "Peace (the Law) was righteousness in action, the practice of justice between individuals and nations."[12]

The Tree of Peace is also a Hoop image, because this Tree has roots that extend to the four cardinal directions, making a mandala. This mandala reaches out as a Hoop of Relationship toward all of humanity. The Peacemaker said, "These roots will continue to grow, advancing the Good Mind and Righteousness and Peace, moving into territories of peoples scattered far through the forest. And when a nation, guided by the Great White Roots, shall approach the Tree, you shall welcome her here and take her by the arm and seat her in the place of council."[13] This is an image of world peace, far ahead of its time.

Deganawidah expressed Hoop values by encouraging the people not to go against the flow of nature but to "dip with the current."[14] He also said, "We bind ourselves together by taking hold of each other's hands so firmly and forming a circle so strong that if a tree should fall upon it, it could not shake nor break it, so that our people and grandchildren shall remain in the circle in security, peace, and happiness."[15] Clearly, this is a Hoop.

The Iroquois mythic Hoop and Tree image gave birth to a civilization that lasted for three hundred years, until it was largely destroyed by the incursions of European settlers. While this civilization was not perfect, it was marked by an emphasis on peace, a representative form of government, a balance of male and female energies, and an ecological orientation to the world. Representatives of the Iroquois Nations (Mohawks, Oneidas, Onondagas, Cayugas, Senecas, and later the Tuscaroras) met at the great council at Onondaga (Syracuse, NY), to manage the affairs of the league. While it was the males who met in council, it was the females who selected who should go. "The office of civil chief was . . . the gift of the suffrages of a definite group of his clanswomen."[16] In each family council the "chief matron" of the family had the deciding voice.[17] The women of marriageable age and the mothers also had the right to hold their own councils for the purposes of nomination of chiefs and to formulate propositions to be brought to the tribal council. The Iroquois believed that it was imperative to recognize both male and female principles in the world.[18]

Balance was also expressed in the structure of the Iroquois three governing principles, roughly translatable as Health, Righteousness, and Power. These principles were structured as balanced pairs: the first principle means sanity of mind and health of the body and also peace between individuals and between groups; the second means righteousness in conduct and its advocacy in thought and speech, and also equity or justice; the third means physical strength or power and also *orenda* or spiritual power.[19]

Deganawidah, the Peacemaker, also taught a principle that has become well known in environmental circles. He said, "When you sit in council for the welfare of the people, think not of yourself, nor of your family, nor even of your generation, but make all of your decisions on behalf of the seventh generation coming."[20]

The ecological orientation of Iroquois culture persists to the present day. Huston Smith tells a story about Oren Lyons, the first Onondagan to attend college. On Oren's first return to the reservation from college his uncle invited him to go fishing on the lake. After they had been fishing for a while out in the middle of the lake, his uncle turned to him and said, "So, Oren, you're probably pretty smart by now, from all they've been teaching you in college. So tell me: Who are you?" Oren didn't know what to say.

> "What do you mean, who am I? Why, I'm your nephew, of course." His uncle rejected his answer and repeated his question. Successively, the nephew ventured that he was Oren Lyons, an Onondagan, a human being, a man, a young man, all to no avail. When his uncle had reduced him to silence and he asked to be informed as to who he was, his uncle said, "Do you see that bluff over there? Oren, you are that bluff. And that giant pine on the other shore? Oren, you are that pine. And this water that supports our boat? You are this water."[21]

How different now might the United States be had the founding fathers adopted from the Iroquois not just a portion of their political structure but an entire worldview? Today we could begin to follow the Hoop-and-Tree model by bringing more ecological and gender balance into our political life and by adopting a "Seventh Generation" amendment to our Constitution.

A study by Harvard University political scientist Robert Putnam gives additional hints about the possibilities inherent in a fully Hoop-and-Tree society. Putnam looked at the development of some twenty regional governments created in Italy in 1970. The formal structures of these governments were identical. Yet some governments were "inefficient, lethargic, and corrupt," while others were dynamic and effective, "creating innovative day care programs and job training centers, promoting investment and economic development, pioneering environmental standards and family clinics." The only set of indicators that consistently differentiated localities with effective governments from those with ineffective governments was the presence of what Putnam refers to as *social capital*: rich networks of nonmarket interpersonal relationships.[22] In other words, the differentiating factor was the presence of Hoop—at least the human ring of the Hoop.

Putnam's research and the history of the Iroquois League imply that much more might be possible if we were to integrate not only the human ring, but also the ecological rings of the Hoop and the full extent of the Tree into the structure of our society.

Bringing the Hoop and Tree into the World

> To fit into the universe, the Indian had to do two
> things simultaneously: be strong as an individual,
> and submerge his personal feelings for the good
> of the tribe.
>
> —Barry Lopez[23]

The inner experience of the fully developed or whole self means nothing if it is not expressed in the outer realms of individual behavior, social relationships, and culture. The Divine manifests not only as inner experience but also through external beauty, interpersonal morality, and scientific truth. As Joseph Campbell says, one of the functions of myth is to teach us how to live a full human life. The Hoop-and-Tree model provides a three-dimensional compass for such a life. It can orient us in psychological space-time and guide our social action and personal development. To work successfully with the Hoop and the Tree is to develop one's innate gifts and then to carry them into the world.

The person who works to manifest the Hoop and the Tree in the world follows the Iroquois Peacemaker's advice to consider the consequences of any decision down through the seventh generation of descendants. A choice to purchase organic foods, for example, would be more supportive of the Hoop and the Tree than the choice to purchase conventionally grown foods. Organic farming does not expose farm workers to toxic chemicals. It also leaves the soil and water without toxic residue to poison future generations of humans or other beings. A choice to limit human population would support the Hoop and the Tree because human population is now exceeding the carrying capacity of the earth.

Work

A great teacher once said, "My work is my altar." Buddha taught that work or "Right Livelihood" is part of the path to enlightenment. The choices we make about work—what work to take and how to do that work—are powerful ways to manifest the Hoop and the Tree. Ideally, work ought to elevate the spirit and deepen the soul along the Tree axis, and simultaneously serve the Hoop.

Hoop-and-Tree behaviors do seem to be emerging in certain sectors of the workplace, especially with regard to the wider environmental Hoop. Companies like Patagonia are beginning to use organic or recycled raw materials in their processes.[24] Others, like Interface Inc., are developing ways to use closed-loop recycling, waste reduction, solar energy, and other emerging technologies in order to become not only ecologically sustainable, but also environmentally restorative.[25] In one of the poorest areas of rural Colombia, the Gaviotas community develops appropriate human- or solar-powered labor-saving technology for the developing world while also restoring the ecosystem *and* supporting the continuity of the local indigenous culture.[26]

In Bangladesh, Muhammad Yunus's Grameen Bank has pioneered a form of lending that has improved morale, sanitation, housing, education, and health for hundreds of thousands of the poorest of the poor. The bank's lending model supports both the Hoop and the Tree. The loans themselves elevate the self-esteem and financial independence of the bank's borrowers (Tree axis). The bank also requires its borrowers to organize themselves into small groups. These groups support their members not only in repaying their loans but also in abiding by positive and environmentally restorative social values (Hoop).[27]

Initiatives like these are encouraging, even inspiring. Yet unless we can make fundamental changes in our economic system, achieving large scale Hoop-and-Tree wholeness in the workplace may be impossible. The focus of global corporations on monetary profits, especially short-term profits, undermines "seventh-generation" decision-making.[28] We need an economic system based on the principles of sustainability.

Fortunately, the fundamental principles of such a system have already been developed. A team of some fifty distinguished scientists headed by Dr. Karl-Henrik Robèrt of Sweden has identified the four underlying principles of an environmentally sustainable society. These principles, called collectively "The Natural Step," are as follows:

1. Substances from the earth's crust—fossil fuels, metals, and other minerals—must not be extracted at a faster rate than their redeposit back into the earth's crust.
2. Substances produced by society must not be produced at a faster rate than they can be broken down in nature.
3. We cannot harvest or manipulate ecosystems in such a way as to diminish their productive capacity, or threaten the natural diversity of life-forms (biodiversity).
4. In order to meet the previous three system conditions, we must meet basic human needs with the most resource-efficient methods possible, including a just distribution of resources.[29]

These are not just high-minded abstractions. By following the precepts of The Natural Step, one company has cut its annual use of plastics by ninety tons, metals by fifteen tons, soap by twenty-five tons, toxic mercury by sixty kilograms, while at the same time improving employee morale and profitability.[30]

According to businessman Paul Hawken, if we are going to reorient our economic system to be sustainable, we will have to start living on our current energy income rather than on our precious "capital reserves" of solar energy stored in oil and coal. We will also have to follow nature's own Hoop design principle that the waste from one process becomes the "food" or input for another. The emerging discipline of industrial ecology, which brings ecological principles to bear on the design of industrial processes and facilities, is a way to start putting this principle into practice on a large scale. Finally we will have to develop new feedback systems to steer the economy in the right direction, so that economic activity tends to restore the earth rather than deplete it.[31] Examples of feedback systems include taxes on pollution or wasteful production, economic incentives for sustainable practices, and also new ways of measuring economic activity.

Standard measurements such as the gross domestic product (GDP) distort our perception of environmental and human well-being, primarily because they make no distinction between harmful and helpful economic activity. In fact the GDP can disguise social and environmental breakdown as economic gain. The production of land mines and concertina wire, the overfishing of the oceans, are all included as "product."

One of several proposed alternatives to the GDP is an indicator called the Genuine Progress Indicator (GPI). Unlike the GDP, the GPI counts the positive contributions of unpaid household and community work. The GPI also subtracts for depletion of natural habitat, pollution costs, and crime. A measurement like the GPI would give us a truer picture of our situation than the GDP now gives us. Although the GDP has been generally rising in the United States, our Genuine Progress Indicator has been declining since the 1970s.[32]

Activism

> At its best, activism comes about as our expanding circles of compassion encounter our capacity for free will.
>
> —*Yes!* magazine[33]

The changes we need to make in the world will come about as a result of individual choices made by you and by me. As we work on reclaiming our inner psychological and spiritual wholeness, we can work to restore the outer world as well.

Our outer work will require from each of us a balance of activism and pacifism. Many spiritual traditions encourage what the Jewish tradition calls *tikkun olam* or healing the world through active social engagement. Because we are all interconnected through the Hoop, we ourselves are healed when we work to heal others. No matter what tradition we are working in, the Hoop-and-Tree model offers guidelines for social action. The model says we should help people and societies grow and deepen on the Tree dimension, and at the same time strengthen all our relationships within the social and ecological Hoop.

We can learn from the Iroquois and actively require that our governments not only have a hierarchy of "chiefs" but also be truly representative and respect the wisdom of nature and the balance of male and female. We can work for "Seventh Generation" processes in all our decision-making. We can ask our educational institutions to foster both Tree "IQ" intelligence *and* Hoop emotional intelligence. We can each ask our own spiritual tradition for its Tree wisdom *and* its Hoop wisdom. We can support bioregional parks and reserves for the living planet. We can work for social justice for all races, creeds, genders, and lifeways of the human ring of the Hoop. We can build "social capital" by actively supporting our own personal and community networks.

The biggest active change we can make is to change the way we think: we need to start thinking as participants within the ecological Hoop rather than as some kind of lords over nature, set apart from it. For how we think determines how we design, and how we design determines what we do with our money and energy. How we think will determine whether we make the exciting and difficult choices needed to steer the world toward regeneration and sustainability and away from dying in a bleak toxic wasteland of our own making.

Many people have been experimenting with techniques that bring more of a Hoop perspective to the work of thinking about the future. By involving all interested parties in the planning process, these approaches avoid some of the problems that occur when plans are made by only a few people.[34] When the "whole system" contributes, the resulting plans are less likely to have blind spots and more likely to be implemented. These techniques even helped bitter antagonists join together to create a shared future in post-apartheid South Africa.[35]

While these more inclusive approaches to planning have yielded promising results, they still limit participation to include only the human ring of the Hoop. The next step is to include the ecological rings. A ritual form known as the "Council of All Beings" moves us in this direction. Each person coming to the council wears a mask and speaks on behalf of Wolf or Spadefoot Toad or Moss or the Delaware River or Tundra.[36] In the course of a council of two or three hours, all the humans behind the masks begin to widen their Hoop consciousness. The "voices" from the Council of All Beings could be invited to participate with the human voices in our decision-making processes.

The ecological ring of the Hoop would really begin to penetrate our thought processes if our legal system began to recognize the inalienable rights of natural objects, such as trees and watersheds. This is not to say that the environment should have the same body of rights as human beings, or that everything in the environment should have the same rights as every other thing. It is simply to recognize in law the Hoop principle that humans are not the owners of the universe. Each animal, plant, spirit, and stone has its own piece of the truth and its own value in and of itself.

Acknowledging legal rights of natural objects is not as far-fetched as it may sound at first. In 2019 the Yurok Tribe declared rights of personhood for the Klamath River, and the voters of Toledo, Ohio, did the same for Lake Erie.[37] In 2018 the Colombia Supreme Court ruled that the Amazon region of that country has rights.[38] A year earlier the New Zealand government gave the Whanganui River its own legal standing in court. And the 2008 Ecuadorean Constitution granted legal rights to nature.[39]

Furthermore, every single day our legal system deals with inanimate nonhuman rights holders such as states, trusts, and corporations. Lawyer Christopher Stone points out in his book *Should Trees Have Standing? Toward Legal Rights for Natural Objects* that "we have become so accustomed to the idea of a corporation having 'its' own rights and being a 'person' and a 'citizen' that we forget how jarring the notion was to early jurists."[40] In fact corporations were originally established only for limited periods of time and only for specific purposes that were deemed to be of benefit to the public, such as building a road. State legislators reserved the right to withdraw the charter of any corporation that didn't serve the public interest. If an intangible mental construct such as a corporation is deserving of legal rights, how much more so are the physical objects, many of them living beings, who are our companions on this earth? In pointing us toward a higher level of consciousness and an expanded Hoop, Stone reminds us that not very long ago such groups as women, Black people, and Native Americans were also denied basic human rights on the ground that they were not quite human.

To redirect our world requires from each of us pacifism as well as social activism. This pacifism includes nonviolent approaches to relationship. It includes willingness to accept from as well as give to our social networks. It also includes willingness on each of our parts to take our fair share and no more. Those of us living in the overdeveloped countries of the world have a distorted view of what constitutes our "fair share." We have been getting more than our fair share for a long time. Our individual choices to "reduce/ reuse/recycle" can help. What is needed is what the Zen tradition calls "enough-mind." The person who practices enough-mind is satisfied with just enough, and finds abundance there.

In practical terms, "enough-mind" can mean the difference between life and death for the earth as we know it. John Ryan and Alan Durning point out in *Stuff: The Secret Life of Everyday Things* that "the United States, with less than 5% of world population, consumes 34% of the world's energy and a similar share of other commodities. . . . For all the world's people to consume at that rate is a mathematical impossibility. It would require four earth's worth of productive land. In other words, we're three planets short. And we're at least nine planets—or atmospheres—short of safely absorbing the greenhouse gases that would result if all the world's people pumped pollution aloft at the North American rate."[41]

Our clear challenge is to manifest and nurture the Hoop and the Tree in the world. The place to start is in our own lives. We can each work to be strong as individuals and, at the same time, work for the good of the whole "tribe" of creation.

The Individual's Journey

> With beauty may I walk.
> With beauty before me, may I walk.
> With beauty behind me, may I walk.
> With beauty above me, may I walk.
> With beauty below me, may I walk.
> With beauty all around me, may I walk.
> In old age wandering on a trail of beauty, lively
> may I walk.
>
> —from the Navajo *Night Chant*[42]

Phra Prajak Kuttajitto, a Buddhist monk, exemplifies someone who first evolved along the Tree dimension and then brought the fruit of his insight back to benefit the Hoop of his community. By happenstance the focus of his work was, quite literally, the Tree.

His story takes place in Thailand, a land once lush with thick forests. Then private and military interests began to rape the majestic Thai teak trees for profit, turning them into lumber and furniture for export to Japan and Europe. By 1994 only a quarter of this country was forest. Without trees to hold moisture, Thailand has endured deadly floods and terrible droughts.[43]

Phra Prajak Kuttajitto began draping many of the giant teak trees in saffron robes and ordaining them as "children of Buddha." Other forest monks began following his example. Since 1987 they have ordained thousands of acres of trees. This tactic succeeds in protecting the forest and the people who depend on it because many potential exploiters are afraid to chop down the "holy" trees and arouse the wrath of Buddha. For a time, at least, Prajak and the other monks have stopped the destruction of the forests.

In addition to protecting the great Tree and wide Hoop, Prajak also strengthened the Hoop of community and the Tree of self-reliance among the local villagers. He set up "buffalo banks" and "rice banks" that foster the cycle of economic energy in the community. Farmers borrow buffalo to till their fields, then give the buffaloes' offspring back to the bank. They borrow rice, then give a portion of their rice crop to the temple, which uses it to feed the elderly. Prajak also taught the villagers meditation. Their alcoholism rate, which had been driven up during government-forced relocation, dropped. "Phra Prajak has helped a lot of people change their opinions about themselves," says a local rice and corn farmer. "He's really improved the quality of our lives and given us hope."[44]

Prajak wasn't always this saintly. His younger years were marked by drinking and gambling. But during an extended hospital stay brought on by his lifestyle Prajak resolved to be reborn. He left the hospital to become a wandering monk. His spiritual attainment eventually led to his work for the benefit of the Hoop—the Hoop of the human communities in the forest and the Hoop of the forest itself. He says:

> I didn't realize how important and vital the forest was until I came here and experienced it for myself. Like most everyone else, I saw the forest in terms of its uses, what you can exploit—wood for homes, or for charcoal. It was a one-sided relationship.
>
> Once I became a monk I came to understand that you can't just take without giving back or it will all dry up and everything will die.[45]

After attaining spiritual insight Prajak worked on his relationship with the natural world, to make it a two-way relationship and not just one-sided. He descended and ascended the Tree, then worked to help the Hoop.

Paths to Wholeness

> The journey of a thousand miles starts from beneath your feet.
>
> —Tao Te Ching[46]

There are two beginning paths toward bringing Hoop-and-Tree wholeness into the world. One or the other of these has been followed by every saint, sage, and savior, every highly evolved person the world has ever known. But you don't have to be a saint to follow either of these paths. Phra Prajak Kuttajitto was a drinker and a gambler in his younger years. Saint Matthew was a tax collector before he was a saint. The women and men in Heath's study of fulfilling lives did not walk on water.

Phra Prajak Kuttajitto followed one of these paths. He plumbed the depths and grew along the Tree axis to greater spiritual awareness, and then brought this awareness into the world to help the Hoop of the human and environmental community. This path might be called the shamanic path. Its movement is first Tree, then Hoop. This is the path of Christ, Mohammed, Moses on Mount Sinai, the !kia healing dance, and the traditional shaman who ascends and descends the Tree in order to bring back spiritual and healing gifts for the benefit of the Hoop of his or her whole tribe. It is the path of the Sufi mystic who ascends progressively higher stations of the path to achieve *ma'rifah* ("interior knowledge," "gnosis") and then returns to this world as a living witness of God. It is the path of Buddha who sat under the Tree of enlightenment and then turned the Hoop of teaching (Wheel of Dharma) for the benefit of all beings.

The other path might be called the path of the Taoist sage. It is first Hoop, then Tree. The sage immerses herself in the way of nature, in the flow, in the web (Hoop), and through this connection attains deep insight and high knowledge (Tree). This person embarks on a vision quest in nature, enters into right relationship with all our relations in the ecological atom, and is gifted with visions from the great mystery.

Dr. Jane Goodall might be said to have followed a Hoop-then-Tree path. In the summer of 1960 Jane Goodall entered the remote

African jungle to begin what was to become the longest continuous field study of animals in their natural habitat. After spending
over thirty-five years learning from chimpanzees, our near kin on
the ecological Hoop, she has broadened her awareness of Hoop
and has begun her Tree work. She acknowledges the broad Hoop
when she says "you gradually realize that as you move out in these
ever-widening circles, that it's all interlinked." Her Fruitful Tree
work is her Roots and Shoots program, which is designed to teach
children how their actions can make a difference in the world: "Its
goal is to educate a new generation and empower young people to
launch 'constructive service' projects in their own communities."[47]

In philosophical terms, this Hoop-then-Tree path has to do
with connecting to life through the principle of *eros*. Eros has nothing to do with the lewd or the vulgar or the merely sensual; it is
the magnetic attraction between two sparks of the Divine embodied
in matter. You connect with the Hoop because you delight in its
beauty and mystery, and serve it because it is holy.

In philosophical terms the other path (Tree-then-Hoop) has to
do with connecting to life through the principle of *logos*. Logos is
"cosmic reason," the thought and will and pattern of the Divine. It
is the electricity of insight. You connect with the Tree because you
delight in its clarity and mystery, and serve it because it is holy.

Both paths are valid routes to wholeness. The Hoop is a way
to the Divine out and through the world, by inclusion and extent;
whereas the Tree is a way to the Divine in and through the core,
by deepening and ascent. The Hoop-then-Tree route leads through
connection and compassion to the ultimate compassion of wisdom;
the Tree-then-Hoop route leads through knowledge and wisdom to
the ultimate wisdom of compassion. *Ultimately both paths become
the same path.*

Ecopsychologist David Abram studied with the shamans of
contemporary Bali. He describes how the shaman works to serve
the Hoop. The shaman

> commonly acts as an intermediary between the human col-
> lective and the larger ecological field, ensuring that there

is an appropriate flow of nourishment, not just from the landscape to the human inhabitants, but from the human community back to the local earth. By their rituals, trances, ecstasies, and "journeys," [Tree work] magicians ensure that the relation between human society and the larger society of beings is balanced and reciprocal, and that the village never takes more from the living land than it returns to it—not just materially, but with prayers, propitiations, and praise.... The medicine person's primary allegiance, then, is not to the human community, but to the earthly web [Hoop] of relations in which that community is embedded—it is from this that her or his power to alleviate human illness derives.[48]

Who Are You, Really? Really?

I am the Tree,
The Tree so strong.
I am within you
All life long.
Look to the top—
No one can see.
All things abiding,
I am the Tree.

Here is the life
That's ever green.
Deep in my roots
I touch the dream.
Around my branches
A crown of light;
The spiral stairway
From day to night.

I am the crossroads
Of East and West.
No one forsaken,

No one the best.
I am within you
Forever still.
Trust in the Tree,
All will be well.

—C. H.

Whatever your starting path, the deep structure of Hoop-and-Tree wholeness lies within you, urging you on.

Imagine yourself as the Hoop and the Tree. This is not extravagance. The Hoop and the Tree describes the innate pattern of sacred life energy possessed by all beings. So imagine yourself as the Hoop and the Tree.

When I imagine myself as Hoop and Tree I find I am surrounded by a great Hoop: the Hoop of all my relations, the ecological atom. Because I am a finite human, I need certain allies to help me relate to this infinite universe. The water of the ocean that I swam in as a child, and a certain smooth round stone help me to connect with the mineral realm. The vegetables I tend in my garden, and a certain pine tree help me to connect with the realm of vegetation. A coyote, an owl, and a bear that have come to me on vision quests guide me into the animal realm. Each of the four cardinal directions also comes to me in the form of a particular animal, whom I honor. These are animals who have chosen me, not I them. In the human realm, I can grow because I am supported by the Hoop of my family and friends. In order to connect with the spirit realm I pray and meditate. All of this is nothing extraordinary. The universe is ready, reaching out. I am just one jewel among the infinite jewels of Indra's net. We each are Hoop and Tree.

As a Tree, my roots reach down to the nourishment provided by my family tree, my ancestors and great ancestors, whose lives made my life possible and who passed their wisdom on to me in family stories. These stories reach way down into the roots of language itself, through the stories told by early speakers of my language. My roots reach down to the underworld of dream which sends messages about the myth or story that is being lived through my life.

My deep taproot touches a being that is at times a dragon and at times a snake. As dragon, this being is like Yggdrasill's dragon Nidhogg, which gnaws on my roots at the places of family hurt; it is partly the unlived life of my ancestors, their unspoken resentments, anger, and suffering. This dragon is also all my unnamable terrors. From time to time I descend to wrestle with this dragon; at times the dragon reaches up to claw me down. When I wrestle successfully the dragon changes for a while into a snake, whose head is half-black, half-white, like the yin-yang t'ai chi. This snake is Kundalini, the mysterious energy of life. It is also an ancestral gift: the snake ring that my grandfather Abuelo bought for me when I was about eight years old and faced with a difficult moral choice. The roots of myself as Tree are watered by tears honoring my ancestors, by the sweat of my wrestlings, by the moisture of dreams, and by the inexhaustible water of the great Hoop-shaped wellspring of life.

As a Tree I am growing toward light—the light of Buddha-nature, of Christ consciousness, and of an image of the Divine that came to me once in a dream. I lift a small bowl to this light, by way of offering of myself. I would become empty so as to receive. I receive the blessings of light from this sun. This bowl is an upper Hoop. I am attempting to grow through skill and power toward knowledge and wisdom. On the Tree of myself there are apples maturing: my son, the books and poetry I am writing, my work in counseling and conflict resolution. I offer this work as all trees lift up their fruit. The story that rises like sap from my roots nourishes the fruit of my limbs and the fruit of my loins. This is nothing special. We are all growing like Trees.

As I reach decision points in life, I look at the Hoop of my relations. Are any relationships in disrepair? Am I returning positive energy to the universe? Am I living my life as a Tree story that connects my roots with my guiding light? Am I, as Joseph Campbell would say, following my bliss?

To imagine oneself as the Hoop and the Tree parallels a Tibetan Buddhist practice of working with an image called a *yidam*,

an image embodying a certain facet of enlightenment.[49] By considering ourselves as an image of wholeness we can see more clearly
what we are and what we are not. We can see where we have not
enough Tree; we can see where we have not enough Hoop. We
also visualize what we can become. It gives us a model, a "future-
focused role-image," which draws us to fullness and health.

Go in Beauty

> Be the change you want to see in the world.
>
> —Mahatma Gandhi

Maturing and integrating the Hoop and the Tree is the work of a
lifetime. Carl Jung once said, "The right way to wholeness is made
up, unfortunately, of fateful detours and wrong turnings. It is a
longissima via, not straight but snakelike, a path that unites the
opposites in the manner of the guiding caduceus, a path whose
labyrinthine twists and turns are not lacking in terrors."[50] Jung is
also saying here that the path to the fully developed Hoop and Tree
is itself in the shape of the Hoop and the Tree: the snake spiraling
up the staff of the caduceus. Gradually, through many repeated lessons at different levels and depths, we learn interdependence and
autonomy, flowing and being, the Hoop and the Tree.

Once when hiking in the wilderness high desert of New Mexico
I came across the Hoop as a wreath of antlers laid on the stony
soil. This Hoop was perhaps twelve or fourteen feet in diameter.
There was a gap in one side of the Hoop, a gap formed by a pair
of carved stone lions, so worn with age that it was hard to tell at
first glance that they were not just two half-buried boulders. Right
next to this Hoop was a Tree. Faded strips of cloth hung from the
branches of this tree, resembling almost exactly the *clooties* tied to
branches by the sacred springs of Celtic Europe. When I think of
the path to the Hoop and the Tree, I imagine a trek deep into the
wilderness of the psyche. After miles of desert and hard walking,
not really knowing what to expect or hope for, suddenly, wonder-
fully, there is the shape of the heart's desire.

Begin where you are. Live as if your life depended on it. In the mythologies, religions, and psychologies of the world there are whole libraries of practices for encountering and nurturing the Hoop and the Tree of the whole self. I have mentioned just a few of these practices in this book. The core practice is a form of quieting: listen to, open up to, give attention to the Divine / Buddha Mind / True Self, and then let your experience of wholeness function from moment to moment to help all beings.

Create and nourish your Hoop. Build a supportive social atom. Especially build relationships with those who will give you a safe space—those who are able to see, hear, feel, and respect you as you truly are. Build relationships with those who respect your boundaries. Let your own boundaries be semipermeable: not too rigid, yet not so tenuous that you become enmeshed with others. Reach out and connect with those who seem different from you.

Build relationships to all the other rings of the ecological atom. Find some way to relate not just to the human world, but also to the animal, vegetable, mineral, and spirit realms. Find allies of the four directions. Center yourself in a living mandala of your own local ecosystem. Behave as though you were part of the web, the great Hoop of all of life, because in fact you are. Live simply and sustainably. Listen for the beat, the rhythm of life, so the music of your actions blends into the vast symphony. The Tree of your self will grow within this Hoop.

Nourish your Tree. Aspire to a high place. Pray. Ascend. Receive the light from on high.

At the same time, be willing to delve into your roots. Acknowledge support from your ancestors, your lineage. Slay the dragon, the frog who poisons or the mouse who nibbles at your roots. Wrestle with the darkness. Be willing to pace the floor of the underground chamber until the ground is quite smooth underfoot. Do the work which Mother Holle requests of you. Discover the gifts below.

Let the nourishing sap of life flow through your veins. As a tree grows, its branches reach out all around. Transcend and include.

As you rise higher, be fruitful. Viewed from a certain perspective the Tree becomes the Hoop of Life. The Tree grows up, matures, yields fruit. The fruit falls and the seed of the fruit enters the earth, which is made of decayed trees and rotted fruit. From this earth the seed sprouts to form a new tree and begin the Hoop of growth, maturation, fruitfulness, and decay all over again. In fruitfulness, decay, and growth lies another secret correspondence between the Hoop and the Tree.

Developing either the Hoop or the Tree can further the development of the other. One may transcend (Tree) to include (Hoop) or include to transcend. As a living tree grows it adds rings. As the inner Tree grows it adds Hoops to the ecological atom. The inner Tree also grows by opening the Hoops of the chakras. The inner Tree grows within the support of nurturing relationships, within the protection of the Hoop. The Hoop nurtures the Tree. The Hoops are also the fruit of the Tree. The fruitful Tree is wholeness, health, enlightenment. The fruitful Tree is the Confucian "profound person," the person of "genius."

In order to be whole we need both the Hoop and the Tree together and in dynamic, living balance. The mature Hoop and Tree is mature androgyny, not a facile blending but real "alchemical" work, which involves full engagement in the experience of life. One could say that the practices for developing the Hoop and the Tree add two more *R*s to the traditional curriculum of Reading, 'Riting, and 'Rithmetic. Hoop adds Relating, and Tree adds Realization.

As we each work on our own journey to wholeness we can remember that everyone—our spouse, parent, child, friend, enemy—has the same shape of wholeness latent within themselves as well. Each being, by his or her own lights, and however imperfectly, is working toward that wholeness. All the world's wisdom points to the same underlying structure of wholeness and health.

On your journey, remember that you are a unique and essential part of the fabric of life of those who surround you. Those who surround you need your help and the gifts you have to offer. In fact you are a unique and essential part of the whole fabric of the universe, of Spider Woman's Web. You are here because the universe needs your creativity, the lusciousness of your fruit.

When you begin to embody the Hoop and the Tree you grow rooted and fruitful, humble and whole. You put yourself at home in the universe, in the flow of life, nurturing, sustaining, and honoring the great mystery, and supported by it. Your life becomes a prayer of gratitude.

Personal Hoop and Tree illustration by Anne Parker, a workshop participant. This is a black-and-white photograph of a very colorful painting.

6

The Hoop and the Tree for Healing and Transformation: A Twenty-Year Perspective

ABOUT TWENTY YEARS AGO *THE Hoop and the Tree* introduced the idea that the deep structure of psychological and spiritual wholeness is well imagined through the visual metaphor of the Hoop and the Tree, and that cultures around the world and throughout history have been pointing, each in its own way, at this deep structure of wholeness. In essence, the Hoop dimension has to do with relationship in all its aspects, including cooperation and working for the collective good, and the Tree dimension has to do with deepening and ascending for psychological and spiritual growth. The Hoop has a female tone and the Tree a male tone. Both dimensions are needed, developed and in balance with each other, for a person or a society to be psychologically and spiritually whole and healthy.

In the intervening years, I have experienced the Hoop-and-Tree image at work in individual counseling, teaching, and organization development. Readers of the book as well as my students, clients, and workshop participants have told me how the image has helped them. Raymond of the Colorado State Patrol put his experience this way: "This model pulls together those many different facets of one's life in order to visualize who we are and how to continue."

Many others have found the Hoop-and-Tree image helpful in their lives and careers and have shared here how it can be applied to organizations and leadership coaching. These examples show the model's usefulness in the current world situation. They also lead us to the crucial importance of initiations on both the Tree dimension and the Hoop dimension.

Reverend Timothy Dobson is an interfaith minister, sacred dance leader, and personal development coach. He says that for him, the Hoop and the Tree serves like a GPS. It is a tool for finding one's present location and then assessing practical paths to move toward the quality of relationship we desire: "As a sacred dance teacher for many years, I see the Hoop-and-Tree image of the whirling dervish, standing boldly as the embodiment of the living axis between self/individuation and community/culture. I have borrowed exercises from the book and incorporated them into dance workshops I lead in Europe."[1]

Jocelyn Gordon is a women's health coach and doula, working in both the United States and New Zealand. She says:

> When *The Hoop and the Tree* came into my life nine years ago as a birthday gift, it was truly life-changing. At the time, I was birthing HoopYogini, a movement meditation that merges hula hooping with Hatha yoga and mindfulness meditation. The book provided context and confirmation of my own deep and transformative experiences in the hoop. The Hoop and the Tree has since been required reading in my two-hundred-hour HoopYogini Teacher Training and continues to be a favorite of our global community of instructors.[2]

For these people and many others, the Hoop-and-Tree model has been a useful compass toward lives of balance and fulfillment. The model resonates with so many because each of us has a deep part of ourselves that yearns for psychological and spiritual wholeness and dares hope that it is possible for ourselves. Our life task is to honor this deep intuition, nurture it, and bring it into full embodied expression. Being alert to Hoop and Tree patterns in life helps with this task.

Though many psychologists have noted the dual aspects of human nature, they have usually privileged one aspect over the other. They have used terms like "communion and agency" or "relatedness and individuality" for what I am calling Hoop and Tree. For a long time, Western psychologists have considered the Tree/agency/individuality aspect as the more important factor in a mature personality. Fortunately, in contemporary psychology the Hoop is starting to come into balance with the Tree, due to the influence of observations of pro-social behaviors in animal species in the wild, as well as a growing respect for feminist and non-Western psychologies and relational Western psychologies (e.g., Rogerian).

What is clear is that we actually have two separate developmental lines or sets of tasks as human beings: a task of developing individuality and a task of developing relatedness. Modern psychology is rediscovering that two tasks support each other: "An increasingly mature sense of self is contingent on interpersonal relationships; conversely, the continued development of increasingly mature interpersonal relationships is contingent on mature self-definition... These two developmental processes evolve in an interactive, reciprocally balanced, mutually facilitating fashion from birth through senescence."[3] And full maturity for both men and women is the integration and consolidation of both lines of development. Overemphasis on either one or the other means missing one's full potential as a human being.

Since publication of the first edition of this book, I have continued to find examples in wisdom traditions around the world and throughout history of the Hoop and the Tree as a template for wholeness. This is reassuring confirmation that anyone working with the Hoop and the Tree is working on a solid footing. A few of the most compelling of these examples follow because they amplify the psycho-spiritual associations of the two dimensions and help us apply them.

Beyond the individual level, the Hoop and the Tree has proven useful in organizations. A professional colleague, Lola Wilcox, uses

the Hoop-and-Tree model in her work as a transformational consultant. She provides this summary and the accompanying chart
to explain how she uses the model for leadership consulting and
organizational diagnosis.[4]

Consider that the Tree represents Hierarchy, and the Hoop
represents Democracy. Some leaders excel at one or the other
approach, most excel at neither; very few are able to move
between the two. A hierarchy by definition is vertical, with the
most powerful decision-maker at the top. Any person further
down the line is in service to the people above. Most vertical
leaders manage a group of people, who might be seen as little
hoops of equals, but who are more likely to be sorted into smaller
hierarchies of supervisors and team or project leads. This type
of organization is a Tree of Responsibility, and functions best
when all, even the smallest twig, has necessary information and
understands who makes which decisions.

Poet and government worker Geoffrey Chaucer (b. 1343,
England) names this model "The Faire Chain of Love," with God
at the top, and wisdom and *caritas* (love for all) flowing down
a human hierarchy from a good king/queen to the animals and
earth. When a thief, drunk, or despot is at the top, however, the
chain has a different binding. This is an organization of secrets;
frequent shifting of positions keeps accountability at a minimum.
The middle management branches are not clear about what is
going on or what they are to do. People in these hierarchies are
seen as human "resources," not human beings; they are used or
disposed of at management's will. Everyone knows not to ask
questions or "make waves." If opposed to an action they silently
drag out implementation time, knowing a new "boss" will bring
another change.

A Hoop is a good image for a democratic system. And, just
as Tree Hierarchies have methods and practices, so do Hoops
know how to engage when every member is equal to the other,
and how to hear and respect each person's opinion. Decisions
are emergent, involving lots of discussion before they are made.
Because decisions are made together each person is responsible

for having accurate information, for presenting it, for stand-ing up for that information while being willing to hear new or conflicting facts and ideas and respond accordingly. In hierar-chies, accountability rests with the individual in charge of that part of the organization or project. There is "one throat to grab" if failure is on the horizon. In Hoop structures all are equally responsible for outcomes.

Democratic processes are essential to complex problem-solving. Whole-systems thinking begins with recognizing every stakeholder. This includes giving a voice to those entities who might otherwise not have a voice. This would mean, for example, assigning a person to attend and speak as a representative and voice for the interests of future or aging generations, or of the ecosystem, the natural world. Other voices could be current economic and political stakeholders, etc. The goal is not to win the conversation, or to subdue all the opposing or tangential points of view. The goal is to engage, seeking solutions outside the participants' current boxes and models.

There are cultures which flourish with this model; the old Norse governing model of the Althing laid the foundation of modern Scandinavia. North American indigenous tribes offered Hoop-and-Tree models to the US Constitution builders. (See chapter 5.) The Society of Friends (Quakers) has many seasoned Hoop processes that can be incorporated into a leader's toolbox.

Hoop structures are vulnerable if a member is more commit-ted to advancing a personal agenda than trusting the group's process. And, always, diverse thinking and feeling is critical, or "groupthink" may lead all in the wrong direction for lack of depth exploration. Weak Hoop structures tend toward compromise or accommodating solutions. Accountability for reaching a decision rests with the group, and some people resist deciding and closure. Many people have experience in hierarchy, but lack training in democratic process skills such as how to reach concordance or consensus—decision-making processes that demand both asser-tiveness and cooperation. Using argumentation instead of these processes slows things down and limits the solution.

Leaders who know how to create and work with Hoops access large amounts of information. In a hierarchical Tree organization, the edge of the organization is the customer-facing employee. In a democratic Hoop organization, the edge is everyone gathering new information, and responding quickly to new situations. New businesses often are Hoop, and military and corporate organizations are usually Tree. The fast-moving and complex current world is fostering more Hoop organizations.

The Hoop and Tree can serve as a diagnostic tool to determine if the individual or group is a Tree in need of a Hoop or vice versa. Listen for the language being used, and the mental model in the structure of the organization. The Hoop and the Tree help identify issues and suggest solutions or new directions. A few examples are suggested in the diagnostic chart that follows; obviously, there are numerous possible situations.

Tree/Hoop Diagnostic Chart
(Examples)

Issue	Hoop, Tree, or?	Action
INDIVIDUAL ISSUES:		
Lonely; lack of connection; lack of information	Tree	Grow Hoop—help individual consciously build sociometric network (*See Social Atom, Chapter 2.*) If person is a social Isolate, connect him/her to an empathetic social Star.
Addiction; abusive Relationships	Tree	"I" alone in the world moves to Hoop community of recovering. *(See discussion of AA Twelve Step process as a Hoop-Tree integration in Chapter 4.)*
Emotional state: lost in overwhelm	Hoop	When given too many goals, timelines, projects, responsibilities Tree structure and ownership helps clarify who owns what.

Emotional state: blame/shame	Tree	Blamer insistence that others are at fault is a Tree response: I'm rooted where I stand. Hoop skills involve the victim in shared problem-solving.
ORGANIZATIONAL / SYSTEM ISSUES:		
Confused by multiple stakeholder demands	Hoop	Develop Tree—use vertical goal structure to aid decision-tree; reasoned choice-making
New or disliked "boss" of family or organization	Tree	Develop Hoop—build mutually supportive relationships by listening, questioning, responsiveness
Ignored safety programs	Tree	Develop Hoop—safety Committees with teaching responsibilities, decision-making permission
Disaster recovery	Both	Initial response is Tree: authority to provide immediate solutions. Long-term recovery is Hoop: democratic processes to recovery, rebuilding, prevention strategies
Economic resilience	Both	Bank loans—Tree, balanced with microlending Hoops

The Hoop and the Tree and Our World Situation

The balanced importance of both Hoop and Tree has implications for social policy. At the individual level it means supporting equal and complementary emphasis on the development of both individuality and relatedness for both men and women. At the level of society, it means recognizing that people need to be interpersonally related (Hoop) as well as having an individual sense of self and purpose (Tree). This recognition could improve how we as a society deal with issues like poverty and crime. Helping people feel interpersonally related with family and community can foster successful development and help prevent psychological and behavioral problems.[5]

In the realm of human society as a whole we face, in addition to conflict and oppression, big problems of climate change and species extinction.[6] It seems to me that one of the reasons for this is that for many years our society has lacked key initiations into full Hoop and Tree maturity, especially on the Hoop dimension. To be fully mature we need not only to "grow up" (Tree) but also to "grow out" (Hoop). I will discuss more about these initiations shortly.

The scale of our problems is almost unimaginable. As I am writing this in 2019 the carbon dioxide in our atmosphere is at a level not seen in eight hundred thousand years. Considering the total weight of the earth's terrestrial vertebrates, humans now account for 30 percent, farm animals another 67 percent, and all the wild animals together only 3 percent. There are half as many wild animals on the planet today as there were in 1970.[7] As of now, humans use the equivalent of 1.7 planet earths to provide the resources we use and absorb our waste. In other words, it now takes the earth one year and eight months to regenerate what we use in a year.[8]

The closest historical analogue to what may be coming is perhaps the early middle ages in Western Europe. This was a period marked by a decline of trade, increased migration, and a scarcity of literary and cultural output. But if we completely tip the environmental balance, we could be dealing with all of that plus drought, flood, famine, conflict, and migration for centuries into the future. We seem to be driving toward a cliff, and the closer we get to it the harder we will have to jam on the brakes to avoid a crash. Life itself will survive in any case. It just may not include human life; or if human, it may not be the life we desire.

The current epoch in the history of our planet has been called the *Anthropocene*, from *anthropos*—human. It refers to the period since the beginning of significant human impact on the earth's geology and ecosystems—roughly since the beginning of the industrial revolution.

Physicians Susan Prescott and Alan Logan describe the Anthropocene this way: "Rather than an easily identifiable era appearing in rock strata, the Anthropocene is more of a diagnostic syndrome, a set of signs and symptoms including climate change, gross biodiversity losses, environmental degradation, and an epidemic of non-communicable diseases. The syndrome is intertwined with politics, economics, and public policies (or lack thereof), social values, and a global push of calorie-dense, nutrient-poor foods and beverages. The healing of Anthropocene syndrome is the grand challenge of humanity."[9]

Hoop-and-Tree practices can help with this healing because the Hoop-and-Tree image of wholeness is *ecopsychological*. That is, it teaches that a person or a society cannot be healthy or whole without a respectful, reciprocal relationship with the natural world of which we are a part.

The Anthropocene makes those of us who believe that the earth is our sacred home feel profoundly distressed when we see places that we love under attack and species and ecosystems collapsing. It erodes our sense of belonging and identity. It produces a psychological experience of desolation, or "lack of solace." The resulting pain or sense of yearning is something environmental philosopher Glenn Albrecht has named *solastalgia*. "Solastalgia," he says, "is a form of homesickness one gets when one is still at 'home.'"[10] The concept is a way to bundle together the emotional costs of ecological decline: anxiety, despair, numbness, a sense of being overwhelmed or powerless, and grief.

Many of us these days also experience a feeling that we do not wish to return to a place that we once loved and enjoyed, when we know that it has been irrevocably changed for the worse.

To heal the Anthropocene, we need to work together to move the world to a new place.

A Dream of the New Earth

Once upon a time
the earth will be new again,
scars healed, roads narrowed,
all life flourishing,
clear-cuts lush with old growth

sustainably harvested,
rivers pure to drink from,
the birds come back, flashing
and speckled fish thronging the seas,
the minefields will be cleared,
the radioactivity gone,
no more stabbings or beatings
or wrongful tears in the night;
the work of humans
will be a few things beautifully made,
humble and fit,
with music, jokes, ceremony,
poetry, and dance in endless abundance
in place of a vomit of stuff
reeking of obsession and bound for the landfill,
humankind scaled back, its factories and cities
no longer a plague
that pimples and blisters the landscape
but a string of jewels
on the body of the earth,
the air fit to breathe again
simple silence available
and billions of stars at night.
O may we weave ourselves
into the fabric of life
and truly feel the path,
smooth or rocky, beneath our feet,
and be worthy of this passage,
long or short,
between the two doorways
where naked we enter
and naked we depart.

—C.H.[11]

The "new earth" will be marked by mutually enhancing relationships between humans, the earth, and the other creatures here on

our planet. Albrecht proposes that we call this positive new epoch the *Symbiocene*.[12]

"Symbiocene" has its root in the word "symbiosis," which refers to any type of a close and long-term biological interaction between two different biological organisms. The rationale, Albrecht says, is that biology "now presents irresistible evidence that the rules of the foundations for life are interconnection, interrelationships, diversity, and cooperation, and that homeostasis between the 'diversity of lives' give the stability that life in general needs to endure. Symboiosis has now emerged as a primary determinant of the conditions of life."[13]

As just one surprising illustration of this, roughly 90 percent of the cells that constitute the human body are actually symbiont bacteria. We have ten times more bacterial cells in us, or on us, than human cells.[14] Microbial ecosystems are an essential part of the many diverse natural systems that sustain human life.[15] Recent studies have found significant interactions of animals and plants with symbiotic microorganisms, to such an extent that the notion of the "biological individual" is an oversimplification of the true state of affairs.[16] Recent studies have also shown that life in nature is marked not solely by competition (Tree) but also by cooperation and symbiosis (Hoop).

In reality everything is dependent on everything else. We are nature and nature is us. We inter-are. This is the concept of *inter-being* from Buddhist monk Thich Nhat Hanh (chapter 2). Many traditional cultures have known this for centuries.

"The Symbiocene," Albrecht says, "begins when recognition by humans of the vital interconnectedness of life becomes the material foundation for all subsequent thought, policy, and action."[17] Our arrival into the Symbiocene depends on full development of the Hoop.

To get there, we can work to let our human population taper down to a size appropriate to the carrying capacity of the earth. Famed naturalist E. O. Wilson recommends that in order to stave off mass extinction we devote half the surface of the earth to nature.[18] We can organize our political subdivisions around bio-regions or watersheds, as Grand Canyon explorer John Wesley

Powell proposed back in the nineteenth century for the western United States as a way to conserve water and reduce conflicts.[19]

We can develop cultural competency to thrive in a diverse tapestry of cultures. We can reimagine our economic system as something not separate from the world but part of a larger enveloping and sustaining whole—the earth with its atmosphere and its ecosystems—and transition to a regenerative economy that restores the earth instead of depleting it.[20] The biggest and most urgent need right now is to stop emitting carbon dioxide and other greenhouse gases into the atmosphere and to start to draw down the excess already there.

Ecophilosopher, Buddhist teacher, and Rilke translator Joanna Macy recommends that we now put the healing of our world at the very center of things.[21] We must not turn away from the suffering world any more than we would turn away from a beloved relative who is dying. Our pain at the suffering of the earth, she says, is simply an indication that we are deeply alive and that our hearts are open.

In essence, as a world society we need to acknowledge and transmute the shadow side of our collective Tree and explore our highest aspirations on the Tree axis and also to expand our Hoop to embrace the reality of our interdependence with other humans and with the entire web of life in all its forms. The organizing principles of much of contemporary society are unfortunately limited to the lower levels of the Tree—especially sexuality and power—and to an exclusionary and constricted Hoop. We need instead to be fully initiated on both dimensions.

Initiations

Human life has an arc. Along this arc from birth to death there are several important inflection points when our consciousness, which had heretofore been adequate for our lives, becomes inadequate due to new life circumstances. The new circumstances may be biological, social, or spiritual. At these points we need to attain a new level of consciousness that is more adequate for the new circumstances.

Some key biological inflection points include puberty and elder-hood. Marriage and parenthood are social inflection points. Any of these, plus others such as death of a loved one or losing a peer group through a move, may trigger a spiritual crisis.

These inflection points always involve some internal struggle, and often some external struggle as well, because each time we are like a caterpillar in a chrysalis, dying to our old selves and then giving birth to our new selves. Our struggle is to find a way to move into increased self-knowledge and a "new life" under the new circumstances.

We humans have used various metaphors to talk about these inflection points. Psychologist Erik Erikson speaks of them in terms of "Eight Ages." As discussed in chapter 3, Erikson's Eight Ages are critical periods, or crises, in the development in the human psyche, each of which can result in a positive forward-trending resolution or a stuck or backward-trending resolution.[22] At each crisis we face a pivotal opportunity.[23]

The very first inflection point occurs during the early period right after birth. Ideally, the infant then acquires a sense that the outer world is trustworthy and that its own inner sensations are acceptable. A mother instills this in her baby by combining sensitive care of the infant with a firm sense of personal trustworthiness. "The infant's first social achievement, then, is his willingness to let the mother out of sight without undue anxiety or rage, because she has become an inner certainty as well as an outer predictability."[24]

So, at the first inflection point we either gain the boon of basic trust, or we get stuck in basic mistrust. This is not to say we can't try again, but basic mistrust is a difficult position from which to live. As discussed in chapter 2, developing a secure sense of attachment with our principal caregiver is essential for our future health and well-being.

The pivotal opportunities of Erikson's Eight Ages continue up the Tree axis of individual development. The rest of them resolve ideally with a preponderance of a sense of autonomy over feelings of shame and doubt (crisis 2), initiative over guilt (3), industry/industriousness over inferiority (4), identity over role confusion (5), intimacy over isolation (6), generativity over stagnation (7), and ego integrity over despair (8). The work at each inflection point is for the individual to achieve and integrate a *favorable ratio* of the tendency toward growth over the tendency toward regression.

The Hindu Kundalini system talks about the inflection points in terms of "opening" the chakras (*chakra* meaning "wheel" or Hoop) rising up along the Tree axis. Each of the chakra levels represents a quality that needs to be made accessible so as to enable the full flourishing of the human spirit. Chapter 3 contains a chart showing how Erikson's ages and the chakras map to each other. For example, having a sense of basic trust (Erikson) gives us a firm root support, which is what the first chakra represents. In mythologist Joseph Campbell's words, each inflection point is "the threshold of adventure."

No matter how they may be named, these inflection points are metaphors for transitions needed in order to achieve a fully mature, whole human psyche and spirit. Each inflection point presents an opportunity for life to move forward and also a risk of life becoming stuck.

Each inflection point involves elements of Tree and elements of Hoop. As consciousness moves to become more adequate to a new situation, it *transcends* (moves up the Tree axis) and *includes* (widens the Hoop to include not only the prior worldview, but more).[25] Erikson acknowledges the Hoop aspect when he says, "The human personality in principle develops according to steps predetermined in the growing person's readiness to be driven toward . . . a widening social *radius*" [emphasis added].[26] The Kundalini system acknowledges this in the very name *chakra* or "wheel." A living Tree grows by adding rings (Hoops).

Even though all the levels on the Tree have Hoop aspects, the strongest Tree connection with Hoop is at the Kundalini heart chakra, which maps to the Eriksonian level of intimacy. For this reason, and also because it is simpler to talk about the Hoop dimension and the Tree dimension separately, I structure my discussions with the Tree intersecting the Hoop at the heart level. (For more on the levels of the Tree, see chapter 3.)

What we know from world cultures is that successful passage through each inflection point in life's arc can be facilitated by a process of initiation. When people think of a "process of initiation," the first image that probably comes to mind is of some sort of coming-of-age or puberty rite of passage into adulthood. (This initiation is usually timed to help resolve the internal struggle of identity versus role confusion.) But because there are many inflection points in life, there are many initiations other than at puberty. And for the most part these all involve aspects of both the Hoop and the Tree. There are three Hoop initiations in particular that seem most relevant to healing our current world situation.

Initiations into the Human Ring of the Hoop

Our first relational or Hoop initiation is our initiation into what it means to be a human being. This formally begins with a birth ceremony (naming ceremony, christening, baby-welcoming ceremony, etc.), some form of which exists in all cultures. This initiation then continues over many years, as our parents or principal caregivers model for us what it means to be a human being. If we are fortunate, they are good at it. They don't need to be perfect, just "good enough."[27] If we are lucky, they are good role models and for the most part they know when and how to use praise and to set limits on our behavior for our own benefit.

The Hoop aspect of the initiation into humanity continues as the growing child expands its awareness beyond the immediate family. The initiators for this task include parents, school, and friends, combined with travel, study, and self-reflection. Hierocles, a Stoic philosopher who lived in the first half of the second century CE, gives a clear prescription for initiation into the human ring of the Hoop. Notice how closely it resembles the "social atom" described in chapter 2.

> Each one of us is as it were entirely encompassed by many circles. . . . The first and closest circle is the one which a person has drawn as though around a center, his own mind. . . . Next, the second one further removed from the center but enclosing the first circle, . . . contains parents, siblings, wife,

and children. The third one has in it uncles and aunts, grandparents, nephews, nieces, and cousins . . . that is followed by
the circle of local residents . . . fellow-citizens . . . people from
neighboring towns, and the circle of fellow-countrymen. The
outermost and largest circle, which encompasses all the rest,
is that of the whole human race. Once these have all been
surveyed, it is the task of a well-tempered man, in his proper
treatment of each group, to draw the circles together somehow
towards the center, and to keep zealously transferring those
from the enclosing circles into the enclosed ones. . . . The right
point will be reached if, through our own initiative, we reduce
the distance of the relationship with each person.[28]

This points to a well-initiated person being one who embraces
the full spectrum of diversity in the human realm.

Initiations into the Ecological Ring of the Hoop

After a person's initiation into the Hoop of humanity has begun,
there are at least two more essential Hoop initiations. Both of these
are initiations into the ecological ring of the Hoop. As with Erikson's
Eight Ages, each of these coincides with a critical period or crisis in
the development of the human psyche. And, as with Erikson's Eight
Ages, each can result in a positive forward-trending resolution, or a
backward-trending resolution, or simply becoming stuck. The first
of these initiations I call the "TEN" initiation; the second I call the
"Kali" initiation.

The Transformative Experience of Nature ("TEN") Initiation

In many traditional cultures, an initiation to the ecological Hoop was
a normal part of growing up. Human children are innately curious.
And when one's family's life is deeply and intimately interrelated
with the natural world, opportunities for connection with and learning from the natural world appear daily.

Initiations were also formally structured. For example, many Native American cultures sent their youth on a ceremonial vision quest.[29] Similarly, young Australian Aboriginal people would go *walkabout*—a ritual journey across the bush for expanding their wisdom and understanding. The essence of a transformative experience of nature is a fundamental shift of consciousness: from viewing ourselves as separate from nature to knowing that we are each a jewellike knot tied into the infinite webbing of Indra's Net, the largest Hoop of all.

Henry David Thoreau came close to the sense of this in his essay "Walking," in which he asks us to regard human beings as "a part and parcel of Nature, rather than a member of society."

Today, we find ourselves greatly impoverished compared with Thoreau, who wrote: "I can easily walk ten, fifteen, twenty, any number of miles, commencing at my own door, without going by any house, without crossing a road except where the fox and the mink do: first along by the river, and then the brook, and then the meadow and the woodside. There are square miles in my vicinity which have no inhabitant . . . In one half-hour I can walk off to some portion of the earth's surface where a man does not stand from one year's end to another."[30] Walking in nature is one of the best ways to open oneself for a potential transformative experience.

In the initiation into the ecological ring of the Hoop, it is often nature herself who performs the initiation, not some human intermediary as is true with the human ring. TEN is a useful mnemonic because the Transformative Experience of Nature frequently, though not always, takes place when a person is about ten years old, give or take a few years. This seems to be the age when the developing psyche is primed for the experience.

Priest and earth scholar Thomas Berry reflects on a profound experience of nature that happened when *he* was about ten years old. It was springtime, early May. He saw a certain meadow for the very first time.

> And that sight, together with the sounds of the insects—the crickets, the birds—all of this somehow struck me in such a way that ever since then that meadow has become my

> norm of reality and value . . . If we don't have certain outer
> experiences, we don't have certain inner experiences or at
> least we don't have them in such a profound way. We need
> the sun, the moon, the stars, the rivers and the mountains
> and the trees, the flowers, the birds, the song of the birds,
> the fish in the sea. All of this evokes something in our
> inner world, evokes a world of mystery. It evokes a world
> of Sacred and gives us that sense of awe and mystery.[31]

There is abundant evidence that having a strong positive childhood experience of nature like this one is key for allowing a person's creativity and full humanness to blossom. Edith Cobb's research documents this thoroughly.[32] Richard Louv gives even more evidence in his book *Last Child in the Woods*.[33] A powerful experience of nature evokes a sense of wonder, which is a prerequisite for creativity. Walt Whitman, in his poem "Out of the Cradle, Endlessly Rocking," describes his own experience of this and says, "My own songs awakened from that hour."

Supplementing the teachings of traditional cultures, many scientific studies establish the connection between "nature relatedness" (affinity to the natural world) and a variety of aspects of physical and emotional well-being (in addition to pro-environmental behavior and empathy).[34] For example, exposing humans to nature has been associated with increases in concentration, increases in self-concept, improvements in student test scores, decreases in the time it takes to recover from surgery, decreases in symptoms of attention-deficit/hyperactivity disorder in children, decreases in aggressive behaviors, and decreases in stress.[35]

At some time in your life you may have taken a walk along an unpopulated water shore or on a path through a mature, undisturbed forest, or you may have sat beside a waterfall, or enjoyed being out on a prairie watching birds in flight. If so, it probably won't surprise you to learn that people who are more connected to nature tend to experience more positive affect, vitality, and life satisfaction compared to those less connected to nature.[36] Even spending just two hours a week in nature can significantly improve one's sense of health and well-being.[37] The Japanese actually have a word for this healing experience of spending time in nature and breathing it in. They call it *shinrin yoku* (literally: "forest bathing").

Since contact with green space and natural environments is a health asset, access to the natural environment is also a social justice issue. We must ensure that all people regardless of socio-economic status have access to nature and opportunities to develop a relationship with earth's natural systems.[38]

Unfortunately, with growing urbanization and increased population, fewer and fewer children have even the opportunity for initiation into the ecological Hoop. Richard Louv warns us that we need to rectify this and save our children from what he calls "nature-deficit disorder."

The importance of initiation into the ecological Hoop raises the question of what happens when "nature-deficit-disordered" children grow into the adults who run society. The answer is, pretty clearly, the disaster of our current environmental crisis.

The "TEN" Initiation: Wonder and Kinship Versus Disrespect

The legend of King Midas with the golden touch is well known as a cautionary tale about greed. Less well known but perhaps even more important these days is the legend of Erysichthon, another ancient king.

Erysichthon had so little respect for the natural world that he cut down all the trees in a sacred grove. The earth goddess Ceres, outraged, summoned the goddess Famine to punish Erysichthon. That very night Famine came while the king was sleeping, wrapped her emaciated body around his, pressed her dry, cracked lips against his, and kissed into him an insatiable hunger.

In his sleep he began to grind his jaws, dreaming of food. After awakening he soon depleted the entire treasury of his kingdom in purchasing feasts that brought no fill. Eventually he sold his own daughter to buy food. When both food and daughter were gone, with no other recourse, he bit his sharp teeth into his own flesh and soon consumed his own body.[39]

Like Erysichthon, in our reckless consumption we in the modern world have been clear-cutting the "sacred groves" of the world (even literally doing so in the Amazon rain forest) and sacrificing the welfare of the next generation ("selling our own daughter"). We have been behaving with disrespect rather than a sense of kinship and wonder. Those in power who are making disastrous decisions for the world's future are setting us up to eat our own flesh.

A successful TEN initiation, the first into the ecological ring of the Hoop, ignites our sense of wonder. Wonder is the prerequisite for creativity. If the heart chakra has been opened and one is therefore available for intimacy (versus isolation), then the TEN initiation also awakens a sense of kinship with the natural world. Kinship naturally evokes a sense of responsibility or care for the natural world, the same sense that one would feel in a relationship with a significant other human being. An unsuccessful or absent TEN initiation results in alienation from, and disrespect for, the natural world. This enables the commodification of it.

Psychotherapist Kaisa Puhakka puts it this way: "It is only when intimacy is felt palpably as no separation that its essential connection with care becomes evident. Thus, a child experiences his finger as inseparable from or of the 'same stuff as,' his self, and were he to stick it in a fire he would spontaneously pull it out without conscious thought. Similarly, indigenous peoples who took their natural environment to be their sustaining mother and themselves of the same flesh as her, showed the same care and concern for their environment as they did for themselves and their families, presumably without the need to be persuaded by argument or evidence." Yet, "contemporary educated, thoughtful folk often find themselves in the curious predicament of being persuaded by evidence and argument from evolutionary biology and ecological science that they are 'part' of nature, yet not feeling a part of nature in their bones and at the basis of their moral compass."[40]

Nature initiated a relationship with Thomas Berry that evoked in him a sense of wonder ("the Sacred," "awe and mystery") and developed into active caring for the environment. It became the basis for his moral compass. Berry is the one who gave us the

Hoop teaching that "the universe is a communion of subjects rather than a collection of objects."[41]

The "Kali" Initiation: Reverence Versus Dread

In *The Heart of the Hunter,* Sir Laurens van der Post (author, war hero, philosopher, friend of Carl Jung, anti-apartheid activist, among other attributes) describes the end of one of his journeys in the wilds of South Africa with these words:

> When one has lived as close to nature for as long as we had done, one is not tempted to commit the metropolitan error of assuming that the sun rises and sets, the day burns out and the night falls, in a world outside oneself. These are great and reciprocal events, which occur also in ourselves. In this moment of heightened sensibility, there on the lip of the pan, I was convinced that, just as the evening was happening in us, so were we in it, and the music of our participation in a single overwhelming event was flowing through us.[42]

This sense of wordless communion between nature and the human psyche that "you and I are one" is the essence of the first initiation into the ecological Hoop. It creates a sense of being held by the natural world, just as good mothering creates the sense of being held safely in the human world and lays the foundation for basic trust in life and the universe. We are opened into wonder and kinship.

But there is at least one other initiation into the ecological Hoop. This is because nature itself is more than human—not *inhuman* but *other than human.* It is the *matrix* (the "womb") within which all life take place. Nature is not only nurturing but also "red in tooth and claw" (Tennyson). Nature includes not only beautiful meadows and sunsets but also hurricanes, earthquakes, wildfires, and avalanches. It includes life feeding on other life—which means death for the other life and, by implication, for ourselves. Kaisa Puhakka suggests that this aspect of nature might be called the "Kali" aspect, after the fierce Hindu goddess of both life and death.

The first Kali initiation occurs at the crisis of death awareness. It seems to continue in increments that arrive more and more frequently as one grows older and has more encounters with the reality of death.

In my case, my most vivid Kali initiation increment thus far came while I was a young man and single, between my first and second marriages. I was skiing with a friend in the Colorado mountains and I was buried by an avalanche, with only my right forearm remaining visible above the snow. Fortunately, my skiing companion persisted in looking and eventually found me and dug me out. Then we had a rather harrowing journey back to a road. It was a close call.

Whether awareness of death arrives through a close call personally or the death of a loved one, it comes as a shock. Having a mythological container for the terror that it engenders is helpful. Joseph Campbell tells us that myth serves four functions, the first of which is the "mystical function" that opens us up to the mystery of the world, including a reconciliation with life and death. "If mystery is manifest through all things," he says, "the universe becomes, as it were, a holy picture. You are always addressing the transcendent mystery through the conditions of your actual world."[43]

With good fortune the Kali initiation happens after the creative, life-opening TEN initiation has happened. This is helpful because the fruits of the TEN initiation, wonder and kinship, are prerequisites for a successful Kali. Like the TEN initiation, the Kali initiation to the ecological Hoop presents a crisis with two potential outcomes.

If a person has some mythological container for the shock of mortality, then the crisis can resolve into a sense of reverence. One's life can move forward. If there is no container, or a weak one, the outcome is a sense of dread. An underlying sense of dread about nature can lead to a stuck life or even lead backward, with an unconscious wish to seek and destroy what one fears.

Thomas Berry did have a mythological container for his profound experience with nature. He says, "A good religion is what enabled me to understand the deep mystery in the meadow."[44]

We could say that all three of these Hoop initiations have to do with developing a sense of care. The first Hoop initiation, into the human world, teaches us to take care of each other. The second, the TEN initiation, teaches us to take care of the earth and her beings. The third opens us up to the cycles of birth and death and teaches us to take care of the generations. We do this by honoring the past generations and uplifting our elders and by safeguarding and teaching our youth and becoming good ancestors for the coming generations, even to the seventh generation coming. This helps us heal intergenerational trauma.

No one is perfect, but a society owes it to itself to ask that its leaders be at least well-initiated on both the Hoop and Tree dimensions. Regardless of politics, we need to choose leaders who have at least done enough inner work to have achieved a positive-trending resolution of most key developmental milestones. Along the Tree axis they should have achieved a preponderance of basic trust (you can't trust anyone who does not himself or herself trust the world), as well as of autonomy, initiative, industriousness, a sense of identity, a capability for intimacy, and an impulse to be generative and foster the next generation.

Along the Hoop dimension they should have achieved the ability to form positive relationships within a wide Hoop in the human world (Hoop 1). They also should have a sense of wonder and kinship with the natural world and demonstrate care for it (Hoop 2/"TEN"). And, independent of religious affiliation or non-affiliation, they should have a sense of reverence for the mystery of life (Hoop 3/"Kali").

The Millennial Adventure of the Soul

To understand initiations better, it helps to have as a framework something known as the hero/heroine's journey.

As we live our lives, we live them in at least two realms. One is the outer realm of life of our family of origin, school, career choice, jobs, grocery shopping, friendships, significant others, perhaps marriage and children of our own, sickness and health, good and bad turns of events, etc. The other is the inner realm. This is the realm of the life that is apparent only to ourselves. It has to do with our core beliefs, our hopes and fears, our inner struggles about making the right choices, our dreams and nightmares, etc. The inner life is where initiations do their work.

The inner life begins with our first glimmerings of consciousness of ourselves as individual beings and stretches perhaps all the way to the end of life, perhaps beyond. This is the life that Joseph Campbell has called "the millennial adventure of the soul."[45]

The two levels are not separate. Indeed, they interact, often in unexpected ways, with outer actions altering the inner landscape and inner promptings influencing outer actions. Sometimes there are coincidences that link inner and outer in some meaningful way, though with no apparent causal connection. Jung named an experience of this a *synchronicity*.

As we live our outer lives, in the inner realm we are yearning for some sense of wholeness, something that perhaps might be called "enlightenment" or "heart's ease" or "redemption." So we undertake an inner journey, with more or less awareness of it, as we continue to lead our outer lives. This inner journey is known as the hero's or heroine's journey. And it tells us in metaphorical language the obstacles to be overcome and the powers of the psyche to be recognized and integrated if we are to become whole.

In his classic *The Hero with a Thousand Faces*, Joseph Campbell describes the basic template for the hero/heroine's journey. This story has been told and retold thousands of ways throughout history and in cultures all around the world. It is the pattern or monomyth that each of us follows in our inner lives if we are to become heroes or heroines of our own life story and reach that inner sense of enlightenment/peace/redemption.

The basic pattern is this: Something unexpected calls us away from, or yanks us out of, our ordinary lives. We are challenged to enter a perilous situation. There we confront some sort of test or ordeal. Successful resolution of this confrontation yields a new insight or power and perhaps a gift symbolic of the new insight or power. Then we must contrive a safe return from the mythological realm to the world of ordinary life. Finally, we need to integrate the new insight or power into our ordinary lives in a way that benefits or blesses the wider community.[46]

This description might sound like just the synopsis of some quest type of computer game. But when we ourselves are living through it, it is a real, emotionally charged, psycho spiritual experience. How real to each of us are our own hopes, fears, desires, neuroses? (It may be, in fact, that the fascination some people have with the quest type of computer game is because it allows them to rehearse for their own hero/heroine's journey.)

At the deepest level, the insight gained through the hero/heroine's journey is a healing of the internal split between the person and their deep true nature. So, for the heroine's journey it is a healing of the internal split between the woman and the deep feminine.[47] For the hero's journey it is a healing of the internal split between the man and the deep masculine. For other gender inflections it is a similar healing of a split. The accompanying gift typically has to do with spiritual wealth—represented by gold—and also often includes a symbol of healing, such as a cloth that will heal any wound or the "water of life." Often, there is also a sense of a sacred marriage, a *heiros gamos*, of masculine and feminine energies that restores wholeness.

The basic pattern of all initiations, both Hoop and Tree initiations, is similar to that of the hero/heroine's journey. In a sense, any single initiation and the hero/heroine monomyth are *fractals*. A fractal is something whose shape at one size or scale is similar to its shape at another size or scale. A classic example is cauliflower. Take a head of cauliflower and snap off a sprig. That little sprig looks very much like a miniature head of cauliflower. (Romanesco broccoli is even more this way.)

The overall arc of one's life can be seen as a hero/heroine's journey, and each step or initiation along the way is itself a hero/heroine's journey.

Every initiation on the Hoop dimension and on the Tree dimension, except perhaps the very first initiation into humanity through relationship with our principal caregiver, involves the same phases of the journey: the call to adventure, separation from the everyday realm, interaction with the primal forces of life and death, and transition back into the everyday realm, bringing back some gift or insight that will be of benefit in the everyday realm.

So, how does the Hoop and the Tree image of wholeness help us navigate the hero/heroine's journey? It is a map or template that shows us how the puzzle pieces of our own journey fit into the big picture of our own wholeness. With the Hoop-and-Tree image we can see how insights from our own personal exploration and themes from myths and fairy tales (the roots of modern psychology) tell us in picture language what our souls need to hear in order to move ahead on our journey.

We have encountered some of these traditional themes before: "Mother Holle" and the story of Inanna's descent to wisdom are heroine stories. "The Woodcutter's Son" and the story of the princesses in the well ("The Gnome") are hero stories. The Greek myth of Psyche and Eros is a heroine story.

One of the most complete stories related to a man's initiation is "Iron Hans" or "Iron John" from the Grimm brothers' collection.[48] One of the most complete related to a woman's initiation is "Vasalisa the Beautiful" or "Vasalisa the Wise" from the Russian/Slavic tradition.[49] Since both of these tales have been ably treated elsewhere, I'll focus on just a few elements most closely related to our theme of the Hoop and the Tree.[50]

"Into the Forest": Descent into the Roots of the Tree

> No tree, it is said, can grow to heaven
> unless its roots reach down to hell.
>
> —Carl Jung[51]

In both the Vasalisa story and the Iron John story, the protagonist at some point must go "into the forest," which is another way of saying "down into the roots of the tree." In Iron John the forest is "full of all kinds of wild animals," and the king has been sending huntsmen one after another into the forest to hunt deer, but none has returned. So the king has stopped sending men into the forest. It is too dangerous.

In Vasalisa, within the forest lies the house of the fearsome Baba Yaga. She travels in a cauldron shaped like a mortar, rowing it with an oar shaped like a pestle, and sweeping out the tracks behind her with a broom made out of a dead person's hair. Her house is surrounded by a fence made of bones topped by skulls that blaze with an inner fire at nighttime. In both tales the forest is not a friendly place. This is picture language telling us what the descent into the roots can feel like.

An introduction to our own depths often comes unbidden. It typically follows fast upon some unexpected and unwanted failure or loss, and we go down into a sense of mourning and confusion. It is the "dark night of the soul," the alchemical *nigredo*, when everything seems bleakest. It can be tempting to try to avoid this experience. Hyperactivity, sleep, and addictions to drugs or sugar or alcohol are common avoidance mechanisms. But as Carl Jung has said, "One does not become enlightened by imagining figures of light, but by making the darkness conscious."[52] So we need to go into the roots.

The descent can be triggered by something that feels like a personal tragedy: the death of a loved one, a serious illness, a betrayal, a humiliating failure or rejection, insolvency, disillusionment with a job or a creed, or simply noticing the cumulative effects of ageing in a human body. It can result from something as debilitating as physical or sexual abuse (abused Hoop) or addiction or trauma leading to PTSD.

Note that Hoop relationship issues can trigger roots work, just as readily as getting stuck at a Tree level or falling down a level (or more) on the Tree axis can trigger it. Any descent is roots work, "in the forest." The descent is not necessarily a one-time journey. Because of the fractal nature of the hero/heroine's journey, it is possible to experience a mini-descent at the onset of every initiation.

When we are drawn into the roots it is helpful to have a wise elder or skilled therapist as an initiator or guide, just as Dante had Virgil as his guide through the depths of Hell. It can also help to have some foreknowledge about some of the energies we might encounter.

In the roots we start to encounter our *shadow*—the whole unconscious part of ourselves that we cannot directly know.[53] Jung used the shadow metaphor because the shadow is what follows behind us when we are walking toward the light of the sun. Robert Bly describes it as the long bag we drag behind ourselves into which we stuff all the parts of ourselves that we don't like and want to pretend are not there.[54] It is our large blind spot. It is the opposite side of the face of the coin that we show to the world. Everything that I say I am not, goes into the shadow.

A person's shadow may include unconscious impulses toward pride, greed, lust, envy, gluttony, wrath, and/or sloth. It can also include elements of exuberance, curiosity, sensuality, and/or joy that may have been part of our original makeup as children, but which we stuffed into our bags when our parents or social milieu expressed disapproval. If we ever find ourselves having an irrationally strong reaction to someone we meet, it may be a hint to look at our own shadow.

Our shadows also include elements of the collective shadow of society. For example, parts of the shadow of a capitalist society are poverty and imperialism. In the United States, all of us, whether we have a white body or a black body, carry as part of our personal shadows the trauma of racism. As therapist Resmaa Menakem says in *My Grandmother's Hands*, "White-body supremacy is part of the operating system of America."[55] This harms everyone, though of course it harms non-white-bodied people to a vastly greater degree.

The work with the shadow in the roots world is to acknowledge and digest some of its contents, to make conscious parts of ourselves that we have split off. If we metabolize them, they become nourishment. And they can lead us to further discoveries of nourishing roots.

This can be difficult work. It can be humbling, and it involves considerable moral effort.[56] It requires slowing down and listening to the signals sent by one's own body. This is because trauma is stored in the body and therefore, under stress, we can find ourselves starting to react in inappropriate or exaggerated ways—to freeze, flee, or fight, for example—before we even know what we're doing or why.

One way to unwind the trauma and prevent new trauma is to stay with the body's sensations and be willing to experience the feelings that arise without acting on them, other than perhaps through energetic discharge by tears, sounds, or safe movement. The body is where the root hairs of our psyche touch materiality and converse with it.

As the work in the forest/roots world progresses we may uncover dirty linen that we'd rather not air in public. But the work rewards us by adding to our resources of energy and restoring to us spontaneity and lost capacities. We become more whole; and by working on ourselves we also make our society more whole.

One way to think about the unconscious is as a protective black dog. The dog is doing the best that it can under the circumstances. But if the dog is unloved or has been abused, it can be vicious and snarl and attack people and cause all kinds of problems for us. If the dog is well treated, it can be a powerful companion that can guide us and expand our consciousness. Psychologist James Hillman often reminds us that the best way to deal with those emissaries from the unconscious that we call dreams is to make friends with them.

We can learn from the example of the full moon how to approach the unconscious. The full moon sheds light, but it is a reflected light and not the direct light of the full sun. To enter into the unconscious is to be reflective about it, rather than drilling into it with the penetrating light of solar consciousness. We replace force with curiosity.

Here among the roots we encounter *archetypes*. These are powerful forces that can pull us off our path of Hoop and Tree development unless we recognize them, acknowledge them, and develop a relationship with them.

An archetype is like a ditch or channel dug into the earth. When rain falls, the water tends to collect in the channels and flow through them. Similarly, archetypes are preexisting channels in the human psyche. When life energy waters that area, it doesn't flow randomly; it flows in the pattern of the channels.

In the roots world there exist a number of different archetypes. One indication that we might have bumped into one of them is the sudden triggering of a powerful pattern of behavior—anger, indignation, depression, selfishness, jealousy, timidity, moodiness, etc.—during which we may feel irrational or "not ourselves." Jung says that in men this sometimes shows up as a cloud of sentimentality or resentment, and in women, as a surge of opinionated views, insinuations, and misconstructions. Contact with an archetype is likely to be the case if our behavior is accompanied by an unshakeable feeling of rightness and righteousness.

One of the most important archetypes is the *contra-sexual archetype*, which usually appears for a man in a female form, the *anima*; and for a woman in a male form, the *animus*. If the anima or animus has lain unrecognized in the shadow area for a long time, when it finally emerges it can appear in an immature and sometimes hostile form. If the anima or animus is not seen as an archetype within oneself but is projected onto a figure in the outer world as a movie is projected onto a screen, the contra-sexual archetype can lead to difficult relationships with the opposite sex. This is one of the many places where inner Tree/roots work and outer Hoop relationship work interact. With successful work in the roots, insight into one's anima or animus can uncomplicate and facilitate relationships in the outer world.

Both the anima and animus also have the positive potential of acting as mediators between the conscious and unconscious parts of ourselves. A male artist's muse would be an example of this.

Another potential mediator is the *wild person* archetype. This is a more-than-human, arcane, strange energy that shakes us awake into awareness that life is bigger and deeper than we ever had imagined. Successful work with the wild person connects us to the deep currents of our own instinctual nature and inner resources. This is one of the treasures chests hidden amongst the roots.

In the Iron John story, the wild man is Iron John himself, all shaggy with rusty red hair and living at the bottom of a deep pool. By the end of the adventure Iron John has helped bring about the young man's sacred wedding and has blessed the young man with "all the treasure" that Iron John possesses. In Vasalisa, the wild woman is Baba Yaga. By the end of the adventure Baba Yaga has given a gift of some of her wildness to the young woman in the form of one of those fiery skulls on a stick, whose fierce gaze then burns the wicked stepmother and stepsisters to cinders. Many of the other archetypal patterns that may be encountered in the roots have been vividly described in the stories of the gods and goddesses of ancient Greece.[57]

Two of the best introductions to this resource that I know of are Jean Shinoda Bolen's books *Goddesses in Everywoman* and *Gods in Everyman*.[58] Other mythologies outside of the Western tradition offer insights to these patterns through the metaphors of other cultures. For people with nonbinary gender identities, there are mythological resources in books such as Judy Grahn's *Another Mother Tongue*.[59]

In terms of Greek god and goddess archetypal patterns, as a man you might find yourself quite introverted, somewhat invisible socially, with perhaps a rich inner life, and a tendency toward depression (the energy of the god Hades). Or perhaps a successful goal-setter who values truth, reason, clarity, and order, an admirer of Thomas Jefferson, with perhaps a tendency to be emotionally distant or arrogant (the energy of the god Apollo). Or perhaps like one of the other gods, or a combination of several of them.

As a woman you might find yourself an "earth-mother" type, nurturing of growth, caring of children, and well-grounded, and with perhaps a tendency to be overprotective, passive-aggressive, or subject to periodic depressions (the energy of the goddess Demeter). Or you might find yourself a sensual, creative, romantic, seductive woman who stimulates growth in others with perhaps a tendency toward vanity or promiscuity (the energy of the goddess Aphrodite). Or perhaps like one of the other goddesses, or a combination of several of them.

Depending on our gender, stage of initiation, and what is happening in the outer world, some other key archetypes that may begin to flow with energy for us include: mother, father, child or adorable little one, friend, enemy, hero/heroine, hunter, alchemist/

magician, wise old man/woman. If we are unconscious about our own archetypal tendencies, we may miss potential traps or hazards in our outer lives. We could be unaware of our own Achilles's heel.

And if we are unconsciously projecting archetypes onto others, we won't really see who they are; we will react only to the "person" we expect them to be. This can lead to, at best, misunderstandings and, at worst, disastrous marriages or business relationships.

If we avoid our work in the roots, we may fail to distinguish between the inner realm and the outer realm, or to mistake the outer for the inner and vice versa. A lot of violence in our world takes place in part because people have inner dragons that they need to slay, inner shadow work that they need to undertake, in their inner hero/heroine's journey and, mistaking the outer for the inner, try to resolve the inner situation through acting in the outer realm.

This is one of the reasons why Jung warns us that when an inner situation is not made conscious, it happens outside as fate.[60]

Ideally, we use our initiatory time "in the forest," in the roots of the Tree, to make the unconscious conscious, and to do it carefully. The ego is like a boat floating on the ocean of the unconscious, and we need to be careful not to fish up more than the boat can carry. The forest/roots work can make us more whole, but only if we do it slowly and with a sense of modesty. Too much too fast can leave us inflated with an exaggerated sense of our own abilities or importance. And without lived integration into our own lives, we can be left with only dry cognition—names and labels but no understanding.

A physical tree stands on its roots and depends upon them for nourishment and stability. We do the same. The root hairs of a physical tree thread through the mystery of matter itself. The tips of our roots thread through the mystery of the unconscious. The journey into our roots, the descent into what might be called the lower shamanic world, offers access to extraordinary resources.

Descent along the Tree axis offers the opportunity to discover hidden treasure, to heal old wounds, to learn more about our life trajectory, to moisten a life that has become dried out, to surrender to humility, to renew one's energy from the ancient inexhaustible source. Our work there is to see deeply into our own nature.

Getting Stuck: Initiation Failures or Regression

As hero of his own adventure, the legendary King Minos had become king of Crete, presiding over a civilization of great wealth and culture. But then he became stuck at a certain level of development because he tried to keep for himself what he had vowed to sacrifice for the general good. After that failure he turned into a tyrant who demanded human sacrifices.

In our own hero/heroine's journey, every developmental stage, every initiation, every inflection point comes with the danger of getting stuck. Life needs to keep moving. Successful initiation means, in essence, dying and being reborn and returning with something in your new personhood that will benefit the Hoop of the world.

In chapter 4 I discuss some of the problems that ensue when the Hoop and/or the Tree is undeveloped. One additional aspect of the undeveloped Hoop has become more apparent to me since writing the first edition. It is the negative or shadow aspect of the powerful human need to belong to at least some kind of Hoop. A good description of this aspect was given by C. S. Lewis in a public lecture at King's College in London. He talked about the "inner ring" of an organization. This is the informal network of people who influence how an organization works. Lacking other Hoop connections or a Tree sense of integrity and agency, a person can almost desperately desire to belong to this inner ring. Lewis said, "Of all passions the passion for the Inner Ring is most skillful in making a man who is not yet a very bad man do very bad things."[61]

This helps explain a recent study of group acceptance that demonstrated that people who identify strongly with a group but feel they are not yet fully accepted are more likely than other group members to engage in extreme behavior in order to gain acceptance.[62] Research on gangs and terrorist organizations show that membership is particularly attractive to those who feel peripheral in society.

Being part of a Hoop is essential for humans. Our biology motivates us to eat and to reproduce. But it is the social world in which we live, not our biological drives, that guides us about *what* and *how* to eat and *with whom* to seek sexual release. As Berger and Luckmann say in *The Social Construction of Reality*, "Society determines how long and in what manner the individual organism shall live."[63] We cannot survive without a social Hoop. Also, we are psychologically disposed to believe that any behavior our social Hoop finds honorable is in fact socially beneficial, and any behavior that we and our peers find base is socially detrimental.[64]

Because humans need to belong to some social group in order to survive, we tend to resist anything that would estrange us from our group. This is why we abide by group norms. This is also one of the reasons that we resist factual information that threatens the defining values of the group to which we belong.

This helps explain a seemingly paradoxical situation: although there is near-unanimous scientific consensus that the earth's atmosphere is warming due to human actions, large numbers of people still refuse to believe it. Positions on issues like climate change have come to signify what kind of person one is and whether one is "in" or "out" with respect to a particular group or community.[65]

The Perilous Return: Gluskabe and the Four Wishes

Attaining some new insight through an initiation can leave us feeling all sparkly with stardust and believing we are somehow "special" or better than we actually are. (Interestingly, the word "glamorous" comes from a root whose original meaning suggests magical enchantment.) Our task at this final stage of an initiation is to navigate successfully the return from the mythic realm to the realm of the everyday. A tale from the Wabenaki tradition illustrates the potential danger here.[66]

After Gluskabe (or Glooscap) had defeated the monster who had tried to keep all the water in the world for himself, and after he had done many other things to make the world a good place, Gluskabe got into his stone canoe and paddled away to a far island, some say off the coast of Maine. Some say that the fog surrounding that island is actually the smoke from Gluskabe's pipe. For a time, he let it be known that anyone who came to him would be granted one wish.

Four young Abenaki men, each desiring something different, decided to join forces to make the difficult and dangerous journey to Gluskabe's island. Toward the end of the story, Gluskabe gave each man a pouch that contained what each had wanted. But Gluskabe warned them not to open their pouch until they were safe at home in their own lodge.

On their separate journeys home, three out of the four men opened their pouches too soon. One man drowned when his canoe became swamped and he became entangled by the very mass of possessions he had so greatly desired. The man who had wanted to be tall was transformed into a tree. The man who had wanted to live forever was transformed into a boulder. These are metaphors for inflation—when receiving the insight from the initiation tempts us to see ourselves as better than we truly are—the "richest," the "tallest," the "longest-lived."

The fourth man, the patient humble one who had desired only to be a good hunter in order to feed his family and village, waited until he was home in his own lodge. When he opened his pouch, he found it to be empty. But then a great understanding filled his mind. He understood the ways of the animals and how to prepare himself for the hunt. From that day forward he was the best hunter, always provided for his people, and never took more game than was needed.

Hoop-and-Tree Aspects of All Initiations

Initiation *outcomes* have both a Hoop aspect and a Tree aspect. As discussed, the Tree outcome is the *transcend* part and the Hoop outcome is the *include* part. The initiation *process* also has elements of both Hoop and Tree. The Hoop element is present in the form of the community that surrounds the individual initiate and holds him or her in its care. The Tree element is present in the form of the elder or elders who guide the process of initiation. The elders are typically older than the initiate, and always more developed on both dimensions.

The wider Hoop community has a vested interest in all initiations because an initiation's success or failure affects the whole community. If an initiation fails, if the individual gets stuck at any of life's inflection points, the community suffers. The community then loses all the future leadership and fruitfulness potential of the stuck individual. In the worst case, when there is a regressive resolution of the crisis, the community may have to devote time and resources to taking care of the failed initiate, or even protecting itself from the damage an uninitiated but physically adult individual could inflict on the community.

When the initiation succeeds, the whole community is revitalized with fresh energy from the initiated individual and from renewed cohesiveness as a community that has successfully pulled off an initiation together. This is why initiations are times for community celebrations. There are feasts. There is singing and dancing. A successful initiation helps bridge gaps between the old and the young and serves to strengthen existing bridges.

Black Elk's extraordinary visionary experience, related in the first chapter, happened when he was about nine years old. It was a TEN initiation . . . and much more. It was so powerful that Black Elk did not speak of it until he was about seventeen. But once he had confided in a wise elder, the whole community came together in a ceremony with costumes and horses and pageantry that helped Black Elk digest and integrate his experience.

The interdependence of the initiate and the community raises the question of what cultural and institutional resources our society currently affords as a framework for initiations. What do we offer as a safe container for the spiritual and emotional energy unleashed in the TEN initiation or any other initiation? What do we offer to help someone navigate and integrate any of life's inflection points?

The initiation into human adulthood is never simple and, depending on cultural context, may be more complex for those in some locations along the gender spectrum, since initiation into adulthood usually include an initiation into a gender identity and is typically conducted by elders of that same gender. Initiating elders are not always available. And for many people, regardless of where they fall on the gender spectrum, initiation into adulthood can be haphazard at best. Fortunately, in recent years, more resources and more support are becoming available for everyone.[67]

A full series of successful initiations leads to full maturity and psycho-spiritual wholeness with both the Hoop and the Tree developed and in balance with each other. For some people the series begins with Hoop and leads to Tree; for others it begins with Tree and lead to Hoop. (For more on this, see chapter 5.)

This correspondence between the Hoop and the Tree is actually exhibited by physical trees in real forests. The Haudenosaunee people honor the Tree of the Great Peace, which reaches out its roots to form a Hoop of relationship (chapter 5). Scientists have learned that physical trees in forests similarly "recognize and talk with their kin, shaping future generations. In addition, injured trees pass their legacies on to their neighbors, affecting gene regulation, defense chemistry, and resilience in the forest community. These discoveries have transformed our understanding of trees from competitive crusaders of the self to members of a connected, relating, communicating system."[68]

Full development on both dimensions enables us, as mature Tree individuals, to make authentic, well-grounded, growth-full choices while being compassionately responsive to the widest possible Hoop of human and ecological communities.

The Hoop and the Tree for Personal Growth

Carl Jung was for many years not only a disciple but also a close friend of Sigmund Freud. Due to a profound disagreement about the nature of the psyche, Jung broke with Freud, and as a consequence lost many of his former friends and acquaintances. Jung then found himself in a painfully confused inner state: "I felt totally suspended in mid-air, for I had not yet found my own footing."[69]

He tried analyzing his dreams and reviewing his own life, but nothing helped. He eventually made the humbling discovery that what was most healing for him was returning to an activity he had enjoyed as a boy: playing with sand, mud, and stones, and from those materials constructing little castles and buildings and small towns. He explored the roots of his Tree.

Jung continued his therapeutic play for some time because it was so healing. He says, "I had . . . the inner certainty that I was on the way to discovering my own myth."[70] Later, Jung's experience with therapeutic play led to the development of a form of psychotherapy known as sandplay, which uses a large tray of sand and a wide variety of miniature figures for the creation of tiny worlds.[71] Free play in a safe environment, with little or no verbal comment from the therapist, allows the person creating the tiny worlds to regress to an earlier stage of development in a way that supports the fundamental psychological drive toward wholeness and healing.

The Power of Images

> You must give birth to your images. They are the
> future waiting to be born. Fear not the strangeness
> you feel. The future must enter you long before it
> happens.
>
> —Rainer Maria Rilke, *Letters to a Young Poet*,
> translated by M. D. Herter Norton

Mental imagery has been called the "the true language of the mind," "the natural language of inner life," and "the intelligence of the heart."[72] "The psyche," says Carl Jung, "consists essentially of images."[73] Mental imagery has been used for centuries, in cultures all around the world, for both psycho-spiritual development and physical healing.

We need look no further than the shrine in most places of spiritual practice to find an image used as a focus of aspiration. The Torah and the New Testament are full of visions and visionary dreams. Other examples from the Christian tradition include Mexican retablos and the religious icons of the Eastern Orthodox Church. Both Hindu and Tibetan Buddhist traditions employ active visualizations of deities for spiritual development. Shamanic healers such as the Kahuna healers of Polynesia also rely on images: "The Kahuna's main technique for dealing with negative habits is *laulele*, or deliberate imagination. It is an imagery pattern to direct thoughts, emotions, and actions into new directions."[74]

The Diné (Navajo) people as well as other First Nations people have used healing imagery for many years in the form of sand paintings as part of their ceremonials. These sand paintings are called "places where the gods come and go" in the Navajo language.[75] The wholistic goal of a sand painting ceremonial is to restore *hózhó*, a difficult to translate term that encompasses beauty, perfection, harmony, goodness, normality, success, well-being, blessedness, order, and the ideal.[76]

Images have the power to represent figures and landscapes of both the inner and outer worlds and can serve to mediate between the two and connect them. Imagery, and art in general, seems to be effective at bypassing defenses, resistances, and the conscious critical apparatus.[77]

Mental imagery can affect not only states of the mind but also states of the body.[78] Modern evidence is emerging that mental imagery can help in treating obesity, insomnia, phobias, anxieties, depression, sexual malfunctions, chronic pain, fibroid tumors, and cancer, among other ailments.[79] In the Western tradition, the use of imagery in medicine goes at least as far back as Asclepius, the ancient Greek god of healing. Temples to Asclepius were also treatment centers where one of the key modes of diagnosis and therapy was dream therapy, or divine sleep, which called forth healing dreams. (As noted in chapter 3, Asclepius carried a rustic staff entwined by a serpent—a Tree entwined by a Hoop—as a symbol of his healing powers.)

As of now, nobody knows exactly how images work their magic. It may be partly because experience in the imagination can seem in many significant respects psychologically equivalent to the actual experience.[80] This is suggested by research studies of *mental practice*. In one study, basketball players who spent twenty minutes a day *imagining* sinking baskets improved almost as much as players who spent twenty minutes *actually* sinking baskets.[81]

Given all this background, it seems reasonable to expect that feeding your soul, your inner life, with nourishing images would be of benefit.

A Playful, Useful Image

I was aware of some of this background about imagery and about play when I first started teaching the Hoop-and-Tree material. I gave my students the capstone assignment of creating their own personal Hoop-and-Tree image. Since none of them were trained artists, I suggested making a collage—an artistic composition made of various images and/or materials (such as paper, cloth, or wood) glued on a surface. But they were free to make their image using any media.

They responded enthusiastically with a beautiful variety of results. There were several collages, some paintings, and at least one three-dimensional construction. One of my students was Anne Parker, professor of environmental studies at Naropa University. Her painting is shown at the beginning of this chapter. (Some images from others are on the hoop-and-tree website, www.hoop andtree.org.) Anne says:

> The archetype of the Hoop and the Tree lives, I feel, in our lineages, in our deep psyches. I felt, as I first encountered the sacred world tree in my European ancestral heritage, like a heart coming home. I think it is important to have this model accessible for those who may not enter via ancient lineages or stories. The Hoop and the Tree offers a clear framework together with stories that magnetize and invite us to into this inner work. Some may thus enter via this model suited to our times—one that joins the psycho-logical with the archetypical stories. It is a model calling us back to wholeness, whether we have lost the connections entirely in modern life or seek to protect and preserve them where they are still alive.
>
> When I went through the process of drawing the entire mandala of my life at that moment inside the Hoop and Tree framework, I noticed a feeling of integration and

location on my path coming clear. The symbols that I drew were for me far more than symbols, they captured initiatory moments: turning points, moments of deep shift of perspective, and instructions from the more-than-human world. Drawing them grounded me in a way that claimed them and acknowledged them as my own in my own visual and verbal discourse. Shaped as I have been by western modern thought, I felt joy on my ongoing path of repair of the internalized oppression I had unknowingly embedded not to "hear" directly from the living earth and life around me because "it is not logical." These moments of seeing and hearing remind us of our urgent invitation to repair our connection to the deep roots, life, earth, and cosmos.[82]

Several years after publishing the first edition, I received a photograph from one of my readers, artist Lynn Weekes Karegeannes, of a collage that she calls "The Hoop and the Tree" (photo available on www.hoopandtree.org). Here is what she told me about her process:

During a year of independent study, I did quite a lot of research on topics related to the mandala or sacred circle in the Christian context. This research included topics as diverse as labyrinths, halos, the thought of Carl Jung, and the sacred geometry of the medieval cathedrals. In my broad-ranging research, a number of times, in completely unrelated contexts, I encountered descriptions or images of mandalas/circles featuring a tree growing up from the middle point. I was struck by this synchronicity and curious as to why I would encounter such an image in such completely unrelated contexts.

I began an online search and I eventually came across a reference to *The Hoop and the Tree*. I immediately ordered the book, feeling as if it might contain the answer to my question.

The book did provide an answer. And the answer was that yes, the image or model of a tree growing from the center of a hoop is an archetypal one. Today, all these many years later, I would still say that this archetypal model is an important one to me. The book introduced me to the idea that a balancing and integration of masculine and feminine energies is necessary and desired for optimal health and wholeness—both for us as individuals and for our world as a whole.

In order to give artistic expression to the model, I created a collage. I studied art history many years ago, so the images representing masculine and feminine that came to my mind emerged from my training in this discipline.[83]

A Rewarding Way to Begin

The Road has two rules only: begin and continue.

—Christmas Humphreys

Consider the following exploration as an opportunity to learn more about yourself and to make your life more fulfilling. Do this for the fun of it. Playing with these images could extend over several days or weeks or months. If at any time the project feels like drudgery, stop. Begin again when you feel interested or intrigued.

If making a whole collage seems like too much work, I'd encourage you to look at the suggestions here and select even just one or two images. Then jump ahead to "Further Exploration" and read on to the end. You can always come back and work on more images when you are ready. Using even one image will deliver great benefit.

You could also proceed by simply visualizing the images one at a time. But the scissors-and-paste method is generally more effective because it tends to bypass censoring or judgment by the rational mind and reaches more deeply into the subconscious.

As an alternative to the collage or as an amplification of it (especially if you are a kinesthetic person and enjoy things like dance, yoga, and t'ai chi), you can respond to the visual prompts below through creative movement with your body. You can use costumes, too, if you'd like. Exploring through movement is the way of working with Hoop-and-Tree material practiced by sacred dance leader Timothy Dobson and HoopYogini creator Jocelyn Gordon.

The playful work with the movement method is to move your body in a way that evokes the experience of the full Hoop dimension and the full Tree dimension. How you move may come to you directly as impulses to move in a certain way, or through images that come to you. My Zen master used to say, "What is your correct function and relationship to each situation as it appears?" This is a clue to Hoop—being in the flow, and in relationship. A clue to the Tree is the "primary point" from which each of us moves. I try to follow my Zen master's instructions and I keep failing at it; but trying and trying again seems to make my life go better.

For many people the most accessible route will be through collage. The great thing about making a collage for yourself is that you don't have to be an artist in order to make one that works. If you like what you make, it's good.

Most of us are not trained visual artists. But all of us can say what images we like and what we don't like; what images make us feel good, or peaceful, or uncomfortable, or needy, or generous, etc. In making a collage for yourself, all you need to do is use your innate hunch or feeling about an image. If it calls to you, just cut it and paste it.

When you work, find a quiet place where you won't be interrupted for at least an hour or so. Do this as a gift for yourself, as you might treat yourself to a nice hot bath or a massage or your favorite recreation or favorite food. Remember times when you enjoyed playing as a child. This is an opportunity to experience that same sort of enjoyment. Your goal should be to create a space for yourself that is both free and protected.[84]* (While this process

---

* Safety is paramount. When working with movement in my sacred dance community, we had several rings of safety around the "inner courtyard," where the most intimate and profound free-form dance work took place. Around the inner courtyard we had a feminine circle, which moved with a three-beat counter-clockwise, facing inward. Outside of that we had a masculine circle, which moved

can be very helpful and rewarding, it is not intended as a substitute for professional counseling. If at any time while working on this you feel distress, please stop and seek professional support.)

Start by making two simple collages on two pieces of paper. I recommend using good quality paper because you will probably want to hold on to your collage for a while. I also recommend using paper at least twenty-two by fifteen inches (about sixty by forty centimeters) in size. Give yourself room to explore. People often find themselves frustrated if they start out too small. If at the end you find you have too much white space, you can always trim it away.

Feel free to take all the time you want with this. Don't try to do it all at once or in just one session. Healing at the unconscious level takes its own time. Some people like to shape this process as a ceremony or a series of ceremonies. Meditation or centering prayer is very helpful before beginning. You could light candles or incense. Some like to have music in the background. But none of this is necessary. It is all up to you.

A good way to prepare is to find a tree—in your backyard, on a nearby street, or in a park—and go be with it. The famous haiku poet Basho said that if you want to learn about the pine, go to the pine; if you want to learn about the bamboo, go to the bamboo.

After you make a respectful approach, stand next to the tree and place your hands on its trunk. Appreciate its strength and firmness. Imagine down into the roots. Look up to where it touches the sky. Then press your back against it and listen. Listen for how the tree responds. Through shade? Through a rustle in the leaves?

---

with a four-beat clockwise, facing clockwise. (Both men and women could dance in either of these circles.) Outside of all of that, witnessing carefully, we had one or more "soul-watchers" who monitored the psychic well-being of the dancers. We also had "outriders" whose job was to deal with any interruptions from the outside world—such as passersby who wondered about all the drumming so late at night. We almost never were interrupted because we danced in relatively isolated locations. But it was a comfort to all to know that everything was being handled so we could enter deeply into our work. (The design of the whole grew out of the pioneering work of Elizabeth Cogburn. See Ross Chapin, "Warriors of the Beauty Way–An Interview with Elizabeth Cogburn," in Context #5 - Art and Ceremony In Sustainable Culture, Spring 1984, 42ff.)

Through the feeling of the trunk against your back? Does it bring an image to your mind? A feeling in your heart? Then continue standing next to the tree or sit quietly under it and visualize hoops widening out from your heart like ripples widening on a pond from where a stone has plunked in. See the hoops spreading out wider and wider, so that they widen to encompass your neighborhood, your community, your country, your island or continent, and eventually the whole globe with all its elements and creatures, human and nonhuman alike.

Be like the Haudenosaunee Tree of the Great Peace with its roots reaching out in the four cardinal directions, making a Hoop mandala, advancing the good mind and righteousness and peace.

About Selecting Images

It is helpful, before you begin, to have at hand a large collection of images from which to choose. These can come from magazines (about nature, spirit, fashion, sports, etc.). You can also have available your own photographs (of family, friends, special places) that you don't mind cutting up. The internet is another, nearly endless, source of images. Search engines like Ecosia and Google allow you to search directly for images after you enter your search term.

As for how to select images, I like the advice of Ami Ronnberg of the Archive for Research in Archetypal Symbolism: "We often find when an image moves us that there is a sense of recognition, a reminder how things can be, almost like return from exile. It may only last for a moment, but there is a feeling of fullness."[85]

Pay attention to the feelings in your body. Does an image change the quality of your breathing or evoke a sensation in any particular part of your body? Does it make you feel tense or relaxed? Take your time. Be playful. The images you choose don't have to make rational sense. In fact, it's probably better if they don't. You may think you "ought" to choose one thing, but something else calls you or intrigues you or makes you feel happy, choose that one. Remember: this is a work in progress. You can always replace this image with another one later.

In choosing images consider not just who you are right now, but who your better, more enlightened self is calling you to become and also what that self might be wanting you to know.

If you don't find an image that resonates with you, leave a blank space and come back to it later. It's OK to leave it blank. This process takes time. And having a blank space is an opening for personal learning that you can step into.

Collage #1: Hoop

Lay out the first piece of paper in landscape view (i.e., long axis horizontal). Using a drawing compass and a light pencil stroke, draw a large circle that almost fills the paper. (If you don't have a drawing compass, you can trace around a dinner plate.)

Using the same center point, draw a second circle about half the diameter of the first circle. This creates two bands or rings around the center point.

Then draw a large plus sign (+) at the center point of the circles so that the ends of the horizontal and vertical lines reach all the way to the circumference of the outer circle.

At the center of the circle, where the lines of the plus sign cross, draw a little heart.

Surrounding this heart, in the inner band or ring (the Human ring of the Hoop), paste pictures of:

- images of people you love (family, friends, etc.).
- an image that represents your "community," however you may define it.

In the outer band or ring (the Ecological ring of the Hoop), paste pictures that represent:

- the mineral realm (e.g., salt, the ocean, a lake or stream, the air, dirt, stars, rocks, etc.)
- the vegetable realm (e.g., food plants, flowers, trees, moss, grasses, etc.)

- the animal realm (e.g., wild animals, birds, fish, sea mammals, etc.)
- a place in nature, untouched by human activity, that is a place where you would feel comfortable and happy. In Spanish, you might call this your *querencia*—the place where you feel at home and where you are your most authentic self; the place from which you draw your strength.

At each of the four places where the plus sign touches the circle, paste four different pictures, each one a picture of a wild animal (bird, mammal, amphibian, etc.) or a plant (herb, flower, food plant, etc.) that appeals to you. Or, if a guardian figure (e.g., a saint) has ever appeared to you in a dream, paste that image. These represent your allies of the four directions.

It's best if you relax and allow the image to choose you, rather than you choosing it. Don't be concerned about whether the plant or animal is as small and as seemingly insignificant as a spider or is as large and seemingly majestic as an elk. Outside of the human realm, every living being in nature has something to teach.

If you find the image of a mandala or medicine wheel that is meaningful for you in some way, paste that image within your wider Hoop.

Collage #2: Tree

Lay out the second piece of paper in portrait view (i.e., long axis vertical).

Find an image of a tree and paste it in the middle of the paper, leaving ample space above and below and to both sides of it.

Near the top of the paper, above the top of the tree, paste an image that represents your doorway to spirit or an image that symbolizes enlightenment or transcendence. Some traditions consider this level beyond imaging. If this is true for you, you could place at the top an image of an Islamic *mihrab*. This is the niche in the wall of a mosque that points in the direction of the Ka'aba and concentrates the mind upon Allah. Or you could use a golden circle to represent the aperture through which one approaches transcendence.

Near the bottom of the paper, below the image of the Tree, place photographs or other images spread out in the area of the roots to represent your ancestors who have passed away and who are important to you.

Find an image of something that would be for you like buried treasure, something that you would be overjoyed to discover in your own backyard. It doesn't have to be a trunk of gold, just something of enormous emotional value to you personally. Paste that image on the paper as though it were underground in the roots of the tree.

This next part may take the most effort. Find an image of something that you are simultaneously fascinated with and repelled by. As you look for this image, remember: This collage is for your own use. You don't have to show it to anybody. When you have found this powerfully ambivalent image, paste it next to the treasure image in the roots of the tree.

Next to these images in the roots of the tree you may want to add the image of a long-standing problem or difficulty in your life. This, too, may be hard to do and may call for several revisions.

Along the trunk of the tree between the roots images at the bottom and the image at the top, with your pencil mark five equally spaced dots. Counting up from the bottom, we'll call these locations number 2, 3, 4, 5, and 6.

At location number 2, paste an image that symbolizes your sexuality. Some starting images you might consider include: The Great Rite, Priapus, Sheela na gig, Ardhanarishvara.

At location number 3, paste an image that reflects your relationship with power and how you assert yourself in the world. A starting image you might want to consider: the Sun, which itself is an image of power and because location 3 in your physical body is at the solar plexus.

At location number 4, draw a little heart. (This location will be where your Tree passes through the Hoop mandala you created in collage #1.)

At location number 5, paste an image that represents your expressive creativity. People can be creative in many different ways. In your physical body this location is in the area of your throat, so naturally one of the possibilities for your creativity is in how you speak and use language. Related to this is creativity in writing. Other ways in which you might be creative include: cooking, woodworking, dance, the visual arts, gardening or agriculture, creative mending of broken things, the healing arts, creative problem-solving, and inventing.

At location number 6, paste an image that for you symbolizes wisdom and self-mastery. You could find an image of a beloved teacher or a wise person from your own culture or one of the other world traditions. This would be someone you admire so much that you would want to be like him or her. The person could be currently living or from world religious or secular history. Alternatively, you could try imagining that you are worthy of wearing a crown or ceremonial headdress or royal diadem. What would it look like?

In the foliage of the tree, or to either side of the foliage, paste images of tangible creations and/or symbols of intangible creations that through your life work you would like to bring into being in order to benefit the world. These are to represent your fruit.

The human world is endlessly hungry. It needs food, clothing, shelter, teachers, healers, farmers, builders, makers of useful implements, foresters, restorers of broken ecosystems, inventors, engineers, musicians, dancers, artists, yoga instructors, caretakers of all kinds, interpreters, bakers, and on and on. And each of us has some gift or talent that, when we use it for the benefit of others, we ourselves feel happy and fulfilled. Our fruit can be found in that sweet spot that is the intersection of the world's hunger with whatever it is that we do that gives us our deepest joy.

When you have finished both collages, appreciate your work. Spend some time looking at your two collages. What did you discover in the process of making them? What appeals to you about them? If you were to change them, how would you do it? What new questions do you have for yourself? What new questions to you have for trusted others about yourself? How will you show up differently now in the world?

When you're ready to proceed, get a bigger piece of paper. Paste the Tree collage (#2) in the middle of the bigger piece of paper. Now cut the Hoop collage (#1) so half of it fits on either side of the Tree collage at the level of location number 4.

Using the questions here and the Hoop-and-Tree diagram for reference (see chapter 1; also available at www.hoopandtree.org /HT_diagram.pdf), together with your own intuitive preferences, find any additional images you need and paste them on this new integrated collage.

Further Exploration

Ask yourself the following questions, one by one. You don't have to take them in order. If nothing comes when you first ask yourself a question, just keep the question open—wonder about it as you move on. The answer may come in your dream tonight, or in a chance encounter tomorrow or perhaps days later. This is part of your growing edge. In answering the questions, consider not just who you are right now, but who your better, more enlightened self is calling you to become.

In responding to your Hoop-and-Tree collage, and in responding to the questions here, what is most important is what your images mean to *you*. This is much more important than any "official" interpretation of an image, or anything a friend might say about it, though these can be helpful.

The images you have selected are clues to your innermost processes. You are the detective most able to follow the clues you yourself have laid down (with the cooperation of your unconscious). The word "clue" is a variant spelling of the now obsolete "clew," meaning "ball of thread." Its current application to "that which helps solve a problem" is based on the notion of using (like Theseus in the Minotaur's labyrinth) a ball of thread to show one the way out of an intricate maze or problem one has entered.

William Blake says:

> I give you the end of a golden string,
> Only wind it into a ball,

It will lead you in at Heaven's gate
Built in Jerusalem's wall.[86]

The Tree as a Whole

> People may spend their whole lives climbing the lad-
> der of success only to find, once they reach the top,
> that the ladder is leaning against the wrong wall.
>
> —Thomas Merton

When you look at the Tree as a whole, do you see blemishes or imperfections that give you character? Are there any wounds along the trunk of the Tree or in the roots or branches? What would need to happen in order to heal them? If you were the orchardist for your tree (and you are) how would you take care of it?

Level 1: Roots, Lineage, and Ancestors

Who were your nourishing ancestors? They may be your parents, grandparents, or farther back.

Who in your early years saw, heard, felt, and respected you for who you truly are? These are people in whose presence you felt safe and understood.

Do you have "unfinished business" with your parents or primary caregivers? Are there issues you need to resolve with them, or things you need to say?

Identify the people who have helped develop your "craft lineage"—what you do for work or who have inspired you in what you do for work or fulfillment.

Identify ancestors who may have been toxic or harmful. These are some of your dragons/your darkness.

What archetypal patterns are powerful in your life?

What are parts of yourself that you are ashamed of or fearful or ambivalent about? These also are some of your dragons/your darkness.

What gifts have you received thus far from working with your darkness?

Level 2: Sexuality

How comfortable are you with your sexuality? What are your sexual fantasies? What is your sexual ideal?

Level 3: Power, Will, and Initiative

In what ways are you powerful?

In what ways do you wish you were powerful?

What manifestations of power scare you?

What fears do you have about stepping into your own power?

If you have not acknowledged or integrated aspects of your own power, it can "leak" out of you without you being conscious of it. When this happens, your power can show up in its shadow form, with destructive results. Shadow expressions of power include gossiping, backhanded compliments, and *triangulation*. Triangulation occurs when person A needs to talk to person B to resolve a conflict, but instead of talking to person B, person A talks to person C and just complains about person B. In extreme cases, triangulation can devolve into the destructive "Victim-Rescuer-Persecutor" Karpman drama triangle.

Like a good king or queen, do you use your power for the benefit of the realm over which you hold sway? Your realm could be, for example, your family or your employees. An exercise: walk through your city or neighborhood as though you were its king or queen. How do you feel? What would you do to improve the lives of your subjects?

Level 4: The Hoop as a Whole

Are there gaps in the Hoop? What would need to happen to fill them?

Hoop Inner Circle: The human ring

What would you say is your community? Or, what are your communities? How do they overlap?

Most of us are parts of many circles of relationship—work, family, clubs, teams, political groups, etc. First: Identify these circles.

Then identify whom you feel closest to in each of these circles. Do these circles overlap or intersect in any way? Who is in your inner circle of close relationships? In other words, who would be difficult or impossible to replace if they were to die or move away?

How are you nourishing these relationships?

Which relationships are broken and need mending?

Is there an empty space in your life of relationships that needs to be filled? If so, what is it and how might you work to fill it?

What relationship actions might you need to take?

Hoop Ecological Circle: The ring of the natural world

> Messages everywhere. Scholars, I plead with you,
> Where are your dictionaries of the wind, the grasses?
>
> —Norman MacCaig, "By the Graveside, Luskentyre"

Before you begin this part, recall any powerful experiences you may have had in the natural world. If you have ever done a vision quest, tap into what you learned on your quest. You might even take a break and go for a walk and rediscover how sensuous of an animal you might be.[87]

If you were a place in the natural world, what place would you be? Where do you feel most at home in the natural world? What ecosystem and key plants and animals are in your ecological circle?

How are you nourishing these relationships?

What relationships are broken and need mending?

What actions are you taking to support and protect the world you live in—its ecosystems, plants, and animals?

In general, the best way to support both the human ring and the ecological ring of the Hoop is to behave in ways that enable all beings to flourish within the carrying capacity of the earth, now and forever. From my research the key behaviors seem to be:

- Making societal choices for prosperity rather than economic growth
- Working to increase social equity

- Reducing our environmental footprint
- Working to restore and maintain ecosystems[88]

Both the ecological Hoop and the human Hoop are involved with environmental justice. Environmental justice is a movement that grows from the recognition that a disproportionate number of environmental burdens fall on certain communities. Environmental justice works to ensure a healthy environment for all regardless of race, nationality, income, gender, or age. What image represents environmental justice to you?

Allies of the Four Directions: Hoop Allies

> Be still with yourself until the object of your attention affirms your presence.
>
> —Minor White, photographer

Who are your allies of the four directions, your guardian spirits? This may be a difficult question. If we are fortunate, we have strong relationships with human allies within the inner circle of our Hoops. It is helpful, though, to have a relationship with more-than-human allies that link us to the more-than-human world. Sometimes such allies take the form of spiritual guardians or saints. Allies often appear in the form of animals because animals carry the instinctive wisdom of nature. Something you might want to try: Go to an open place in nature—hilltop, meadow, forest clearing, a peaceful place in a park. Then face each cardinal direction in turn and watch and listen for what happens.

If an animal appears, be sure to thank it. Get to know it. Every being, no matter how small or apparently insignificant, has something to teach. Also, watch your dreams.

If an animal or plant has appeared to you as an ally, you now have a responsibility to reciprocate and to honor it. You do not eat it or harm it in any way. Instead, you work to protect it and its ecosystem.

Practices for Hoop Development

The essence of the Hoop dimension of wholeness is the ability to build and maintain relationships both with the human circle and with the ecological circle of the Hoop. Chapter 2 describes the four essential processes for building and maintaining relationships. Those processes are foundational.

I would like to suggest here two additional practices from the world's vast literature on relationships. One or both of these might be of value to you.

Naikan is a Japanese word that means "looking inside" or "seeing oneself with the mind's eye." It is also the name for a method of self-reflection that helps us understand our relationships. It is widely used in Japan and Europe in a variety of settings including mental health counseling, addiction treatment, schools, and businesses. It is perfectly applicable both to the human ring of the Hoop and also to beings from the ecological ring (plants, animals, ecosystems, the ocean, rivers, air, etc.). The method is based on three powerful Hoop questions that can be employed by anyone at any time:

1. What have I received from _____?
2. What have I given to _____?
3. What troubles and difficulties have I caused _____?

Pondering these questions can promote new appreciations and changes in behavior toward the object of the questioning.

The second practice is primarily applicable to the human ring of the Hoop. As discussed in chapter 2, traditional cultures strengthen relationships between individuals and between communities through the practice of giving gifts. Much of the time, this giving is not a simple exchange, but a practice of "paying it forward." The recipient of the gift at some later time gives a gift to a third party. When this practice functions well, the gift economy "circulates" (from "circle"—i.e., Hoop) the gift energy throughout the wider community or communities. This strengthens the web of relationships. In his book *The Gift*, Lewis Hyde shows that a cardinal property of gifts is that the gift must always move.[89]

The following gift practice is inspired by Native American give-away ceremonies and potlatches. In this practice you give gifts to your inner circle of best friends and family without expecting anything immediately in return. The gifts you give should not be yard-sale items that you are trying to get rid of but rather things that have meaning for you. Things like ceremonial items, small heirlooms, souvenirs from travel, items from your childhood, or things you have made are excellent options. They don't need to have a large monetary value, but they each should have a story. When you give each away, tell its story to the recipient.

Don't overdo it. Don't give away anything you would resent giving away. Do select items that would be meaningful to the recipient and also that have been important enough to you in the past that you will want to be sure they have good new homes. You might even feel a bittersweet pang in giving them away.

The giveaway is like a birthday party in reverse. It is you giving the presents to others, not others giving the presents to you. And your own birthday celebration is also an excellent opportunity to have a giveaway (and request that the invitees do not bring presents).

Level 5: Creativity, Generativity, and the Fruits of Your Tree

What do you want to produce as the fruit of your creativity? What fruits do you wish to bear for the benefit of all? What accomplishments or achievements or gifts that you have given to the world would you like to have acknowledged in your obituary?

Related to creativity is what psychologist Erik Erikson calls generativity (see chapter 3). Erikson says that generativity "is primarily the concern in establishing and guiding the next generation."[90]

A wonderful Tree story related to helping the next generation is the scientific finding that exposing small seedlings to the microbiome-rich leaf litter derived from adults of the same species protects the young and increases their chances of thriving.[91]

Level 6: Self-Mastery and Wisdom

In your own life, who has served in the role of wise old man and/ or wise old woman?

How do you recognize self-mastery and wisdom in others?

Level 7: Aspiration and Divine Union

How do you visualize your highest aspiration or ideal beyond self-mastery or wisdom? To whom or what do you pray? If you were to have an inner shrine for your life, what image would be on it?

The Whole Image, The Whole Self

Now look again at your whole Hoop-and-Tree image. How do you feel about what you see in the whole image? Are there any cravings/ attachments/desires related to any level or ring that would lead to suffering for yourself or others? If so, what are they? What healing is needed at this level or ring?

Consider the pictures you have pasted at each level on the Tree and on each ring of the Hoop. Do you want to change any of the images? What changes might you want to make in your life?

Your personal Tree image within the image of your Hoop or medicine wheel is a very approximate mirror of your own potential wholeness. It points toward what is possible when both dimensions are developed and in balance with each other. It is a glimpse of the Self, the alchemists' famous philosopher's stone that turns lead into gold, the mysterious conjunction of opposites, the mystical wedding of male and female in spiritual (not physical) androgyny.

When this image matures and blossoms within us it becomes a portable, weightless, indestructible, inalienable shrine of the heart.

Full development on both dimensions allows us to stand in our own identity, while fruitfully relating to the rest of creation and to the cycles of life.

Once You Have "Finished": Growing with It

Now is the time to let your work sink into your psyche. Once you have a tentative image of your own unique sense of wholeness, sit with it. Do not judge it—especially do not judge it as "good art" or "bad art." Just observe what has come out of your conscious and unconscious processes. Even if you have not done so previously, now would be the time to offer incense and candles and meditate on the image.

At least half of the personal transformation comes not from the finished product but from the process of creating it. The balance of the transformation comes from carrying the imagery into your life. In order to do that, you need to see it clearly.

Depending on your phase of life, you may find you frequently want to modify your Hoop and Tree collage; or you may be satisfied with it for long periods of time and then make important changes.

Sooner or later you will most likely come across better images than the ones you've already chosen. Just go ahead and replace the old images with the better ones. This will happen because (1) you have found an image that more closely resembles what you are trying to express, and/or (2) just by creating the collage, you have increased your self-awareness and need to update your images.

When this happens, be glad. You are healing and growing. You may have grown a wider, more inclusive Hoop, or realized the need to sever a toxic relationship, or have found a new fondness in the natural world. You may have made new discoveries in your deep roots through dreams or meditation or suffering consciously endured. You may have developed new aspirations on the Tree axis.

Often, working with images in this way, people find themselves creating a series of images that becomes almost like a healing dream, needing time to work itself out to a satisfying conclusion.

I strongly recommend hanging your finished collage in a place where you can see it every day—maybe next to your home shrine if you have one, or on the wall in your bedroom, or perhaps inside your closet door so you can see it before you get dressed to go out to face the world.

When you feel ready you may want to show your finished collage to someone you trust to receive it without judgment. Be very careful whom you choose; do not rush to do this. The witnessing and acceptance, in and of itself, can be powerful. You may also, if you wish, talk to that person about its meaning for you.

Sharing your collage with a trusted other is also a way to strengthen your own interpersonal Hoop. It is an opportunity to practice the key behaviors for building relationships (chapter 2) as well as to exercise your emotional intelligence (chapter 4) by putting into words your innermost feelings, hunches, and thoughts.[92]

Getting Down to Work

With the degree of dysfunction in the world today and our many social and environmental challenges, we need everyone living at their fullest potential. This also means everyone living the most fulfilled lives they can live. My hope is that the Hoop-and-Tree image of wholeness offers something to you for your own benefit and for your use in helping heal the wounded world.

So may your life be nourished and fruitful and may you bring your own unique gifts into the world for your own joy and the blessing of all. May your Hoop be whole and your Tree flourish. May you truly inhabit every moment and have a rich and full experience of being alive.

This concluding poem was inspired by the wisdom of the Haudenosaunee people. This is the same civilization that produced the inspiring Hoop-and-Tree integration of the Tree of the Great Peace with its roots reaching out to the Hoop of all humanity. It addresses the work to be done.

Getting Down to Work

As we gather here together
may we be mindful that we all
have limited life spans and energies,

that every one of us desires happiness
for ourselves and for those we love,
that despite our powers
we are utterly dependent on the well-being
of the earth, our home,
on her soils, her waters, her green life forms,
and all her other creatures.

May the wisdom of the four directions
steady our thoughts.
May the inner light
of high promise inspire us.
May the work we engage in today
be worthy of blessing from our ancestors
and be a source of eternal gratitude
from our descendants.

With full awareness of our imperfections,
we make our hearts and minds as one
to honor the web of trustful relationships
that holds us together as a people.

Now let us work to create
the simple beauty of what is needed.

Acknowledgments

PROFOUND THANKS

To the Hoop and to the roots of my Tree, in particular . . .

to Carl Hollander for encouragement and support, especially at the earliest, tender stage of the writing;

to Bob Rehm, for several readings of the manuscript, including the first rough draft. His comments and insights have been extremely useful. His belief in me and in the model helped more than I can say;

to Zen master Seung Sahn, Dae Soen Sa Nim;

for inspiration and role-modeling, to the masters who have taught me in person or through their books: Robert Bly, Joseph Campbell, Walker Evans, Ben Lo, Theodore Roszak, Robin Williamson;

to Keith Andresen, Janice Bartholomew-Turner, Chip Clark, Randy Compton, Francesca Howell, Steve Jones, and Susan Secord for their thoughtful readings of all or parts of the manuscript at various stages; and for the new chapter 6, once again to Lola Wilcox, Randy Compton, Steve Jones, and Susan Secord, and also to Richard Prée, Anne Parker, and Lynn Weekes Karegeannes;

extra special thanks to my colleague and friend Lola Wilcox, who helped me present the first glimmerings of the Hoop and the Tree at the ACI annual retreat and later invited me to present the Hoop and the Tree at the Naropa Institute, and who with her husband, Charles Wilcox, Shakespearean actor, provided not one but two thorough critiques of the original manuscript at different phases in its development. Lola's ongoing support as well as her insightful suggestions on content and style have been invaluable;

to Brenda Rosen, for wise editorial guidance and compassionate encouragement when I needed it most;

to dharma sister Deborahann Smith, for support in presenting the manuscript to publishers, and for good wishes;

to my family Hoop and family Tree: Susan Secord, Benjamin Sequoia Secord Hoffman, Charles Harry Hoffman, Louise Williams Hoffman, Jennifer Lee, Molly Watson, and the rest, extended through space and time;

to the staffs of Norlin Library at the University of Colorado in Boulder and of Boulder Public Library. I am grateful for the public support provided to make these institutions possible; also to the helpful staff of The Tattered Cover bookstore in Denver;

to Mary Ann Hamm for a few small but crucial pieces of research assistance;

to my skilled original editor, Kevin Bentley, and all the other helpful people at Council Oak Books;

to other teachers and friends, too numerous to mention, but including elder dharma brother Stephen Mitchell, William Meredith, George Moffat, Casimir France, Herbert Hahn, Paul Oertel, Allegra Ahlquist, Sandra Ebling, Jed Swift, Pam Sherman, Barry Bloom, Keith Andresen, Evan Hodkins, Elizabeth Roberts, Cass Adams, Vivianne Crowley, Renee Kutash, Denise Kale, Loraine Masterton, the Hoop of Cloud Pond, the Tree who was my t'ai chi teacher at Fresh Pond, Cambridge, and the helpful stranger.

Notes

1. The Shape of All Shapes

1. Neihardt, John G. *Black Elk Speaks*. New York: Pocket Books, 1972, p. 36; Black Elk's actual words were not as succinct and poetic as the familiar passage developed by Neihardt, Black Elk's interviewer. Neihardt tried to represent what Black Elk would have said if he had understood the concept of literature and if he had been able to express himself in English. Many would agree that in this case Neihardt succeeded admirably. For the most original records of Black Elk's teachings available see DeMallie, Raymond J. *The Sixth Grandfather*. Lincoln, NE: University of Nebraska Press, 1984, pp. xxii, 129–130. See also Holler, Clyde. *Black Elk's Religion*. Syracuse, NY: Syracuse University Press, 1995, pp. xx–xxi, 1, 7.

2. Jung, C. G. "Commentary." In Wilhelm, Richard. *The Secret of the Golden Flower*. New York: Harcourt, Brace & World, 1962, p. 100; Lewis, Samuel L. *Spiritual Dance and Walk*. Seattle/Fairfax, CA: PeaceWorks, 1990.

3. Jung, C. G. *Aion*. (*Collected Works*, Volume IX). Princeton, NJ: Princeton University Press, 1959, pp. 223–224.

4. Ross, Anne, and Don Robins. *The Life and Death of a Druid Prince*. New York: Summit, 1989.

5. Patnaik, Naveen. *The Garden of Life*. London: HarperCollins/Aquarian, 1993, p. 37; Newberry, John. *The Indus Script of the Mohenjo-Daro Shamans* (monograph). Victoria, BC: John Newberry, 1980.

6. Cox, Harvey. "Christianity." In Sharma, Arvind, ed. *Our Religions*. San Francisco: HarperSanFrancisco, 1993, p. 404.

7. Frazer, Sir James George. *The Golden Bough* (abridged edition). New York: Macmillan, 1963, pp. 139–146.

8. "Shamanic Counseling and Ecopsychology: An Interview with Leslie Gray." In Roszak, Theodore et al., eds. *Ecopsychology: Restoring the Earth, Healing the Mind*. San Francisco: Sierra Club Books, 1995, p. 173.

9. Eliade, Mircea. *Shamanism*. Princeton, NJ: Princeton University Press, 1964, p. 259.

10. Halifax, Joan. *Shamanic Voices*. New York: E. P. Dutton, 1979, p. 17.

11. Harner, Michael. *The Way of the Shaman*. New York: Bantam, 1982, p. xv.

12. Landaw, Jonathan, and Andy Weber. *Images of Enlightenment: Tibetan Art in Practice*. Ithaca, NY: Snow Lion Publications, 1993, p. 42.

13. Shore, Eliezer. "The Tree at the Heart of the Garden." *Parabola* XIV, no. 3, August 1989, pp. 38–43.

14. Katz, Richard. "Education for Transcendence: !Kia-Healing with the Kalahari !Kung." In Lee, Richard B., and Irven De Vore, eds. *Kalahari Hunter-Gatherers.* Cambridge, MA: Harvard University Press, 1976, p. 297.

15. Starhawk (Miriam Simos). *The Spiral Dance.* San Francisco: Harper & Row, 1979, pp. 44, 128–133; Adler, Margot. *Drawing Down the Moon.* New York: Penguin/Arkana, 1986, pp. 109–110.

16. Zolbrod, Paul G. *Dine bahane: The Navajo Creation Story.* Albuquerque: University of New Mexico Press, 1984.

17. Cushing, Frank Hamilton. *Zuni Fetishes.* Las Vegas: Facsimile Editions by K C Publications, Box 14883, 1974, p. 13 (reproduced from *Second Annual Report of the Bureau of Ethnology, 1880–1881.* Washington, DC: US Government Printing Office, 1881).

18. Waters, Frank. *Book of the Hopi.* New York: Penguin, 1977.

19. Erdoes, Richard, and Alfonso Ortiz, eds. *American Indian Myths and Legends.* New York: Pantheon, 1984, p. 98.

20. Waters, Frank. *Masked Gods: Navaho and Pueblo Ceremonialism.* Chicago: Swallow Press, 1950, p. 174.

21. Freud, Sigmund, cited in Erikson, Erik H. *Childhood and Society.* New York: W. W. Norton, 1963, pp. 264–265.

22. Jung, C. G. *Alchemical Studies* (*Collected Works*, Volume XIII). Princeton: Princeton University Press, 1967, p. 253.

23. Angyal, Andras. *Foundations for a Science of Personality.* Cambridge, MA: Harvard University Press, 1967 (first published: New York: Commonwealth Fund, 1941), pp. 172–173.

24. Laszlo, Ervin. *The Systems View of the World.* New York: George Braziller, 1972, p. 48.

25. Laszlo, *Systems View of the World*, p. 67.

26. Alighieri, Dante. *The Paradiso.* Translated by John Ciardi. New York, Mentor, 1970, p. 365.

27. Yeats, William Butler. Letter to Lady Elizabeth Pelham, January 4, 1939.

28. *Dhammapada*, first verse.

29. Bandler, Richard, and John Grinder. *The Structure of Magic.* Palo Alto, CA: Science and Behavior Books, 1975, p. 18.

30. Polak, Fred. *The Image of the Future.* Translated by Elise Boulding. San Francisco: Jossey-Bass, 1973, p. 300.

2. All My Relations: The Hoop

1. Buck, William. *Ramayana.* Berkeley: University of California Press, 1976, p. 315.

2. Adler, Ronald B., Lawrence B. Rosenfeld, and Neil Towne. *Interplay: The Process of Interpersonal Communication.* Fort Worth, TX: Harcourt Brace College Publishers, 1995, p. 4. (Citing Duck, S. "Staying Healthy. . .With a

Little Help from Friends?" In Duck, S. ed. *Human Relationships: An Introduction to Social Psychology*, Newbury Park, CA: Sage, 1991; and Ruberman, R. "Psychosocial Influences on Mortality of Patients with Coronary Heart Disease." *Journal of the Americal Medical Association* 267, January 22/29, 1992, pp. 559–560.)

3.   Myers, David G. *Psychology*. Holland, MI: Worth Publishers, 1995, p. 83–85.

4.   Ainsworth, Mary. "Infant-Mother Attachment." *American Psychologist* 34, 1979, pp. 932–937, cited in Myers, *Psychology*, p. 98; van den Boom, Dymphna. "Preventive Intervention and the Quality of Mother-Infant Interaction and Infant Exploration in Irritable Infants." In Koops, W., H. J. G. Soppe, J. L. van der Linden, P. C. M. Molenaar, and J. J. F. Schroots, eds. *Developmental Psychology Behind the Dikes: An Outline of Developmental Psychology Research in The Netherlands*. Utrecht, NL: Uitgeverij Eburon, 1990. See also Hazan, C., and P. R. Shaver. "Deeper into Attachment Theory." *Psychological Inquiry* 5, 1994, pp. 68–79, cited in Myers, *Psychology*, p. 98.

5.   Bowlby, John. *Separation: Anxiety and Anger*. New York: Basic Books, 1973, p. 322.

6.   Myers, *Psychology*, pp. 99–100.

7.   Hale, Ann E. *Conducting Clinical Sociometric Explorations*. Roanoke, VA: Royal Publishing Co., 1981, p. 23.

8.   www.oilspill.state.ak.us/nwhistory.html.

9.   Gallagher, Winifred. *The Power of Place*. New York: Poseidon Press, 1993, p. 224.

10. Lame Deer, John (Fire), and Richard Erdoes. *Lame Deer: Seeker of Visions*. New York: Simon & Schuster/Touchstone, 1972, p. 112.

11. Mullett, G. M. *Spider Woman Stories*. Tucson, AZ: University of Arizona Press, 1984, p. 16.

12. There are echoes of Indra's Net elsewhere in Indo-European myth: in the motif of the spinning of the three Fates (Greek mythology) and in the web of *wyrd* (Anglo-Saxon mythology), both of which are related to the Hoop of Energy or karma. See Branston, Brian. *The Lost Gods of England*. New York: Oxford University Press, 1974.

13. Hillman, James. "A Psyche the Size of the Earth," in Roszak, *Ecopsychology*, p. xxi.

14. Ittelson, William H., Harold M. Proshansky, Leanne G. Rivlin, and Gary H. Winkel. *An Introduction to Environmental Psychology*. New York: Holt, Rinehart, and Winston, 1974, pp. 12–14; Gibson, Eleanor, J. "The Ecological Approach: A Foundation for Environmental Psychology." In Downs, Roger M., Lynn S. Lieben, and David S. Palermo. *Visions of Aesthetics, The Environment & Development*. Hillsdale, NJ: Lawrence Erlbaum Associates Inc., 1991 (Conference Papers, Pennsylvania State University), p. 94.

15. Perls, Frederick, Ralph E. Hefferline, and Paul Goodman. *Gestalt Therapy*. New York: Dell, 1951, p. 228.

16. Searles, Harold, cited in Nixon, Will. "How Nature Shapes Childhood." *The Amicus Journal*, Summer 1997, pp. 31–35.

17. Ulrich, Roger S. "Natural versus Urban Scenes: Some Psychophysiological Effects." *Environment and Behavior* 13: 523–556.

18. Myers, *Psychology*, p. 518.

19. Carrington, Damian. "Fishery Collapse 'Confirms Silent Spring Pesticide Prophecy.'" *Guardian*, October 31, 2019, https://www.theguardian.com /environment/2019/oct/31/fishery-collapse-confirms-silent-spring-pesti cide-prophecy; Branch, John, and Brad Plumer. "Climate Disruption Is Now Locked In. The Next Moves Will Be Crucial." *New York Times*, September 22, 2020, https://www.nytimes.com/2020/09/22/climate/climate-change-future. html?auth=login-google&searchResultPosition=6.

20. Kaplan, Rachael, and Stephen Kaplan. *The Experience of Nature*. Cambridge, UK: Cambridge University Press, 1989, p. 162; Gallagher, *The Power of Place*, pp. 210, 213.

21. Ulrich, Roger S. "View through a Window May Influence Recovery from Surgery." *Science* 224, no. 4647, April 27, 1984, pp. 420, 421, cited in Perlman, Michael. *The Power of Trees*. Dallas: Spring Publications, 1994, p. 157.

22. Fisk, Sarah. "Healing Through Restoration." *The Ecopsychology Newsletter*, no. 5, Spring 1996, pp. 5–6; Powch, Irene G. "Wilderness Therapy: What Makes It Empowering for Women?" *Women and Therapy* 1994, vol. 15, pp. 11–27; Hartig, Terry, Marlis Mang, and Gary W. Evans. "Restorative Effects of Natural Environment Experiences." *Environment and Behavior* 23, no. 1, January 1991, pp. 3–26.

23. Sakaki, Nanao. *Break the Mirror: The Poems of Nanao Sakaki*. San Francisco: North Point Press, 1987, pp. 12–13.

24. Eaton, Evelyn. *The Shaman and the Medicine Wheel*. Wheaton, IL: Theosophical Publishing House, 1982, p. 50.

25. Fox, Matthew. *Illuminations of Hildegard of Bingen*. Santa Fe, NM: Bear & Co., 1985, p. 76.

26. Bowman, George. Essay in "Tying the Knot: An Album of Buddhist Weddings." *Tricycle: The Buddhist Review* VII, no. 3, Spring 1998, p. 33.

27. Tanahashi, Kazuaki, ed. *Moon in a Dewdrop: Writings of Zen Master Dogen*. San Francisco: North Point Press, 1985, p. 70.

28. *The Bhagavad Gita*. Translated by Eknath Easwaran. Tomales, CA: Nilgiri Press, 1985, p. 107.

29. *Utne Reader*. July/August 1992, p. 59.

30. Markham, Edwin. *Poems of Edwin Markham, Selected by Charles L Wallis*. New York: Harper & Brothers, 1950, p. 18.

31. Weil, Simone. "Reflections on the Right Use of School Studies with a View to the Love of God." In Panichas, G., ed. *The Simone Weil Reader*. New York: David McKay, 1977, pp. 44–52.

32. McLuhan, T. C. *Cathedrals of the Spirit*. Toronto: HarperCollins, 1996, p. 181.

33. Bureau of American Ethnology. *Forty-Seventh Annual Report—1929–1930*. Washington, DC: US Government Printing Office, 1932, pp. 783–784.

34. Johnston, Basil. *Ojibway Ceremonies*. Lincoln, NE: University of Nebraska Press, 1982, pp. 109–110.

35. Matthews, Caitlin. *Elements of the Celtic Tradition*. Rockport, MA: Element, 1989.

36. Starhawk, *The Spiral Dance*, pp. 55–56.

37. Gray, William G. *Qabalistic Concepts*. York Beach, ME: Samuel Weiser, 1997, pp. 60–62.

38. Waters, *Book of the Hopi*, p. 35.

39. Jung, C. G. *Analytic Psychology: Its Theory and Practice*. New York: Vintage, 1968, p. 17.

40. Storm, Hyemeyohsts. *Seven Arrows*. New York: Ballantine, 1972, pp. 6–7.

41. *The Bhagavad Gita*, pp. 62–63.

42. See also Adler, *Drawing Down the Moon*, p. 148.

43. Paterson, Jacqueline Memory. *Tree Wisdom: The Definitive Guidebook*. London: Thorsons, 1996, p. 22.

44. Halevi, Z"ev ben Shimon. *Kabbalah: Tradition of Hidden Knowledge*. New York: Thames & Hudson, 1992, p. 29; Cooper, Rabbi David A. *The Mystical Kabbalah* (audiocassettes). Boulder, CO: Sounds True Audio, 1994.

45. *Chuang Tsu: Inner Chapters*. Translated by Gia-Fu Feng and Jane English. New York: Vintage, 1974, p. 123.

46. Gyatso, Tenzin, the Fourteenth Dalai Lama. *The Meaning of Life from a Buddhist Perspective*. Boston: Wisdom Publications, 1992.

47. Thich Nhat Hanh. *Being Peace*. Berkeley: Parallax Press, 1987, p. 85.

48. Sandner, Donald. *Navaho Symbols of Healing*. New York: Harcourt Brace Jovanovich, 1979, pp. 159–160.

49. Harner, *The Way of the Shaman*, p. 76; Matthews, John. *Taliesin*. London: HarperCollins/Aquarian, 1991, p. 318.

50. Abramovitz, Janet N. "Learning to Value Nature's Free Services." *The Futurist*. July–August 1997, pp. 39–42.

51. Buchmann, S. L., and G. P. Nabhan. *The Forgotten Pollinators*. Washington, DC: Island Press, 1996.

52. Hyde, Lewis. *The Gift*. New York: Vintage, 1983, p. 4.

53. Hyde, *The Gift*, p. 15.

54. Campbell, Joseph. *The Way of the Animal Powers*. San Francisco: Alfred Van Der Marck/Harper & Row, 1983, pp. 152–153; Rockwell, David. *Giving Voice to Bear*. Niwot, CO: Roberts Rinehart, 1991, p. 183; and Campbell, Joseph. *The Power of Myth*. New York: Doubleday, 1988, pp. 76–78.

55. Kaptchuk, Ted J. *The Web That Has No Weaver: Understanding Chinese Medicine*. New York: Congdon & Weed, 1983, pp. 6–7.

56. Klein, Bob. *Movements of Magic: The Spirit of T'ai-Chi-Ch'uan*. North Hollywood, CA: Newcastle Publishing Co., 1984, p. 91.

57. *Chuang Tsu: Inner Chapters*. Translated by Gia-Fu Feng and Jane English. New York: Vintage, 1974, p. 74.

58. Moreno, J. L. *Who Shall Survive? Foundations of Sociometry, Group Psychotherapy, and Sociodrama*. Beacon, NY: Beacon House, 1953, pp. 42, 722.

59. Mitchell, Stephen. *Tao Te Ching: A New English Version*. New York: Harper & Row, 1988, pp. 15, 27, 28, 22.

60. Buddhadasa Bhikkhu, Ajahn [Phra Thepwisutthimethi (Nguam)]. *Heartwood of the Bodhi Tree*. Boston: Wisdom Publications, 1994.

61. Cooper, *The Mystical Kabbalah*.

62. Wing, R. L. *The I Ching Workbook*. Garden City, NY: Doubleday, 1979, p. 8.

63. Wing, *The I Ching Workbook*, p. 14.

64. Bohart, Arthur C., and Judith Todd. *Foundations of Clinical and Counseling Psychology*. New York: HarperCollins, 1988, p. 137; Rogers, Carl. *On Becoming A Person*. Boston: Houghton Mifflin, 1961.

65. Miller, Scott, Mark Hubble, and Barry Duncan. "No More Bells and Whistles." *Family Therapy Networker* 19, no. 2, March/April 1995, pp. 53–63.

66. Lame Deer, *Lame Deer*, pp. 177–178.

67. Jung, C. G. *Psychology and Alchemy* (*Collected Works*, Volume XII). Princeton, NJ: Princeton University Press, 1968, pp. 107–109, 217; Cornell, Judith. *Mandala: Luminous Symbols for Healing*. Wheaton, IL: Quest Books, 1994, p. 6.

68. Sandner, *Navaho Symbols of Healing*.

3. The Holy Tree

1. King, Martin Luther, Jr. *The Autobiography of Martin Luther King, Jr.* Edited by Clayborne Carson. New York: Warner Books, 1998.

2. Angyal, *Foundations for a Science of Personality*, pp. 174–175.

3. Martinson, Harry. "Hades and Euclid, (first version)." Lines from Bly, Robert. *Friends, You Drank Some Darkness: Three Swedish Poets*. Boston: Beacon Press, 1975, p. 57.

4. Sen Gupta, Sankar, ed. *Tree Symbol Worship in India*. Calcutta: Indian Publications, 1965, p. 3; Martin, E. Osborn. *The Gods of India*. Delhi: Indological Book House, 1972 (Indian reprint), p. 235.

5. Frazer, Sir James George. *The Golden Bough* (abridged edition). New York: Collier Books (Macmillan), 1963, p. 349.

6. Altman, Nathaniel. *Sacred Trees*. San Francisco: Sierra Club Books, 1994, p. 51.

7. Altman, *Sacred Trees*, pp. 9, 205.

8. Perry, Donald R., cited in Perlman, *Power of Trees*, p. 77.

9. Frazer, *The Golden Bough*, p. 126.

10. McLuhan, *Cathedrals of the Spirit*, p. 66.

11. van Renterghen, Tony. *When Santa Was a Shaman*. St. Paul, MN: Llewellyn Publications, 1995.

12. McLuhan, *Cathedrals of the Spirit*, p. 48.

13. Altman, *Sacred Trees*, pp. 23–35, 174.

14. Jung, *Psychology and Alchemy*, p. 28; von Franz, Marie-Louise. "The Process of Individuation." In Jung, Carl, ed. *Man and His Symbols*. New York: Dell, 1964, p. 161. Humans have a profound visceral response to the death of trees. See Perlman *Power of Trees*, pp. 26–27.

15. Kaufman, Bobbie, and Agnes Wohl. *Casualties of Childhood*. New York: Brunner/Mazel, 1992, p. 25.

16. Altman, *Sacred Trees*, p. 75; Jung, *Alchemical Studies*, p. 337.

17. Carl Hollander, PhD, personal communication.

18. Jung, *Alchemical Studies*, pp. 272–273, n.; Altman, *Sacred Trees*, p. 4.

19. *The Upanishads*. Translated by Swami Prabhavananda and Frederick Manchester. New York: Mentor, 1957, p. 23.

20. King, *The Autobiography of Martin Luther King, Jr.*, p. 78.

21. Nasr, Seyyed Hossein. "Islam," in Sharma, *Our Religions*, p. 453.

22. Maslow, Abraham H. *Toward a Psychology of Being*. New York: Van Nostrand Reinhold, 1968, p. 97.

23. Halevi, *Kabbalah: Tradition of Hidden Knowledge*, p. 4.

24. The Pseudo-Chrysostom. Sermon VI for Holy Week, *Patrologia Greaca*, IX, 743–746. In de Lubac, Henri. *Catholicism*. New York: Longmans, Green & Co., 1950, p. 279, cited in Kuntz, Marion Leathers, and Paul Grimley Kuntz. *Jacob's Ladder and the Tree of Life*. New York: Peter Lang, 1987, p. 327.

25. Kuntz, *Jacob's Ladder and the Tree of Life*, p. 326.

26. Kuntz, *Jacob's Ladder and the Tree of Life*, p. 72, 154.

27. Ozaniec, Naomi. *The Elements of the Chakras*. Rockport, MA: Element, 1990, p. 13.

28. Ozaniec, *The Elements of the Chakras*, p. 110.

29. Ozaniec, *The Elements of the Chakras*, p. 42.

30. Ozaniec, *The Elements of the Chakras*, p. 67.

31. Angyal, *Foundations for a Science of Personality*, pp. 218–220.

32. Ozaniec, *The Elements of the Chakras*.

33. Ozaniec, *The Elements of the Chakras*, p. 11.

34. Zimmer, Heinrich. *Myths and Symbols in Indian Art and Civilization*. New York: Pantheon, 1946.

35. Waters, *Book of the Hopi*, pp. 9–11; Halevi, *Kabbalah: Tradition of Hidden Knowledge*, p. 12.

36. Erikson, Erik H. *Childhood and Society.* New York: W. W. Norton, 1963, p. 247.

37. Erikson, *Childhood and Society*, p. 268.

38. Maslow, A. H. *Motivation and Personality* 2nd edition. New York: Harper & Row, 1970.

39. Kuntz, *Jacob's Ladder and the Tree of Life*, pp. 54, 325.

40. *Mathnawi*, IV, 521, s. In De Vitray-Meyerovitch, Eva. *Rumi and Sufism.* Translated by Simone Fattal. Sausalito, CA: The Post-Apollo Press, 1987, p. 112.

41. Levertov, Denise. *The Stream & the Sapphire.* New York: New Directions, 1997, pp. 67–68.

42. Matthews, Caitlin. *Elements of the Celtic Tradition.* Rockport, MA: Element, 1989, p. 35.

43. Wilber, Ken. "The Great Chain of Being." *Journal of Humanistic Psychology* 33, no. 3, Summer 1993, p. 58.

44. Koestler, Arthur. *The Ghost in the Machine.* New York: Macmillan, 1967, p. 48.

45. Wilber, Ken. *A Brief History of Everything.* Boston: Shambhala, 1996, p. 67.

46. Wilber, *A Brief History of Everything*, p. 282.

47. Differentiation and integration is a fundamental dynamic of growth, present at a primitive cellular level in the process of mitosis, as well as in the psychological dynamics of group development.

48. Somé, Malidoma Patrice, presentation at Naropa Institute, Boulder, CO, June 16, 1995.

49. Jung, *Alchemical Studies*, p. 302.

50. All Bible quotations are from *Revised Standard Version.* New York: Thomas Nelson, 1953.

51. Freud, Sigmund. *Introductory Lectures on Psycho-Analysis.* New York: W. W. Norton, 1966.

52. Fordham, Frieda. *An Introduction to Jung's Psychology.* Baltimore: Penguin, 1968, pp. 76–77.

53. Frankl, Viktor E. *Man's Search for Meaning: An Introduction to Logotherapy.* New York: Pocket Books, 1972, pp. 153–154.

54. Jung, *Alchemical Studies*, p. 195.

55. Harner, *The Way of the Shaman*, p. 32.

56. Kurtz, Ron. *Hakomi Therapy.* Boulder, CO: Hakomi Institute, 1984; "Shamanic Counseling and Ecopsychology," pp. 172–182.

57. von Franz, Marie-Louise. *Alchemy.* Toronto: Inner City Books, 1980, p. 162.

58. von Franz, *Alchemy*, p. 147.

59. http://www.jazzcentralstation.com/jcs/station/featured/srollins/fabest.html; Avakian, George. "The Bridge—Sonny Rollins." Liner notes, RCA stereo record, LSP-2527 (rereleased as APL1-0859), April 1962.

60. von Franz, *Alchemy*, p. 104.

61. Jung, Carl, cited in Peck, M. Scott. *The Road Less Traveled.* New York: Simon and Schuster/Touchstone, 1978, p. 17.

62. Walker, Barbara G. *The Women's Encyclopedia of Myths and Secrets.* New York: Harper & Row, 1983, pp. 1067–1068.

63. Kramer, Samuel Noah. *From the Poetry of Sumer.* Berkeley: University of California Press, 1979, cited in Diane Wolkstein and Samuel Noah Kramer. *Inanna: Queen of Heaven and Earth.* New York: Harper & Row, 1983, p. xv.

64. Wolkstein, Diane, and Samuel Noah Kramer. *Inanna: Queen of Heaven and Earth.* New York: Harper & Row, 1983, p. 5.

65. Wolkstein, *Inanna: Queen of Heaven and Earth,* p. 156.

66. Wolkstein, *Inanna: Queen of Heaven and Earth,* pp. 54–55.

67. Wolkstein, *Inanna: Queen of Heaven and Earth,* pp. 57–58.

68. Wolkstein, *Inanna: Queen of Heaven and Earth,* p. 60.

69. Perera, Sylvia Brinton. *Descent to the Goddess.* Toronto: Inner City Books, 1981, p. 25.

70. Perera, *Descent to the Goddess,* p. 13.

71. Perera, *Descent to the Goddess,* p. 45.

72. Estés, Clarissa Pinkola. *Women Who Run with the Wolves.* New York: Ballantine, 1992, p. 134.

73. Webster, Daniel, cited in American Genealogical Research Institute Staff. *How to Trace Your Family Tree.* New York: Main Street Books, 1973, p. 1.

74. Somé, Malidoma Patrice. *Of Water and the Spirit.* New York: Tarcher/Putnam, 1994.

75. Somé, Malidoma Patrice, presentation at Naropa Institute, Boulder, CO, June 16, 1995.

76. von Franz, *Alchemy,* pp. 146–147.

77. von Franz, *Alchemy,* p. 37.

78. Roszak, Theodore. *The Voice of the Earth.* New York: Touchstone, 1993, p. 290.

79. Eliott, T. S. *The Complete Poems and Plays.* New York: Harcourt Brace & World, 1962, p. 119.

80. Donne, John. "A Valediction: Forbidding Mourning." In *Donne* (The Laurel Poetry Series). New York: Dell, 1962, p. 60.

81. Kerenyi, C. *The Gods of the Greeks.* New York: Thames & Hudson, 1979, p. 124.

82. Tanahashi, Kazuaki, ed. *Moon in a Dewdrop: Writings of Zen Master Dogen.* San Francisco: North Point Press, 1985, p. 72.

83. Levine, Stephen. *Who Dies?* New York: Anchor Books, 1982, pp. 4–5.

4. The Hoop and the Tree: The Deep Structure of the Whole Self

1. Bly, Robert. *Selected Poems of Rainer Maria Rilke.* New York: Harper & Row, 1981, p. 13.

2. Erikson, *Childhood and Society*, pp. 97–106.

3. Tannen, Deborah. *You Just Don't Understand*. New York: William Morrow and Co., 1990.

4. Thorne, Barrie. *Gender Play: Girls and Boys in School*. New Brunswick, NJ: Rutgers University Press, 1993.

5. Kegan, Robert. *The Evolving Self*. Cambridge, MA: Harvard University Press, 1982, pp. 107–108.

6. Angyal, *Foundations for a Science of Personality*, pp. 175–177.

7. Csikszentmihalyi, Mihaly. *Flow: The Psychology of Optimal Experience*. New York: Harper & Row, 1990, p. 41.

8. Csikszentmihalyi, *Flow: The Psychology of Optimal Experience*, p. 42.

9. Shepard, Paul. *Nature and Madness*. San Francisco: Sierra Club Books, 1982. See especially Chapter 6: "The Dance of Neoteny and Ontogeny."

10. Shepard, *Nature and Madness*, p. 111.

11. Shepard, *Nature and Madness*, pp. 7–10.

12. Shepard, *Nature and Madness*, p. 113.

13. Williamson, Robin. *The Craneskin Bag*. Edinburgh: Canongate, 1989, p. 79.

14. Thoreau, Henry David. *Walden and Other Writings*. New York: Modern Library, 1950, pp. 102, 194.

15. Plato. *Apology*.

16. Cobb, Edith. *Ecology of Imagination in Childhood*. New York: Columbia University Press, 1977, cited in LaChapelle, Dolores. *Sacred Land Sacred Sex*. Silverton CO: Finn Hill Arts, 1988, p. 136; Edith Cobb. *The Ecology of Imagination in Childhood*. Dallas: Spring Publications, 1993, p. 44.

17. Lakoff, George, and Mark Johnson. *Metaphors We Live By*. Chicago: University of Chicago Press, 1980.

18. Cobb, *Ecology of Imagination*, p. 102.

19. Cobb, *Ecology of Imagination*, p. 88.

20. Van Doren, Mark, ed. *Wordsworth: Selected Poems*. New York: Modern Library, 1950, pp. 193–194 (lines 562–564, 586–587).

21. *In Praise of the Baal Shem Tov*. Translated by Dan Ben-Amos and Jerome R. Mintz. Bloomington, IN: Indiana University Press, 1970, p. 12.

22. Berenson, Bernard. *Sketch for a Self-Portrait*. Toronto: Pantheon, 1949, p. 18, cited in Cobb, *Ecology of Imagination*, 1993, p. 32.

23. Matarazzo, Joseph D. *Wechsler's Measurement and Appraisal of Adult Intelligence*. Baltimore: Williams & Wilkins, 1972, p. 79.

24. Anastasi, Anne. *Psychological Testing* 5th edition. New York: Macmillan, 1982, p. 331.

25. Goleman, Daniel. *Emotional Intelligence*. New York: Bantam, 1995.

26. Goleman, *Emotional Intelligence*, pp. 43–44.

27. Goleman, *Emotional Intelligence*, p. 97.

28. Goleman, *Emotional Intelligence*, pp. 27–28.

29. Minuchin, Salvadore. *Families and Family Therapy*. Cambridge, MA: Harvard University Press, 1974.

30. Bowen, Murray. *Family Therapy in Clinical Practice*. New York: Aronson, 1978.

31. Angyal, *Foundations for a Science of Personality*, pp. 179–180.

32. *Diagnostic and Statistical Manual of Mental Disorders, Fourth Edition (DSM-IV)*. Washington, DC: American Psychiatric Association, 1994.

33. Hillman, James, et al. *Puer Papers*. Irving, TX: Spring Publications, 1979.

34. Real, Terrence. *I Don't Want to Talk About It: Overcoming the Secret Legacy of Male Depression*. New York: Fireside/Simon & Schuster, 1997, p. 290.

35. Wegscheider-Cruse, Sharon. *Choicemaking*. Deerfield Beach, FL: Health Communications, 1985, p. 2.

36. *The Twelve Steps and Traditions*. New York: Al-Anon Family Group Headquarters (P.O. Box 182, Madison Square Station, NY, 10159-0182).

37. "Towards an Ecological Self: An Interview with Theodore Roszak." *AHP Forum*. May/June 1993, p. 14.

38. Conn, Sarah A. "When the Earth Hurts, Who Responds?" In Roszak, *Ecopsychology*, p. 162; see "Affluenza," a PBS special from KCTS/Seattle and Oregon Public Broadcasting, coproduced by John de Graaf and Vivia Boe.

39. Jung, *Psychology and Alchemy*, pp. 167, 419.

40. Eliade, Mircea. *Images and Symbols*. Translated by Philip Mairet. New York: Sheed and Ward, 1969, p. 14, cited in Monick, Eugene. *Phallos: Sacred Image of the Masculine*. Toronto: Inner City Books, 1987, p. 24.

41. Monick, *Phallos: Sacred Image of the Masculine*, p. 16.

42. Danielou, Alain. *Shiva and Dionysus: The Religion of Nature and Eros*. Translated by K. F. Hurry. New York: Inner Traditions International, 1984, p. 56, cited in Monick, *Phallos: Sacred Image of the Masculine*, p. 29.

43. Blake, William. Letter to Thomas Butts, November 22, 1802, second letter, lines 87–88.

44. Lubell, Winifred Milius. *The Metamorphosis of Baubo: Myths of Woman's Sexual Energy*. Nashville, TN and London: Vanderbilt University Press, 1994.

45. *The Siva Samhita*. Translated by Rai Bahadur Srisa Chandra Vasu. Delhi: Sri Satguru Publications, 1979, pp. 18–19.

46. Starhawk, *The Spiral Dance*, p. 176.

47. Eliade, Mircea. *Mephistopheles and the Androgyne*. New York: Sheed and Ward, 1965, pp. 98–100.

48. Singer, June. *Androgyny: The Opposites Within*. Boston: Sigo Press, 1989, pp. 107–120.

49. *The Gospel According to Thomas*, Established and translated by A. Guillaumont, H.-CH. Puech, G. Quispel, W. Till, and Yassah Abd Al Masih. San Francisco: Harper & Row, 1959, pp. 17–19.

50. Jung, *Psychology and Alchemy*, p. 232; Jung, C. G. *Mysterium Coniunctionis* (*Collected Works*, Volume XIV). Princeton, NJ: Princeton University Press, 1963, pp. 457–459.

51. Heath, Douglas H., and Harriet E. Heath. *Fulfilling Lives: Paths to Maturity and Success*. San Francisco: Jossey-Bass, 1991, pp. 18–19.

52. Heath, *Fulfilling Lives*, p. 19.

53. Heath, *Fulfilling Lives*, p. 17.

54. *Dropping Ashes on the Buddha: The Teaching of Zen Master Seung Sahn*. Compiled and edited by Stephen Mitchell. New York: Grove Press, 1976, pp. 131–132.

55. Maslow, Abraham H. "On Self-Actualization." In Cooney, William, and Barry Trunk. *Ten Great Thinkers*. Lanham, MD: University Press of America, 1990, p. 92 (reprinted from Maslow, Abraham H. *New Knowledge in Human Values*. New York: Harper & Row, 1959).

56. Maslow, *Toward a Psychology of Being*, p. 76.

57. Maslow, "On Self-Actualization," in Cooney, *Ten Great Thinkers*, p. 96.

58. Uyeshiba, Morihei, cited in Heckler, Richard Strozzi. *The Anatomy of Change*. Boulder, CO and London: Shambhala, 1984, p. 134.

59. Einstein, Albert, cited in Sogyal Rinpoche. *The Tibetan Book of Living and Dying*. San Francisco: HarperSanFrancisco, 1992, p. 98.

60. Nasr, "Islam," in Sharma, *Our Religions*, p. 463.

61. Eckhart, Meister, cited in Roberts, Elizabeth, and Elian Amidon, eds. *Earth Prayers*. San Francisco: HarperSanFrancisco, 1991, p. 251.

5. Go in Beauty

1. von Franz, *Alchemy*, p. 165.

2. Sturlson, Snorri. *The Prose Edda*. Translated by Jean I. Young. Berkeley: University of California Press, 1954, pp. 56, 89.

3. Angyal, *Foundations for a Science of Personality*, p. 222.

4. Bly, Robert. *The Sibling Society*. Reading, MA: Addison-Wesley, 1996.

5. See, for example, the work of sociologist Ferdinand Toennies (1855–1936). Toennies developed an influential typology of societies that contrasted so-called "primitive" communities (*gemeinschaft*) with modern industrial (*gesellschaft*) societies. Community (*gemeinschaft*) is characterized by close personal bonds and kinship relationships; and society (*gesellschaft*) by a predominance of more impersonal or bureaucratic relationships.

6. Eisler, Riane. *The Chalice and the Blade*. San Francisco: Harper & Row, 1987, p. xvii.

7. Eisler, *The Chalice and the Blade*, pp. 13–14.

8. Eisler, *The Chalice and the Blade*, p. 37.

9. Eisler, *The Chalice and the Blade*, p. 50.

10. Wallace, *The White Roots of Peace*. Saranac Lake, NY: The Chauncy Press, 1986, p. 3 (originally published by University of Pennsylvania Press, Philadelphia, 1946).

11. Wallace, *The White Roots of Peace*, p. xvi.

12. Wallace, *The White Roots of Peace*, pp. 7–8.

13. Wallace, *The White Roots of Peace*, p. 45.

14. Wallace, *The White Roots of Peace*, p. 59.

15. Wallace, *The White Roots of Peace*, p. 34.

16. Hewitt, J. N. B. "A Constitutional League of Peace in the Stone Age of America." In Tooker, Elisabeth ed. *An Iroquois Source Book, Volume 1: Political and Social Organization*. New York: Garland Publishing, 1985, p. 543.

17. Hale, Horatio, ed. *The Iroquois Book of Rites*. Toronto: University of Toronto Press, 1963, p. 29.

18. Hewitt, "A Constitutional League of Peace in the Stone Age of America," in Tooker, *An Iroquois Source Book, Volume 1: Political and Social Organization*, pp. 531, 543.

19. Hewitt, "A Constitutional League of Peace in the Stone Age of America," in Tooker, *An Iroquois Source Book, Volume 1: Political and Social Organization*, p. 541.

20. Oren Lyons, Faithkeeper of the Turtle Clan of the Onandaga Council of the Haudenosaunee, presentation at Naropa Institute, Boulder, CO, September 15, 1995.

21. Smith, Huston. *The World's Religions*. San Francisco: HarperSanFrancisco, 1991, p. 371.

22. Putnam, Robert D. "The Prosperous Community: Social Capital and Public Affairs." *The American Prospect* 13, no. 2, Spring 1993, cited in Korten, David C. *When Corporations Rule the World*. San Francisco: Kumarian Press/Berrett-Koehler, 1995, pp. 278–279.

23. Lopez, Barry Holstun. *Of Wolves and Men*. New York: Charles Scribner's Sons, 1978, p. 104.

24. Patagonia website. http://www.patagonia.com.

25. Off the Record, a web-based radio show for business and technology professionals, interview with Ray Anderson, April 1996, http://www.mediapool.com /offtherecord/ray_tran.html. Also: Interface website. http://www.ifsia.com /ecosense/menu.htm.

26. Weisman, Alan. "¡Gaviotas! Oasis of the Imagination." *Yes! A Journal of Positive Futures*, Summer 1998, pp. 36–40; Weisman, Alan. "¡Gaviotas! Oasis of the Imagination, Part 2." *Yes! A Journal of Positive Futures*, Fall 1998, pp. 45–49; and Weisman, Alan. *¡Gaviotas! A Village to Reinvent the World*. White River Junction, VT: Chelsea Green, 1998.

27. Counts, Alex. *Give Us Credit*. New York: Times Books, 1996.

28. Korten, *When Corporations Rule the World*.

29. Robèrt, Karl-Henrik. "Answering the King's Challenge." *In Context* no. 35, Spring 1993, p. 6; "The Natural Step: The Science of Sustainability" (Interview with Dr. Karl-Henrik Robèrt). *Yes! A Journal of Positive Futures*, Fall 1998, pp. 50–54.

30. Nattras, Brian. "Scandic's Natural Step." *Yes! A Journal of Positive Futures*, Fall 1998, pp. 52–53.

31. Hawken, Paul. *The Ecology of Commerce*. New York: HarperCollins, 1993.

32. Abramovitz, Janet N. "Learning to Value Nature's Free Services." *The Futurist*, July–August 1997, pp. 39–42.

33. *Yes! A Journal of Positive Futures*. Fall 1999, p. 12 (sidebar to article by Alice Walker, "A Daring Compassion").

34. Weisbord, Marvin R., ed. *Discovering Common Ground*. San Francisco: Berrett-Koehler, 1992.

35. Robert Rehm, international organizational consultant, 303-499-1607, participate@earthlink.net, personal communication.

36. Seed, John, Joanna Macy, Pat Fleming, and Arne Nass. *Thinking Like a Mountain: Towards a Council of All Beings*. Philadelphia: New Society Publishers, 1988, p. 97.

37. Smith, Anna V. "The Klamath River Now Has the Legal Rights of a Person." *High Country News*, September 24, 2019, www.hcn.org/issues/51.18 /tribal-affairs-the-klamath-river-now-has-the-legal-rights-of-a-person?utm _source=wcn1&utm_medium=email; Conley, Julia. "In 'Historic Vote,' Ohio City Residents Grant Lake Erie Legal Rights of a Person." *Common Dreams*, February 29, 2019, www.commondreams.org/news/2019/02/27 /historic-vote-ohio-city-residents-grant-lake-erie-legal-rights-person.

38. "Press Release: Colombia Supreme Court Rules That Amazon Region Is 'Subject of Rights.'" Community Environmental Legal Defense Fund, April 5, 2018, https://celdf.org/2018/04/press-release-colombia-supreme-court-rules-that -amazon-region-is-subject-of-rights.

39. Smith, "The Klamath River Now Has the Legal Rights"; Constitution of the Republic of Ecuador, http://pdba.georgetown.edu/Constitutions/Ecuador /english08.html.

40. Stone, Christopher. *Should Trees Have Standing? Toward Legal Rights for Natural Objects*. Los Altos, CA: William Kaufmann Inc., 1974, p. 5.

41. Ryan, John C., and Alan Thien Durning. *Stuff: The Secret Life of Everyday Things*. Seattle: Northwest Environment Watch, 1997, p. 67. See also their article in *The Futurist*, March 1998, p. 28.

42. Cronyn, George W., ed. *American Indian Poetry*. New York: Liveright, 1934, p. 93 (originally published under the title *The Path on the Rainbow*).

43. Magagnini, Steve. "If a Tree Falls . . . A Monk's Blessing for Thailand's Forest." *The Amicus Journal*, Summer 1994, pp. 12–14.

44. Magagnini, "If a Tree Falls," pp. 12–14.

45. Magagnini, "If a Tree Falls," pp. 12–14.

46. Mitchell, Stephen. *Tao Te Ching: A New English Version*. New York: Harper & Row, 1988, p. 64.

47. "Jane Goodall Moves from Jungle to City to Help Save Her Beloved Chimps." *Christian Science Monitor*, Wednesday, March 4, 1998, p. 13.

48. Abram, David. "The Ecology of Magic," in Roszak *Ecopsychology*, pp. 304–305.

49. Wallace, B. Alan. *Tibetan Buddhism From the Ground Up*. Boston: Wisdom Publications, 1993, p. 190.

50. Jung, *Psychology and Alchemy*, p. 6.

6. The Hoop and the Tree for Healing and Transformation: A Twenty-Year Perspective

1. Personal communication.

2. Personal communication. Jocelyn Gordon can be reached via her website: www.HoopYogini.com and www.JocelynGordon.com.

3. Guisinger, Shan, and Sidney J. Blatt. "Individuality and Relatedness." *American Psychologist* 49, no. 2, February 1994, pp. 104–111.

4. Personal communication. Lola Wilcox can be reached via her website: https://lolawilcox.com.

5. Biglan, Anthony, Brian R. Flay, Dennis D. Embry, and Irwin N. Sandler. "The Critical Role of Nurturing Environments for Promoting Human Well-Being." *American Psychologist* 67, no. 4, May–June 2012, pp. 257–271.

6. Intergovernmental Panel on Climate Change. Global warming of 1.5°C. Geneva: IPCC, 2018, https://report.ipcc.ch/sr15/pdf/sr15_spm_final.pdf; Kolbert, Elizabeth. *The Sixth Extinction*. New York: Henry Holt, 2014; and Diaz, Sandra, Josef Settele, and Eduardo Brondízio, et al. *Summary for Policymakers of the Global Assessment Report on Biodiversity and Ecosystem Services of the Intergovernmental Science-Policy Platform on Biodiversity and Ecosystem Services* (Advance Unedited Version). IPBES, May 6, 2019, www.ipbes.net/sites/default/files/downloads/spm_unedited_advance_for_posting_htn.pdf.

7. McKibben, Bill. *Falter: Has the Human Game Begun to Play Itself Out?* New York: Henry Holt, 2019, p. 12.

8. Global Footprint Network. Ecologial Footprint. https://www.footprintnetwork.org/our-work/ecological-footprint.

9. Prescott, Susan L., and Alan C. Logan. "Down to Earth: Planetary Health and Biophilosophy in the Symbiocene Epoch." *Challenges* 8, no. 2, 2017, p. 19, doi:10.3390/challe8020019.

10. Albrecht, Glenn. "'Solastalgia.' A New Concept in Health and Identity." *PAN: Philosophy Activism Nature*, no. 3, 2015, pp. 41–55.

11. Hoffman, Chris. *Cairns*. 3rd edition. Bloomington, IN: iUniverse, 2013, p. 41.

12. Albrecht, Glenn A. *Earth Emotions: New Words for a New World*. Ithaca, NY: Cornell University Press, 2019, p. 102; a similar idea appears in Swimme, Brian, and Thomas Berry. *The Universe Story: From the Primordial Flaring Forth to the Ecozoic Era—A Celebration of the Unfolding of the Cosmos*. San Francisco: HarperSanFrancisco, 1992.

13. Albrecht, *Earth Emotions*, p. 97.

14. Albrecht, *Earth Emotions*, pp. 142–143.

15. Prescott, Susan L., Ganesa Wegienka, Alan C. Logan, and David L. Katz. "Dysbiotic Drift and Biopsychosocial Medicine: How the Microbiome Links Personal, Public and Planetary Health." *BioPsychoSocial Medicine* 12, no. 7, 2018, https://doi.org/10.1186/s13030-018-0126-z.

16. Gilbert, Scott F., Jan Sapp, and Alfred I. Tauber. "A Symbiotic View of Life: We Have Never Been Individuals." *The Quarterly Review of Biology* 87, no. 4, December 2012, pp. 325–341, https://www.jstor.org/stable/10.1086/668166; Margulis, Lynn. *Symbiotic Planet: A New Look at Evolution*. New York: Basic Books, 1998.

17. Albrecht, *Earth Emotions*, p. 104.

18. Wilson, Edward O. *Half Earth: Our Planet's Fight for Life*. New York: Liveright, 2016. See also https://eowilsonfoundation.org/half-earth-our-planet-s-fight-for-life.

19. Powell, J. W. *Report on the Lands of the Arid Region*. Washington, DC: Government Printing Office, 1879; Worster, Daniel. "Landscape with Hero: John Wesley Powell and the Colorado Plateau." *Southern California Quarterly* 79, no. 1, Spring 1997, pp. 29–46.

20. Daly, Herman, and Joshua Farley. *Ecological Economics: Principles and Applications*. Washington, DC: Island Press, 2004.

21. Macy, Joanna, and Chris Johnstone. *Active Hope*. Novato, CA: New World Library, 2012, p. 211.

22. Erikson, *Childhood and Society*.

23. After Erikson's death, his widow and longtime partner in his work, Joan Erikson, described a ninth stage of development from her husband's notes and from her own observations of living into her late eighties. For more on this, see Erikson, Erik. *The Life Cycle Completed—Extended Version with New Chapters on the Ninth Stage of Development by Joan M. Erikson*. New York: W. W. Norton, 1997.

24. Erikson, *Childhood and Society*, p. 147.

25. See chapter 3; see also Wilber, *A Brief History of Everything*, p. 67.

26. Erikson, *Childhood and Society*, p. 270.

27. Winnicott, D. W. *Playing and Reality*. London: Tavistock Publications, 1971.

28. Long, A. A., and D. N. Sedley. *The Hellenistic Philosophers*, vol. 1. New York: Cambridge University Press, 1987, p. 349.

29. Neihardt, *Black Elk Speaks*; Brown, J. E. *The Sacred Pipe: Black Elk's Account of the Seven Rites of the Oglala Sioux*. New York: Penguin, 1979; Hallowell, A. I.

"The Role of Dreams in Ojibwa Culture," in von Grunebaum and Caillio, eds. *The Dream and Human Societies*. Berkeley: University of California Press, 1966.

30. Thoreau, Henry David. *Walden and Other Writings*. New York: Modern Library, 1950, p. 603.
31. Berry, Thomas. *The Great Story* in *Heron Dance* 35, 2002, pp. 25–26. *The Great Story* is available from www.bullfrogfilms.com.
32. Cobb, *Ecology of Imagination*, p. 44.
33. Louv, Richard. *Last Child in the Woods: Saving Our Children from Nature-Deficit Disorder*. Chapel Hill, NC: Algonquin Books, 2005.
34. Martyn, Patricia, and Eric Brymer. "The Relationship Between Nature Relatedness and Anxiety." *Journal of Health Psychology* 21, no. 7, 2016, pp. 1436–1445, doi: 10.1177/1359105314555169 hpq.sagepub.com; Craig, Jeffrey M., Alan C. Logan, and Susan L. Prescott. "Natural Environments, Nature Relatedness and the Ecological Theater: Connecting Satellites and Sequencing to Shinrin-Yoku." *Journal of Physiological Anthropology* 35, no. 1, 2016, doi: 10.1186/s40101-016-0083-9.
35. Reese, Ryan F., Todd F. Lewis, Jane E. Myers, Edward Wahesh, and Rachel Iversen. "Relationship Between Nature Relatedness and Holistic Wellness: an Exploratory Study." *Journal of Humanistic Counseling* 53, no. 1, April 2014.
36. Capaldi, Colin A., Raelyne L. Dopko, and John M. Zelenski. "The Relationship Between Nature Connectedness and Happiness: a Meta-Analysis." *Frontiers in Psychology*, 2014, doi: 10.3389/fpsyg.2014.00976.
37. White, Mathew P., Ian Alcock, James Grellier, Benedict W. Wheeler, Terry Hartig, Sara L. Warber, Angie Bone, Michael H. Depledge, and Lora E. Fleming. "Spending at Least 120 Minutes a Week in Nature Is Associated with Good Health and Wellbeing." *Nature Scientific Reports* 9:7730, June 2019, doi.org/10.1038/s41598-019-44097-3; https://www.nature.com/articles/s41598-019-44097-3.pdf.
38. Prescott, "Dysbiotic Drift and Biopsychosocial Medicine."
39. Ovid. Translated by Rolfe Humphries. *Metamorphoses*. Bloomington, IN: Indiana University Press, 1963, pp. 204–208.
40. Puhakka, Kaisa. "Intimacy, Otherness, and Alienation: The Intertwining of Nature and Consciousness." In D. A. Vakoch, and F. Castrillón, eds. *Ecopsychology, Phenomenology, and the Environment: The Experience of Nature*. New York: Springer, 2014, p. 11, 12, doi: 10.1007/978-1-4614-9619-9_2.
41. Swimme, Brian, and Thomas Berry. *The Universe Story: From the Primordial Flaring Forth to the Ecozoic Era—A Celebration of the Unfolding of the Cosmos*. San Francisco: HarperSanFrancisco, 1992, p. 243.
42. van der Post, Laurens. *The Heart of the Hunter*. New York: Harvest/Harcourt, 1980, p. 93.
43. Campbell, *The Power of Myth*, p. 31.
44. Berry, *The Great Story*, pp. 25–26.
45. Campbell, Joseph. *The Hero with a Thousand Faces*. Princeton, NJ: Princeton University Press/Bollingen, 1973, p. 251.
46. Campbell, *Hero with a Thousand Faces*, pp. 245–246.

47. For more on the heroine's journey, see Murdock, Maureen. *The Heroine's Journey*. Boston: Shambhala, 1990.

48. Grimm, Jacob, and Wilhelm Grimm. *The Complete Grimm's Fairy Tales*. New York: Random House/Pantheon, 1972, p. 612–620.

49. Guterman, Norbert, trans. *Russian Fairy Tales*. New York: Random House/Pantheon, 1973, p. 439–447.

50. For the man's story, see Bly, Robert. *Iron John: A Book about Men*. Reading, MA: Addison-Wesley, 1990. For the woman's story, see Estés, Clarissa Pinkola. *Women Who Run with the Wolves: Myths and Stories of the Wild Woman Archetype*. New York: Ballantine, 1992.

51. Jung, C. G. *Aion: Researches into the Phenomenology of the Self*. Princeton, NJ: Princeton University Press, 1978, p. 43.

52. Jung, *Alchemical Studies*, pp. 265–266.

53. von Franz, Marie-Louise. *Shadow and Evil in Fairy Tales*. Dallas: Spring Publications, 1974, p. 5.

54. Bly, Robert. *A Little Book on the Human Shadow*. San Francisco: Harper & Row, 1988.

55. Menakem, Resmaa. *My Grandmother's Hands*. Las Vegas: Central Recovery Press, 2017, p. 268.

56. Jung, *Aion*, p. 8.

57. Hillman, James, ed. *Facing the Gods*. Dallas: Spring Publications, 1980.

58. Bolen, Jean Shinoda. *Goddesses in Everywoman*. New York: Harper & Row, 1984; Bolen, Jean Shinoda. *Gods in Everyman*. New York: Harper & Row, 1989.

59. Grahn, Judy. *Another Mother Tongue: Gay Words, Gay Worlds*. Boston: Beacon Press, 1984.

60. Jung, *Aion*, p. 71.

61. Quoted in Jacobs, Alan. *How to Think*. New York: Currency, 2017, p. 56.

62. Goldman, Liran, and Michael A. Hogg. "Going to Extremes for One's Group: the Role of Prototypicality and Group Acceptance." *Journal of Applied Social Psychology* 46, 2016, p. 551.

63. Berger, P. L., and T. Luckmann. *The Social Construction of Reality: A Treatise in the Sociology of Knowledge*. Garden City, NY: Anchor Books, 1966, pp. 163–183.

64. http://www.culturalcognition.net.

65. Kahan, Dan. "Why We Are Poles Apart on Climate Change." *Nature* 488, August 16, 2012, p. 155.

66. Bruchac, Joseph. *Gluskabe and the Four Wishes*. Dutton, NY: Cobblehill Books, 1995.

67. Mahdi, Louise Carus, Steven Foster, and Meredith Little, eds. *Betwixt and Between: Patterns of Masculine and Feminine Initiation*. LaSalle, IL: Open Court, 1987; Mahdi, Louise Carus, Nancy Gever Christopher, and Michael

Meade, eds. *Crossroads: The Quest for Contemporary Rites of Passage.* Chicago: Open Court, 1996.

68. Simard, Suzanne. "Notes from a Forest Scientist." In Wohllenben, Peter. *The Hidden Life of Trees.* Vancouver, BC: Greystone Books, 216, p. 249.

69. Jung, Carl. *Memories, Dreams, Reflections.* New York: Vintage, 1963, p. 170.

70. Jung, *Memories, Dreams, Reflections,* pp. 174–175.

71. Weinrib, Estelle L. *Images of the Self: The Sandplay Therapy Process.* Cloverdale, CA: Temenos Press, 2004.

72. Epstein, MD, Gerald. "Mental Imagery: The Language of Spirit." *Advances in Mind Body Medicine* 20, no. 3, Fall 2004, pp. 4–5.

73. Jung, C. G. *The Structure and Dynamics of the Psyche.* Collected Works 8, paragraph 618, quoted in Edinger, Edward F. *The Mysterium Lectures.* Toronto: Inner City Books, 1995, p. 19.

74. Sheikh, Anees, Robert G. Kunzendorf, and Katharina S. Schiek. "Healing Images: Historical Perspective." In Sheikh, Anees, ed. *Healing Images: The Role of Imagination in Health.* Amityville, NY: Baywood Publishing Co., 2003, p. 6.

75. http://navajopeople.org/navajo-sand-painting.htm.

76. Kahn-John, Michelle (Diné), and Mary Koithan. "Living in Health, Harmony, and Beauty: The Diné (Navajo) Hózhó Wellness Philosophy." *Global Advances in Health and Medicine* 4, no. 3, May 2015, pp. 24–30.

77. Sheikh, "Healing Images: Historical Perspective," p. 22; Farrelly-Hansen, Mimi. *Spirituality and Art Therapy.* Philadelphia: Jessica Kingsley Publishers, 2001, p. 14.

78. Velmans, Max. "How Could Images Heal Anything?" In Sheikh, Anees, ed. *Healing Images: The Role of Imagination in Health.* Amityville, NY: Baywood Publishing, 2003, p. 54.

79. Sheikh, "Healing Images: Historical Perspective," p. 3.

80. Sheikh, "Healing Images: Historical Perspective," p. 21.

81. Samuels, MD, Mike, and Nancy Samuels. *Seeing with the Mind's Eye: The History, Techniques and Uses of Visualization.* New York: Random House, 1975, pp. 166–167.

82. Personal communication. For more about Anne Parker, see www.naropa.edu/faculty.

83. Personal communication.

84. Weinrib, *Images of the Self,* p. 29.

85. Ronnberg, Ami. "Images from ARAS: Healing Our Sense of Exile from Nature." In Cowan, Lyn, ed. *Barcelona 2004: Edges of Experience: Memory and Emergence: Proceedings of the 16th International Congress for Analytical Psychology.* CD version. Einsiedeln, CH: Daimon Publishers, 2006, p. 398.

86. Blake, William. *Jerusalem,* Part Four. In Frye, Northrop, ed. *Selected Poetry and Prose of William Blake.* New York: Modern Library, 1953, p. 302.

87. Farrelly-Hansen, Mimi. *Spirituality and Art Therapy.* Philadelphia: Jessica Kingsley Publishers, 2001, p. 145.

88. Hoffman, Chris. "Three Behaviors that Can Save Us: The Social Psychology of Planetary Survival," 2012, https://www.hoopandtree.org/other_pubs_pdf/3_Behaviors.pdf.

89. Hyde, *The Gift.*

90. Erikson, *Childhood and Society*, p. 267.

91. Christian, N., E. A. Herre, L. C. Mejia, and K. Clay. "Exposure to the Leaf Litter Microbiome of Healthy Adults Protects Seedlings from Pathogen Damage." *Proceedings of the Royal Society B*, 284: 20170641, 2017, http://dx.doi.org/10.1098/rspb.2017.0641

92. Effective interpersonal communication is beyond the scope of this book, but is an essential life skill. Two good resources are: Patterson, Kerry, Joseph Grenny, Ron McMillan, and Al Switzler. *Crucial Conversations: Tools for Talking When the Stakes Are High.* New York: McGraw-Hill, 2002; and Rosenberg, PhD, Marshall B. *Nonviolent Communication: A Language of Life.* Encinitas, CA: Puddle-Dancer Press, 2015, https://puddledancerpress.com.